DATE DUE

FROM
AIRSHIPS
*TO*AIRBUS

Proceedings of the International Conference on the History of Civil and Commercial Aviation
W. David Lewis, General Editor

The International Conference on the History of Civil and Commercial Aviation was held in August 1992 at the Swiss Transport Museum in Lucerne. Organized cooperatively by aviation historians at Auburn University, the National Air and Space Museum of the Smithsonian Institution, and the Swiss Transport Museum, the conference focused attention on the political, economic, social, and cultural aspects of commercial flight, and on the influence of such contextual forces throughout civil aviation history.

FROM
AIRSHIPS
ᵀᴼ AIRBUS

THE HISTORY OF CIVIL
AND COMMERCIAL AVIATION

Volume 2 ☆ Pioneers and Operations

EDITED BY
WILLIAM F. TRIMBLE

SMITHSONIAN INSTITUTION PRESS
WASHINGTON AND LONDON

Copy Editor: Tom Ireland
Production Editor: Jenelle Walthour
Designer: Kathleen Sims

Library of Congress Cataloging-in-Publication Data
International Conference on the History of Civil and Commercial
    Aviation (1992 : Lucerne, Switzerland)
      From airships to airbus : the history of civil and commercial
    aviation.
          p.   cm. — (Proceedings of the International Conference on the
      History of Civil and Commercial Aviation ; v. 1–2)
      Includes bibliographical references.
      Contents: v. 1. Infrastructure and environment / edited by William
    M. Leary—v. 2. Pioneers and operations / edited by William F.
    Trimble.
      ISBN 1-56098-467-8 (v. 1 : alk. paper). — ISBN 1-56098-468-6 (v.
    2 : alk. paper)
      1. Aeronautics, Commercial—History—Congresses.   2. Private
    flying—History—Congresses.   I. Leary, William M. (William
    Matthew), 1934–   . II. Trimble, William F., 1947–   . III. Title.
    IV. Series: International Conference on the History of Civil and
    Commercial Aviation (1992 : Lucerne, Switzerland). Proceedings of
    the International Conference on the History of Civil and Commercial
    Aviation ; v. 1–2.
    TL515.I53   1992
    387.7'09—dc20   94-26006

British Library Cataloguing-in-Publication Data is available

Manufactured in the United States of America
02 01 00 99 98 97 96 95   5 4 3 2 1

Contents

PART TWO. Flight and Society

PART THREE. Connections between Military and Commercial Aviation

 **PART ONE**

Logistics and Routes

 Wolfgang Meighörner-Schardt

Introduction

The history of aeronautics up to the present is overwhelmingly the history of "lighter-than-air" flight. Only comparatively recently has the principal emphasis been on the airplane and heavier-than-air flight. Moreover, when we think of aeronautics, we forget all too quickly that the major developments in aerodynamics, in the growth of air travel, and in all aspects of technological change in aviation demanded an immense logistical effort—not just in the advanced stages of technical development, but from the very beginning. As an example of this connection, let me remind you that Jean Baptiste Marie Meusnier conceived simultaneously of the airship and the hangar.

The knowledgeable opening chapter by Dr. Alfred Waldis, who was the director of the Swiss Transport Museum in Lucerne for many years, clearly shows how important logistical support was for early air travel. This chapter also makes it apparent that even before World War I a considerable role was given to the tourist side of aviation, along with its obvious military applications. This development was evident in Germany in 1909 with the founding of DELAG, the first airline company in the world. Dr. Waldis's comments also make it clear

that even though Count Zeppelin's airship developments were certainly domi-
nant at the time, other systems were being used successfully during this early
period. An example was the semirigid airship of the French entrepreneur Henri
Julliot, whose *Le Jaune* of 1902–3 was at least on a par with those of the more
famous German count. The significance of the establishment of an airship station in Lucerne is evident in the participation of one of the great promoters of
aviation, Henri Deutsch de la Meurthe; the assumption is not true that the use
of a French airship and the presence of Deutsch de la Meurthe were the result of
anti-German feelings. After all, people in Lucerne had been impressed by Zeppelin's flight to Switzerland. During this time, Count Zeppelin had flatly denied
various foreign inquiries concerning the adoption of his airship designs to safe-
guard them for political reasons. The widely visible "exclamation marks," or
remains of airship hangars, some of which are still present today in a few isolated areas, demonstrate how extensive the requisite logistical efforts were for
airships and lighter-than-air travel.

John Provan's diligence has produced an account of the distribution and diversity of types of German airship hangars. Naturally, these hangars were widely distributed, especially during World War I. They represented the German
commitment to this promising but very demanding type of weapon from the
logistical point of view. The indisputable role in aeronautics of the airship hangars ultimately became clear after the end of the unfortunate war, when the victorious Allies demanded the demolition of the hangars along with the surrender
of the airships. They saw correctly that in so doing the Germans would have a
difficult time reviving a weapon which, ironically, had not proved its military
worth during the war. This rather emotional reaction of the Allies was finally
underscored by the decision to give the United States a Zeppelin airship as
compensation for those deliberately destroyed by the Germans at the close of
the war.

Although heavier-than-air flying machines required a less extensive infrastructure than did airships, their shorter range meant that routes had to be carefully planned and airfields had to be sited along the way. Alexandre Herlea's
work about the French-Balkan airline Franco-Roumaine shows that these
routes, which were supposed to be laid out economically, were also characterized by fierce struggles for shares of the early airline market. The intense

efforts of planning new routes, obtaining the right equipment, and establishing regular service illustrate that the "Golden Age" of aviation had long since passed and that this was now a business totally lacking the playful aura of the pioneer era. Between success and failure there now often lay economic blunders and political errors.

"Logistics and routes" are today more complicated, more demanding, and more expensive than they were earlier in the century; however, the groundwork that was laid during those early days, when one could only speculate about improvements in flight performance, was in the truest sense of the word essential for the development of air transportation. And now, as far as the early years of aviation are concerned, we must dismiss the warmly nurtured idea that the technology developed in a free, unfettered, and frivolous manner. Aviation was then, and remains today, firmly rooted on the ground.

Alfred Waldis

Airship Station Lucerne

The Birth of Commercial Aviation in Switzerland

"Since last Friday, when our Lucerne compatriots paid us a friendly visit in their dirigible giant gondola, nothing can stand in the way of a regular and developing air service between Lucerne and Zürich, there and back," the *Zürich Weekly Chronicle* informed its readers on October 8, 1910. Although the excessive optimism of the journalist is evident in this report, the statement nevertheless accurately reflects the euphoria that characterized the aviation scene in those days.

The enthusiasm in Lucerne for aviation was inspired by the visit to Switzerland of the airship LZ 4 on July 1, 1908. With this flight, Count Ferdinand von Zeppelin wanted to prove that the rigid airship system, tested by him eight years before, was capable of greater achievements than the nonrigid dirigible airship in use at that time.

The impression that Zeppelin's airship made on the citizens of Lucerne was profound. Lucerne was already one of the most popular holiday resorts in our country, and those responsible for tourism saw in the "dirigible balloon," as the novel aerial vehicle was also called, a potentially great attraction for the visitors. In October 1909, this enthusiasm increased when, in connection with the international James Gordon Bennett Races in Zürich-Schlieren, the German nonrigid airship *Parseval 1* undertook a number of flights. It was the star of the show, a real sensation, and the first airship to land and take off on Swiss soil.

The first call for establishing air transportation came from the aviation pioneer Martin Hug, at that time living in Lucerne. As early as March 21, 1909, in a newspaper article, he demanded the setting up of an aviation service. He thought it should also be possible to organize airship flights from Lucerne, similar to the services already existing at Pau in France and Friedrichshafen in Germany. Hug, one of the first to promote aviation tourism over the Swiss lakes, was likewise active in the cause of establishing a Swiss aircraft industry.

Hug's call found a ready response from the Lucerne hoteliers and the Kur Committee. In those days the airship was the only type of flying machine that was practicable for a regular passenger transport service. At its meeting on April 5, 1909, the Kur Committee decided that it was necessary for Lucerne to have an airship station. This decision was reinforced by a report in the *New York Herald Tribune* about a planned (although never realized) airship service linking American cities. On April 8, a Lucerne delegation arrived in Friedrichshafen to discuss with the airship construction firm of Luftschiffbau Zeppelin (LZ) the possibilities of regular flights between the two cities. As soon as May 1, during the return visit to Lucerne of the Zeppelin representatives, conditions for the proposed air link were determined.

However, Deutsche Luftschiffahrt Aktien Gesellschaft (DELAG), the German commercial airship line, would have had to provide the capital—3¹/₂ million marks—for the production of the airship. Further, it was proposed that a commission be set up to organize an air service between Friedrichshafen and Lucerne.

The negotiations with DELAG, whose managing director, Alfred Colsman, was at the same time commercial director of Luftschiffbau Zeppelin, broke down during the summer of 1909. One of the main reasons for this failure was the opposition of German cities that were likewise trying to establish airship stations and services. (To complete the story, it should be mentioned that the first airship ordered by DELAG, the LZ 7 *Deutschland,* carried out its first flight on June 19, 1910. After World War I, regular service between Friedrichshafen and Berlin was renewed with the LZ 120 *Bodensee,* which carried out 78 flights before the connection was closed down at the end of 1919. With this, the service of the world's first airline company came to an end. Altogether, between 1910 and 1919 more than 17,000 passengers had been transported.)

In September 1909, a delegation of the official Kur Committee Lucerne visited the International Luftschiffahrt Ausstellung (ILA, or International Airship Exhibition) in Frankfurt am Main to obtain further information about the possibilities of operating an airship service. Besides DELAG, among the other enterprises interested in developing such a project were the Berlin Aircraft Company, Ltd., which used Parseval nonrigid airships, and the French Société Aéronautique Astra from Billancourt/Paris. In establishing contacts with the Lucerne body in November 1909, both companies showed their keen interest in establishing passenger airship lines. The Lucerne authorities decided in favor of the French enterprise, whose subsidiary, the Compagnie Générale Transaérienne, had airships such as the *Ville de Paris* already in service and could offer more favorable terms.

On February 3, 1910, the Kur Committee signed a contract with the French company. In this agreement the company bound itself to provide a regular service from the airship station at Lucerne with two airships, one with a 4,500-cubic-meter capacity and room for eight passengers, the other—never delivered—with a 7,500-cubic-meter capacity and room for fifteen passengers. In addition, there were to be such aeronautical events as air shows and the ascent of spherical balloons. Furthermore, the French company had to provide the working capital, making their financial involvement, according to the terms of the contract, 650,000 francs. The Lucerne partners were obliged to provide the land and the airship hangar with all necessary "appurtenances" for an estimated 250,000 francs.

To fulfill these obligations, the cooperative Aero Association was founded on February 12, 1910. The association obtained the contractually agreed means by issuing share certificates of 200 francs each, which were quickly bought up: The municipality of Lucerne purchased 250 shares, and the Hotel Association paid out 50,000 francs. The statutes contained the proviso that in the case of liquidation and after the repayment of the association's capital, any eventual surplus would be used towards promoting Lucerne's tourist industry.

The site chosen for the hangar was Tribschenmoos, a swampy area on the left bank of the lake, not far from the Richard Wagner Museum. Because the hangar was to accommodate the two airships foreseen in the contract, it was built on an appropriately generous scale: length 96 meters, width 45 meters, height 30 meters. The total area under roof came to 4,000 square meters, and the total volume 112,000 cubic meters, of which 75,000 cubic meters could be utilized. The Lucerne building was, apart from the Zeppelin hangars in Germany, the largest hangar for nonrigid airships, of which France alone had 11.

Construction started on March 14, 1910. Bad weather conditions caused delays, and because of flooding, the limited work possible on the site had to be done from boats. But thanks to the efforts of an army of workers—up to 240 men—the hangar was completed in the astonishingly short time of 107 days.

1.1. As many as 240 men worked on the construction of the airship hangar at Tribschenmoos on Lake Lucerne in 1910. Timber piles were used in the foundation, and the superstructure was a latticework of 24 upright posts and 12 bowstring girders. A sliding door in the facade was 24 meters wide. (Courtesy of the Swiss Transport Museum)

On July 22, 1910, two days before the official inauguration, it was handed over to the Aero Association.

The total costs of the installations Lucerne was responsible for came to 219,000 francs. The great hangar, the largest single item, cost 182,000 francs. Besides the hangar it was also necessary to build a plant for producing hydrogen gas, which was needed to operate the airships. By the middle of July the buildings were completed. Additional expenditure of 117,000 francs was required for the two jetties, among other items, which was contributed by the city of Lucerne. In justifying this extra financial outlay, the authorities explained that an airship station in a tourist center such as Lucerne would be an important attraction, bringing more guests to the area, and thus benefiting all, not merely a few individuals. Moreover, the Lake Lucerne Shipping Company brought two new motorboats, the *Astra* and the *Aero,* into service.

In France at that time several enterprises were engaged in the construction of "dirigible balloons." Among the best known were those built following the design of Charles Renard and Arthur Krebs, who had delivered the *France*, the first airship in the French army. Another was the balloon manufacturer Surcouf, founded by the Astra Association and located in Billancourt/Paris. Henri Kapferer designed and constructed airships for Surcouf; the engines were the product of Clément-Bayard Motor Works, which likewise undertook the production of similar airships. The airship destined for Lucerne carried out its maiden voyage on April 2, 1910. At first it flew under the name *Ville de Pau*, after the southern French spa, well known for its flying school. In June it was transported by rail to Lucerne, where it arrived on the twenty-first and was rechristened *Ville de Lucerne*.

In contrast to the Zeppelin construction, the semirigid airship possessed a supporting framework attached beneath the envelope. The inflated form was maintained by an internal ballonet (air bag), filled by a ventilator with atmospheric air. The distinguishing mark of these "ballonet airships" was the long gondola-framework, 30 meters in length. Besides accommodating crew and

1.2. The French-built airship *Ville de Lucerne* first flew in April 1910 as *Ville de Pau*. It made its maiden flight with its new name in Lucerne in July 1910. (Courtesy of the Swiss Transport Museum)

Luzern. Luftschiff »Ville de Lucerne«. Luftschiffpark u. Halle.

1.3. This postcard shows the *Ville de Lucerne* with the airship hangar in the background. (Courtesy of the Swiss Transport Museum)

passengers, its function was to stiffen the airship body and distribute the load equally. Moreover, the gondola was suspended immediately under the balloon envelope, which meant that the fixing ropes could be short, minimizing air resistance. A further characteristic was the pear-shaped, gas-filled stabilizers fitted at the tail. The airship possessed dual controls: an elevator control in both the front and rear third of the gondola. The rudder was mounted on the tail. A wooden propeller with a diameter of 6.5 meters was mounted on the end of the gondola-framework: The original is on display in the Hall of Aviation and Astronautics of the Swiss Transport Museum. The engine capacity was approximately 110 horsepower, designed to give a maximum speed of 45 kilometers per hour, although it is unlikely that the airship ever achieved more than 40 kilometers per hour in actual practice. The gondola had room for a five-man crew and eight passengers. The airship was 61 meters long, had a maximum diameter of 12.5 meters, and a volume of 4,500 cubic meters. (This compares with the later LZ 127 *Graf Zeppelin:* length, 236 meters; maximum diameter, 30.5 meters; total volume, 105,000 cubic meters.)

On July 24, 1910, came the great day. At the opening ceremony, the march "Propeller Beat," specially composed for the occasion, had its first perfor-

1.4. Gondola-framework of the nonrigid airship *Ville de Lucerne*. In nonrigids, the pressure of the lifting gas maintained the shape of the envelope. (Courtesy of the Swiss Transport Museum)

mance. The report of the most famous Zürich newspaper, the *Neuen Züricher Zeitung,* expressed the euphoric mood of the time. Its editor, Willi Birbaum, wrote:

> The tension mounted as the seconds ticked by. The chimes from the bell-towers of Lucerne announcing noontime had just died away as the engine was started up; slowly the "Ville de Lucerne 1" rose from the ground and, to the sounds of the Swiss national anthem, prepared itself for flight. At 4 minutes past twelve, the engine thundered in full-throated harmony, the propeller began its furious dance, steam hissed and sprayed from the exhaust pipes and triumphantly the airship ascended.

The first trip of the *Ville de Lucerne* lasted 24 minutes. On board, besides the crew under the command of the constructor and director of the Astra Association, Henri Kapferer, the sole passenger was a great patron of aviation, Henri Deutsch de la Meurthe, who in 1901 had offered a prize of 100,000 francs to the first aviator to fly around the Eiffel Tower.

1.5. The march "Propeller Beat" was composed to commemorate the opening of the airship station in July 1910. The sheet music for the composition is shown here. (Courtesy of the Swiss Transport Museum)

1.6. *Ville de Lucerne* emerging from the hangar, 1910. (Courtesy of the Swiss Transport Museum)

1.7. *Ville de Lucerne* taking off at the airship station, 1910. (Courtesy of the Swiss Transport Museum)

During the following weeks, weather permitting, the airship was seen every day over Lucerne. A "pleasure trip"—as it was advertised in the newspapers—of 20 minutes in the immediate vicinity cost 100 francs; a longer excursion, to the Rigi or Pilatus, 200 francs. For long-distance flights, an agreed-upon price would be arranged. The airship park in Tribschenmoos also enjoyed great popularity with those who came there just to see the airship. In the beginning visitors had to pay five francs (the usual daily wage of an employee) for the first row of seats and two francs for the second.

Meanwhile, interest in aviation steadily grew in Switzerland. Only a few months previously—in February 1910—the first motorized flight over Swiss territory had been made (the German Captain Paul Engelhardt in a Wright biplane over Lake Saint Moritz). This prompted the Lucerne committee to organize an "Aeroplane Competition" as a follow-up to the traditional International Horse Race in the autumn of 1910. It was expected, as the newspapers stated, that "the dramatic show of aeroplane flights in connection with the regular service of the airship will again bring many spectators to Lucerne." In the organized event from September 10 to 15, designated the "First International Flight Meeting of Switzerland," three French aviators and one Swiss pilot took part. There were more "short hops" than flights to be seen, and crashes were the order of the day. But there was one success: The Frenchman René Vallon in his "Sommer-monoplane" carried out the first flight over a Swiss town and simultaneously the first flights in Switzerland with a passenger, namely his wife. But the airship display did not take place as planned because of technical difficulties.

In the middle of August 1910 the airship service had to be suspended because the craft's load-carrying capacity had continuously decreased. The reason for the loss of gas was leakage in the balloon envelope. Then towards the end of August a new balloon envelope arrived from Paris. It had a greater diameter (14 meters) than the previous one, as well as greater capacity (5,000 cubic meters), and its shape was better.

After a test flight of the airship with the new envelope on September 23, regular operations were resumed. Particularly worth mentioning was the flight to Zürich on September 30, 1910—the first air connection between two Swiss cities. The start in Lucerne was at 10:50 A.M.; at 12:03 P.M. the airship flew over the city of Zürich, having covered a distance of about 50 kilometers. Because a strong wind came up, the landing had to be made on the Allmend (the Common) of the suburb Wollishofen. At 12:25 the airship landed safely, and the cadets of the Officers' School who were present "made themselves," in the words of a

Zürich newspaper, "uncommonly useful in the cordoning-off work." After the official reception, the airship was refilled with hydrogen gas, which had to be transported by horse-drawn vehicles from Lucerne to Zürich because the Federal Railways had refused to carry such a dangerous load.

On October 9, the first season came to an end; in all, 66 flights carrying 235 passengers had been made in 30 days. But the first operational year ended with a deficit. Although the Compagnie Générale Transaérienne had only partly fulfilled its obligations, the contract was renewed at the beginning of 1911, because Lucerne, as the Kur Committee wrote, was able to negotiate "extremely favorable terms." The French company committed itself to resuming the airship service with the *Ville de Lucerne* on May 13, 1911, and to have a replacement envelope available in Lucerne by that date. In addition, on July 15, a new airship, larger than the *Ville de Lucerne* and fitted with two engines, was to go into service. There would then be two airships in use at the same time. The French company decided on this new contract, which made great demands on both its technical and financial capacities, because it wanted to prove the economic utility of airship travel; furthermore, during the trial operations in the summer of 1910, the company had come to the conclusion that for this purpose Lucerne was ideally suitable as an international tourist center.

It was further agreed that Transaérienne would make two airplanes available at all times at the airship station. These were amphibians, constructed for operations from land and water. This innovation received widespread publicity in the press. In the *Berliner Tagblatt* of May 20, 1911, appeared a notice whose more than optimistic contents reflected then-current attitudes:

> A taximeter-aircab, in fact the first ever, is promised for Lucerne. Entrepreneur of this traffic novelty is the "Transaérienne" in Paris, which is expediting a biplane equipped with a chronometer to Lucerne. The airplane is to carry passengers on cross-country flights at a price that will be calculated according to the number of kilometers registered on the dial of the taximeter. According to calculations the air-taximeter will, in the last analysis, prove to be a much cheaper form of transport than the street-cab, as it can go as the crow flies and, besides, will have far fewer traffic obstacles to reckon with.

But the reality of 1911 was very different. The service did not begin until June 21, five weeks later than intended, and had to be suspended once more from July 17 on, after 41 flights with 46 passengers, because of gas leakage in the airship's envelope. Substitute ascents were not possible because the second airship, guaranteed in the contract, never appeared in Lucerne.

LUZERN ERSTE SCHWEIZ. LUFTSCHIFF-STATION
·TÄGLICHE AUFSTIEGE·

1.8. This postcard depicts the *Ville de Lucerne* in flight over the city and the airship hangar in the center background. Lucerne's interest in the development of commercial aviation was largely due to efforts to stimulate tourist trade in the area. (Courtesy of the Swiss Transport Museum)

Nevertheless, Transaérienne's chief pilot, Maurice Herbster, undertook several flights with the two airplanes, a Wright and a Farman biplane, mainly starting from the airship hangar. When operations ceased in September, 42 flights had been made.

As a further attraction of the 1911 season, the airship *Schwaben* made flights from Friedrichshafen to Lucerne. On July 20 the airship took off at 7:00 A.M. from Friedrichshafen, arrived at 9:45 A.M. over Lucerne, did "a big loop and . . . disappeared in the direction of the Rigi, because, as could be read in Count Zeppelin's personal, handwritten message thrown down from the airship over Tribschenmoos, a landing manoeuvre had to be dispensed with as a result of the delayed start."

In spite of unpleasant experiences and financial setbacks, the people of Lucerne still believed in a future for commercial aviation. They found a new partner in the Aerial Traffic Company, Ltd., in Berlin, which operated a service with Parseval airships. These nonrigid airships, built by the Bavarian Major

1.9. Aviator Maurice Herbster in Transaérienne's Farman biplane, summer 1911.
(Courtesy of the Swiss Transport Museum)

August von Parseval since 1905, were used for commercial as well as military purposes.

The airship destined for Lucerne, the PL VI, had carried out numerous passenger and advertising flights in Germany since the autumn of 1910. With a length of 70 meters and a maximum diameter of 12.3 meters, it had a volume of 6,800 cubic meters. The 10-meter-long gondola could accommodate up to 16 persons, including the four-man crew; two 120-horsepower engines mounted on the sides of the gondola enabled a maximum speed of 55 kilometers per hour. A specialty of the PL VI airship was its electrical lighting installation with projectors mounted on both sides of the gondola so that pictorial advertisements could be flashed onto the envelope. Lucerners paid 125 francs for an evening flight.

From August 26 until September 25, the airship made 24 ascents on 21 days, with trips lasting between 20 and 130 minutes. With a total of just over 20 hours flying and having covered a total distance of 870 kilometers, it had transported 160 passengers. In spite of all the efforts to increase the frequency of use, such as cutting the fares by half towards the end of season, this airship enterprise also ended with a considerable deficit.

1.10. The Parseval PL VI in flight over Lucerne, 1912. The airship was built by August von Parseval, a Bavarian. (Courtesy of the Swiss Transport Museum)

1.11. Gondola-framework of the Parseval PL VI. (Courtesy of the Swiss Transport Museum)

1.12. Another view of the Parseval PL VI over Lucerne, 1912. (Courtesy of the Swiss Transport Museum)

The airship did not arrive in Lucerne until August 21. Meanwhile, because it was felt necessary to offer the public some form of flight experience, airplanes of Transaérienne were once again in service during the summer, and the Aviatik-Company in Mülhausen was engaged to operate a flight service. In 93 flights, 250 passengers were carried. Within the framework of this aeronautical activity was the Aviation Meeting of September 15, in which, as a special attraction, an airship, a biplane, and a balloon could be seen in flight simultaneously.

The failures of airship operations caused the Aero Association to turn its attention to airplanes for its future air services. Again it was Transaérienne and the Aviatik-Company who sent equipment and pilots to Lucerne, among the former the Voisin floatplane *Icarus*. This "gigantic machine," as it was considered at the time, with its 22-meter wingspan, was sent back to France, however, after several unsuccessful attempts to fly. The passenger trips were well received on the whole, and during the summer season, 406 persons were transported with 250 flights. The longest flight lasted 62 minutes.

The Aero Association decided to continue passenger transport by the two companies in 1914, also. A highlight of the season was the air show starting on July 5, in which, among others, the Frenchman Etienne Poulet performed loops and other aerial acrobatics for the first time. Noteworthy was the greater achievement of the pilot Charles Ingold, who, on July 8, flew to Mülhausen with one passenger in a flight lasting one hour and 40 minutes. The outbreak of World War I shortly afterwards put an abrupt end to this civilian aviation enterprise.

By the summer of 1913 it was already evident that the Aero Association would not be able in the long run to sustain this kind of service. The enterprise sought, therefore, to employ the empty airship hangar for other purposes, and in August 1913 it was the venue for an impressive Wagner concert.

From 1915 to 1919, the hangar was rented out to the Defense Department for the storage of straw, and at times it was used as an ice-skating rink. The fittings and operational equipment were sold off a little at a time. Renovation of the hangar for other purposes was not considered, and at the end of April 1921 it was sold for 10,000 francs. At a meeting on February 16, 1922, the Kur Committee decided to accept 126,709 francs to fulfill the obligations of the Aero Association. The final liquidation took place on January 11, 1923.

The Aero Association Lucerne was the first aviation enterprise in Switzerland, and, after the German DELAG, earned the distinction of being the second passenger airline in the world. It can certainly be claimed as a success that in five years of operation, from 1910 to 1914, a total of 883 passengers were transported without any accidents whatever—441 in 121 airship flights, and 442 in 385 airplane flights.

1.13. The floatplane *Icarus* was used for sightseeing flights at Lucerne in the summer of 1913. (Courtesy of the Swiss Transport Museum)

In assessing the enterprise, one must always keep in mind the particular conditions of the period. The airship in 1910 had not yet proved its worth as a means of transport, and only a few months before, in February 1910, the Swiss had seen the first motorized aircraft in flight. If the Aero Association's undertaking was an economic failure, its pioneering work gave the concept of commercial aviation a boost that should not be underestimated. In addition, the experience led most to recognize that the future of air traffic lay with the airplane.

Aeronautical activity made Lucerne the birthplace of Swiss aviation tourism and for a short time an internationally known airship station. The bond between Lucerne and flying carried over into the 1920s. In 1925 contracts were signed with Balair concerning an air link between Basel and Lucerne, in which the Lucerners agreed to pay two francs per kilometer flown. Similar agreements were made with Zürich Ad Astra, and, after the fusion of these two airlines into Swissair in 1931, Lucerne continued to pay for some years an annual subscription of 3,000 francs to the national airline corporation, in order, as the Kur Committee protocol tells us, to be included as a landing site in the service timetable. It was a perceptive decision that has lost none of its worth to this day.

SOURCES

Neuen Züricher Zeitung, July 25, 1910.
S.L., published by Aero-Club of Switzerland, 1941–42.
Protocol of the official Kur Committee of Lucerne.
Reports and motions of the Lucerne City Council.
Various Lucerne newspapers.

John Provan

The German Airship Sheds

A Problem in Architecture and Logistics

The history of the German airship is fundamentally the story of the rapid development of a military weapon under the pressures of World War I. Unlike that of any other weapon or mode of transportation, the development of airships progressed hand in hand with the architectural requirements of housing them.

The unusual logistical problems involved with the construction and maintenance of German airship sheds have not been dealt with in any depth by historians. Although a wide selection of literature has been written on airships, mainly regarding the German airship program, only a few books examine the architectural and logistical aspects, among them, *Luftschiffhallenbau*, by A. Hänig, published in 1910; and *Anlage und Betrieb von Luftschiffhäfen*, by G. Christians, which appeared in 1914. These books, however, examine projects that were never completed. The Architectural Association School of Architecture in London presented the worldwide phenomena of airship shed construction in a display, "Housing the Airship," held between April and May 1989. The catalog to the exhibition was the first attempt to review historically the topic of airship sheds in general.

The primary dilemmas of designing airship sheds have always been related to their size. Increasing the lift and useful load of a rigid airship requires either a lighter framework, which is only possible to a certain degree, or an increase in size. This ever-increasing requirement for size and space necessitated structures capable of housing them. The cost factor, though, often mandated a smaller configuration. The scale of development in size can best be understood when one considers that Count Zeppelin's first airship had a capacity of 11,300 cubic meters of hydrogen gas, while LZ 130, the last rigid built, had 200,000 cubic meters. Within a period of less than 40 years, the size of rigid airships had multiplied almost 20 times. Therefore, during the development of airship sheds, there was a conflict among present projects, future requirements, cost effectiveness, and available funding.

An understanding of the reasoning behind shed locations and their unique architectural and logistical complications provides insight into the difficulties of effective rigid airship operations. These factors led to the termination of military airship use in World War I, laid the foundation of continued passenger airship service thereafter, and provided Germany with many airport locations still in use today.

A working definition of the term *airship* is necessary to better consider the subject. There are generally three types of airships: nonrigid, semirigid, and rigid. Nonrigids are the smallest type, with one gas cell or compartment in which lifting gas is kept under pressure to maintain the ship's form. This type of airship has remained useful to the present day because of its relatively inexpensive operating costs and suitability for advertising. Semirigid airships tend to be larger because of the rigid underframe, to which one or more gas bags are connected. A rigid airship has a framework of wood or aluminum alloy, in which a number of gas cells are filled with lifting gas. The largest airships ever built, they are commonly known as "Zeppelins" or dirigibles. Although Germany built and developed all three types, this chapter is concerned with the large rigid airships because the smaller airships could always be housed in the Zeppelin sheds, but not vice versa. The difference can easily be understood by comparing the size of the shed in Köln for the nonrigid Clouth airship, which was 40 meters long and 16 meters wide, with the larger Zeppelin sheds at Ahlhorn, which measured 260 meters long and 75 meters wide.

Sheds for nonrigid, semirigid, and rigid airships differed mainly in size. A *shed* is a structure or hangar in which one can house or store an airship. There are two categories of sheds: those for construction and those for the operation of airships. Construction sheds tend to be somewhat larger and have several neighboring buildings, required for fabricating parts or sections, storage facilities, and offices. Operational sheds are used to house a completed airship and usually have small repair shops, offices, and quarters for crews, but tend to have few neighboring buildings. For the purpose of this study, I will consider both categories, while concentrating on rigid airships in general.

German airship shed construction progressed through many stages of development. The forerunners of these buildings were huge iron railroad bridges, the central train stations of many cities, large factories, and the exhibition halls of the world's fairs (such as the Crystal Palace in London) built before the turn of the century.[1]

The first period, from 1899 to 1907, was primarily developmental. During this time the first airship sheds were built. Count Zeppelin built his sheds at Manzell, and Parseval and Gross/Basenach used the sheds at Tegel, Berlin. These early structures were constructed of wood and, in the case of Manzell, were located in the waters of Lake Constance. This floating shed could turn in the direction of the wind, which assisted the maneuvering of the airships.

The initial success of these airships encouraged a second period, between 1908 and 1911. The Parseval Company built construction sheds in Bitterfeld, the Siemens-Schuckert Company erected a revolving shed in Biesdorf, Schütte-Lanz built a tent shed in Mannheim-Rheinau, and the Zeppelin Company built the first double shed in Friedrichshafen. Each company had unique solutions to its problems. Important during this period was the architectural competition that occurred during the ILA (International Luftschiffahrt Ausstellung, or International Airship Exhibition) in Frankfurt am Main in 1909. Architects envisioned projects that were never to be realized, such as round sheds or sheds in which the roof opened.

DELAG (Deutsche Luftschiffahrt Aktien Gesellschaft) was created on November 16, 1909, becoming the first nationwide airship service and possibly the world's first airline. The shed at Metz (today in France) was also built in 1909 for the military, whose interest in airships increased as their size reached more useful capacity. This shed had structural problems and had to be redesigned while under construction. The military also experimented with portable tent sheds during this period. Three tent sheds were used by the military from 1909 until 1913, primarily during maneuvers. Another tent shed was erected in Frankfurt am Main during the ILA but was used only once because of its extremely small size. A fifth tent shed was erected in Friedrichshafen and used temporarily until the large double shed was completed. These tent sheds proved too small and impractical, and their use was discontinued.

The third period, which began in 1910 and lasted until 1914, witnessed the construction of many sheds as part of the foundation of DELAG. The Zeppelin company built sheds at Baden Oos and Frankfurt-Rebstock. Privately funded sheds were also constructed at Düsseldorf, Dresden, Gotha, Hamburg, Johan-

2.1. The large airship shed at Metz under construction, 1909. (Luftschiff Zeppelin Collection, John Provan)

nisthal, and Leipzig as part of the DELAG service. A bimonthly magazine, *Die Luftschiffhalle (The Airship Shed),* published between December 1909 and December 1910, was instrumental in presenting new concepts and proposals on shed construction during this period.

The military erected a shed at Königsberg and small sheds for nonrigid airships at Strasbourg and Thorn. The army was uncertain which type airship would function best under wartime conditions and therefore experimented with nonrigid, semirigid, and rigid airships until 1911 and 1912.

By mid-1913, the military buildup within Europe affected the construction of German airship sheds. During this time, the navy began construction of its first shed at Nordholz. The army airship service built sheds at Allenstein, Liegnitz, Löwenthal, Posen, Darmstadt, Mannheim-Sandhofen, and Trier. At the last three locations, sheds of a new type, known as the standardized shed, were built for the most part by Zeppelin Hallenbau GmbH (a subsidiary of the Zeppelin company) and Arthur Müller Ballonhallenbau, both headquartered in Berlin. The need for a significant number of sheds to be built quickly could only be met with structures of standardized sizes and shapes, which at the same time decreased construction costs. Sheds 184 meters long, 35 meters wide, and 28 meters high were standard for this period, and their length could be easily in-

2.2. The DELAG shed at Baden Oos was built during the third phase of shed construction. (Deutsche Zeppelin Reederei postcard, Luftschiff Zeppelin Collection, John Provan)

2.3. The DELAG shed at Hamburg was typical of the early sheds used by the German airship line. (Deutsche Zeppelin Reederei postcard, Luftschiff Zeppelin Collection, John Provan)

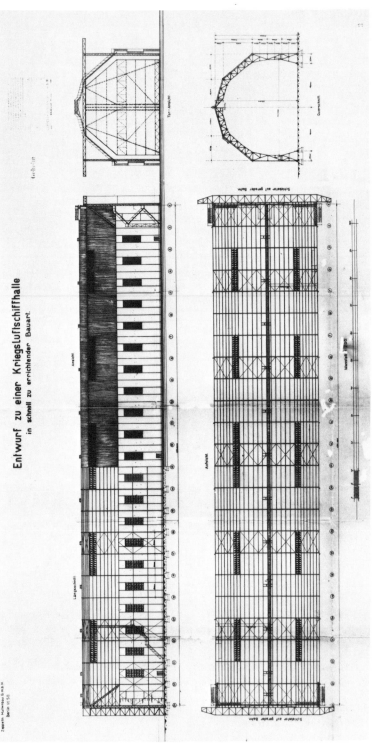

2.4. The standardized single airship shed design was intended to decrease costs and construction time and increase the number of sheds available. (Luftschiff Zeppelin Collection, John Provan)

creased by adding one or more arches. These sheds cost approximately 450,000 reichsmarks, could be completed within an average period of four to six months by a construction crew of 200 men, and required no scaffolding. These small standardized sheds were also built during the fourth construction period.

The fourth building period, between 1914 and 1918, saw the construction of several types of structures. Small standardized sheds were built for the army in Dresden, Düsseldorf, Hannover, Lahr, Schneidemühl, and Spich. The navy continued construction of standardized sheds in Jüterbog, four sheds in Hage, and two each in Nordholz and Tondern. By mid-1916, however, new rigid airships, 198 meters long, made these small standardized sheds obsolete.

The concept of transportable structures led to the construction of sheds in Namur, Düren, and Schaulen. These sheds were designed for temporary deployment at several locations, but only the shed at Schaulen was transported and rebuilt at Warsaw. Like the tent sheds, they proved impractical.

The construction of large standardized double sheds took place during the second half of the fourth period and is the principal factor differentiating the third period from the fourth. The army built only one double shed, at Düs-

2.5. The interior of the standardized shed at Trier following World War I. (Luftschiff Zeppelin Collection, John Provan)

2.6. One of three temporary, transportable sheds was erected at Namur. The concept of transportable sheds proved impractical. (Luftschiff Zeppelin Collection, John Provan)

seldorf, which was never used because it was too far from the front. The navy considered double sheds to be advantageous and built four of them in Ahlhorn in 1916, and two more there in 1917. One double shed was constructed in Nord-holz in 1916, two more at that location in 1917, and one double shed each in Seddin, Seerappen, and Tondern. The army had a total of 41 usable sheds, with space for 49 airships; the navy, on the other hand, had only 37 sheds, but room for 54 airships. These figures demonstrate a significant difference between the two military branches. The advantage of the double shed was that two airships could be housed in a single building, and construction time was only slightly longer than it took to build one airship in a single shed. This was cost effective and yet provided the possibility that if future airships outgrew the length of a double shed, they could still be housed in a sideways position.[2]

The fifth and final period of airship shed construction occurred after World War I, between 1930 and 1938, and witnessed the construction of five clamshell-door airship sheds. The birth of intercontinental passenger airship service and the formation of the Deutsche Zeppelin Reederei (along with Lufthansa) in

1935 necessitated the new design. These clamshell sheds were built in 1930 in Friedrichshafen; 1931 in Löwenthal (about two miles from Friedrichshafen); 1935 in Santa Cruz, Brazil; and in 1936 and 1938 at Rhein-Main Airport (near Frankfurt am Main). The clamshell doors were a major improvement in design because they prevented unwanted air turbulence in front of the structure, which helped ensure the safe maneuvering of airships. The development of clamshell doors began during the second period of airship shed construction in Germany, with the sheds at Liegnitz, Posen, and the city shed in Dresden. German engineers working for the Goodyear-Zeppelin Corporation, which built the huge, 358-meter-long shed in Akron, Ohio, continued the concept.[3] This period is also noted for the development and use of such ground handling equipment as mooring towers and tracks, which reduced the need for the huge landing crews.

Airship shed construction had to meet two different types of requirements during these periods: economic and military. During the second, third, and fifth periods, the economic requirements of airship passenger service often determined the location of a shed. Certain common factors remained for all shed sites, such as the necessity of flat terrain with no neighboring obstacles, and, preferably, a nearby water supply or hydrogen-producing facility. The passenger service claimed that the economic requirement of a nearby affluent pop-

2.7. The clamshell design of the shed doors at Rhein-Main Airport reduced air turbulence in front of the structure. (Luftschiff Zeppelin Collection, John Provan)

ulation that could afford the fares of airship flights should not be overlooked. The early DELAG flights, between 1910 and 1914, and 1919 and 1921, cost between 100 reichsmarks (for a one-hour flight) and 200 reichsmarks, far more than the average monthly income of a German worker. Passengers on board these airships were often well-to-do foreigners who could afford such a flight. The shed in Potsdam was located near the capital of Berlin; the shed in Baden Oos served a famous health spa for the wealthy; the sheds in Düsseldorf and Hamburg were located in prosperous industrial areas. The requirement for large open areas, the price of land, and high labor costs within major cities meant that the airship sheds were placed outside the city, but still close enough for effective operation.

The same economic considerations held true for intercontinental airship service between 1930 and 1937, when a single flight cost 1,000 to 1,400 reichsmarks for the journey between Germany and North or South America. Friedrichshafen was used as an operating base between 1929 and 1935, but it was soon determined that a new base was imperative. The two sheds at Rhein-Main were uniquely located in central Germany, with excellent rail and road connections and an airport providing domestic air travel. These factors virtually guaranteed a successful operation. In considering sites of sheds for passenger airship service, it was necessary to recognize that nearby cities had to have a population that could afford such service.

The demands of military conflict also determined certain elements of location. To support airship attacks on England, sheds were required along the coast so the flight range of airships could be maximized and the success of the raids enhanced. These airship sheds had to be near the front lines, but not too close for fear of enemy attack. An airship was most vulnerable while on the ground and in its shed. Many German airships were lost because their sheds were too near the front lines. The use of the shed at Metz was terminated, for example, because it was within French artillery range. LZ 25 was destroyed in its shed at Düsseldorf; LZ 38 was devastated in the Brussels-Evere shed; and LZ 99 and LZ 108 were destroyed at Tondern by enemy aircraft attacks. These considerations were taken into account for most military shed sites during the third and fourth periods of construction.

Military sheds were usually situated on government-owned land, either by the military or the German civil authorities. In some cases, municipal property was acquired. The land was frequently part of an already existing military base, such as a practice area or maneuver grounds. Because nearby military units were helpful in handling rigid airships, especially in emergency situations, the location of such units played a role in the location of sheds and in the reduction of manpower and housing requirements.

These sheds tended to be located on flat areas, requiring a minimum of expensive ground excavation and construction. The flat surface included not only the structure itself but also a large surrounding area. A wide, open space is necessary for the safe landing and operation of rigid airships, with no obstacles such as factory chimneys, towers, trees, and mountains. An airship making an aerodynamic takeoff (usually due to being overweight) will fly at a 10-percent incline and reach an altitude of only 50 meters in a 600-meter-long open field. Valleys were poor shed locations due to gusty winds, one of the principal reasons Trier was seldom used. Sandy fields were also a disadvantage because heat radiating from sand during the summer months can cause a rapid altitude increase and possible control loss of the airship. The ground also had to be stable enough to support the foundations of the airship shed, especially revolving sheds, which placed enormous pressures upon their foundations.[4]

Water (a river, lake, or stream) was often adjacent to the sheds to supply hydrogen-producing plants. Although these plants were not built at each location, such considerations were definitely taken into account.

Nearby railroad lines were essential to erect a building with the dimensions of an airship shed within the required period of three to four months. Rail lines provided fast transportation of all building materials to the construction site. Likewise, the great quantities of hydrogen required could be easily transported by rail cars. Therefore, the determination of an airship shed site took into account the feasibility of laying a short track to the adjoining rail line.

The altitude of a given site was also important. An airship lost 1 percent of its lift for every 80 meters that the airship shed was located above sea level. The sheds along the coast, closest to sea level, thus provided a maximum of lift. At a shed in Friedrichshafen, for example, with an altitude of 400 meters, airship load capacity was reduced by 5 percent. An airship such as L 71, with a capacity of 68,500 cubic meters, lost 2.55 tons in lift taking off from Friedrichshafen.[5]

When the military necessities were fulfilled and the other aspects considered —available government land, flat terrain, water sources, and most important, the mandatory nearby rail link—it was possible to establish shed locations. At that point, weather considerations became a factor in choosing a location.

It was important to determine the average yearly wind direction at a given site. During the period before World War I, several aero clubs had formed throughout Germany, and they provided the necessary weather information. Sixteen shed sites were erected accordingly, most notably at Bitterfeld, Darmstadt, Düsseldorf, and Frankfurt. The nationwide weather service, especially during the war period, could not provide average wind direction information in every case, resulting in expensive mistakes. The airship shed at Lahr was never used, and those at Spich and Trier were used only rarely because they had been erected in windy areas or faced in the wrong direction.[6] It was impossible during the World War I period to bring an airship safely into a shed with sidewinds. When airship operations required that a shed stand in the correct direction, the early morning and late afternoon hours were optimal. The general weather situation of a given site—for example, how often fog or storms occurred—was also considered. Airship commanders refrained from landing at incorrectly sited sheds.[7]

Several attempts were made to solve this problem. Towards the beginning of World War I, the navy built the large, revolving double shed at Nordholz known as Nobel. The concept of land-built revolving sheds derived from the Siemens-Schuchert shed built at Biesdorf in 1911. Although a much smaller shed, only 135 meters long, it demonstrated the usefulness of revolving sheds.[8] The Nordholz shed, begun in 1913, was ready for temporary use by August 20, 1914, and was totally completed by November 6, 1914. This shed could only house older-model airships until the end of the war.[9] The original length of 182 meters was increased during the winter of 1916–17 to 213 meters.

The army airship service had ambitious plans to build revolving single sheds at three locations: Düsseldorf, Sandhofen, and Schneidemühl. Apparently only the shed at Düsseldorf was begun. The frames were completed, but the struc-

2.8. The small turning shed at Biesdorf was built in 1911. The entire shed revolved while an airship was brought in or out, thus avoiding crosswinds. (Luftschiff Zeppelin Collection, John Provan)

2.9. The large turning shed at Nordholz was completed in 1914. High costs and long construction time precluded the erection of additional revolving sheds. (Luftschiff Zeppelin Collection, John Provan)

ture was not finished, and it was torn down before the end of the war. Because these army revolving sheds had a length of only 182 meters, they would have been obsolete by mid-1916 anyway. The exceptionally long construction period and high costs of building these revolving sheds made them impractical under wartime conditions.[10]

During the final construction period, 1930–38, the plans for the airship station at Rhein-Main called for a revolving shed within a group of three sheds forming a quarter circle. After an airship landed it could be brought into the revolving shed, regardless of wind direction. Once the airship was inside the revolving shed, the shed turned, allowing the airship to move into one of the three other sheds—much like the locomotive roundhouses used by European and American railroads. The second shed built at Rhein-Main was to have been part of this planned group of sheds, but the project never developed further.

The army airship service solved weather problems by building single sheds at many different locations. The army had 41 sheds at 38 different locations, and if poor weather conditions prevailed at one location, the airship commanders could divert to another. However, this involved a large manpower requirement, because landing crews of up to 200 men were required at each location.

A more practical solution was the creation of bases where a number of sheds stood in different directions. The early naval airship bases at Hage, Namur, and Tondern had several sheds standing in the same direction. Thus, if unfavorable weather conditions prevailed, the use of all sheds was hampered. This situation was corrected at Nordholz and Ahlhorn, where sheds stood in several directions. The naval airship base policy led to the building of 37 sheds in only 16 different locations.

The navy made one dramatic mistake in the construction of Ahlhorn. The Ahlhorn airship base was begun in August and September 1915 with the construction of four large double sheds in two parallel pairs standing in two directions. A third group of two parallel double sheds was completed in April and July 1918. The headquarters of the Naval Airship Division moved to Ahlhorn on July 25, 1917. At 5:25 P.M. on January 5, 1918, two soldiers were cleaning L 51 when they noticed a fire. It soon engulfed the entire airship. The explosion of L 51 detonated L 47, which was in the same shed. The explosions from these two airships threw burning wreckage into the shed standing parallel, which ignited and destroyed L 58. Hot debris, blown over 600 meters in all directions, set fire to the second group of sheds, which caused L 46 and SL 20 to explode. During the chain reaction, five airships, most of them the latest versions, were lost within moments. Four huge double sheds were totally destroyed, 14 men killed, and 156 men injured.[11]

2.10. The parallel navy sheds at Ahlhorn were destroyed by explosion and fire on January 5, 1918. The fire destroyed four large sheds and five airships. (Luftschiff Zeppelin Collection, John Provan)

2.11. The remains of sheds number 1 and 2 at Ahlhorn, January 5, 1918. (Luftschiff
Zeppelin Collection, John Provan)

Two errors had occurred at Ahlhorn: First, because double sheds were more
cost effective, the navy had failed to realize that in the event of attack or mishap,
two airships would be lost simultaneously. Second, by building these sheds parallel and too close to one another, the entire group of buildings had been placed
in danger. The disaster at Ahlhorn, the loss of five airships during a raid against
England on October 19, 1917, and later the loss of Captain Peter Strasser (the
strong-willed commander of the Naval Airship Division) on board L 70 during a
raid on August 5–6, 1918, brought an end to the effective use of airships in
World War I.

Architectural deficiencies in airship sheds also hampered the airship services
and contributed to the end of the airship as a weapon in World War I. The architectural problems associated with building these airship sheds were unique.
Considerations of cost-effectiveness and speedy construction, as well as lack of
experience, led to several mistakes. The fundamental architectural problem in
designing airship sheds is the necessity to span large areas without central supports, resulting in a building capable of sustaining not only its own structural
weight but also the weight of snow and one or even two empty airships during
winter. It must also have the ability to withstand wind forces during storms. The

small wooden shed for nonrigids in München, built in 1910, collapsed under the weight of snow in the winter of 1912.[12] The shed in Leipzig, built in 1913 as a DELAG shed and capable of housing two airships, experienced a similar fate. The Schütte-Lanz company obtained use of the shed in mid-March 1915 and built six airships there: SL 6, SL 8, SL 9, SL 11, SL 13, and SL 16. SL 13 had only recently been completed but was returned for modifications to the Leipzig shed, and SL 18 was placed in the second bay, still under construction. Apparently a heavy snow caused an arch to collapse on January 8, 1917, at about 1:00 P.M., which ignited SL 13 and totally destroyed both airships and the shed. In a study completed by the Seibert company, the apparent cause of the mishap was the weak arch, which could not support the combined weight of airships and snow.[13]

The winter months were a severe test of these structures. The gas bags of the airships were often removed during repair because military and passenger operations were hampered by weather conditions anyway. Although blocks supported the airships from underneath, without their inflated gas cells they would collapse under their own weight. Airships, therefore, had to be hung from the ceilings of the sheds for additional support. This was a tremendous weight for any arch to sustain, especially combined with the snow load that accumulated during the winter months. Crews were often sent on top of the shed roofs to

2.12. The Leipzig shed collapsed under the weight of snow in January 1917. (Luftschiff Zeppelin Collection, John Provan)

sweep the snow off, and there were instances when workers fell off and were killed.

Structural engineers had little experience with the problems of airship sheds. Friedrich Ritter von Loessel in 1896 wrote the earliest publication on wind-stress factors, "Die Luftwiderstandgesetze, der Halle durch die Luft und der Vogelflug." The wind-stress factors to which these buildings were exposed were only partially studied or understood. The form of airship sheds was quite different from anything that had been built to date. Train stations, for example, were long, wide, basically flat structures on which the wind had relatively little effect. The height of airship sheds, along with their large, flat wall surfaces, presented a totally new dilemma. Gustave Eiffel wrote the first detailed study of the effects of wind on airship sheds in his book *Nouvelles recherches sur la résistance de l'air et l'aviation faites au laboratoire d'Auteuil (New Experiments on Wind Resistance and Flight),* published in 1914 and translated into German the same year. Eiffel used the French airship shed in Belfort and the German shed in Hamburg as the basis for his study and demonstrated, using models and the laboratory wind tunnel in Auteuil, the effects of wind on an airship shed structure. Eiffel confirmed that it was not only the wind force against a surface that caused the stress on sheds. Rather it was the vacuum effect caused by wind flowing over a large surface and creating almost twice the amount of pressure as the direct force of the wind alone.[14] The north shed and ring shed at Staaken were heavily damaged by a storm on December 18, 1921, because of these forces.[15]

The doors of airship sheds can be generally considered separate structures. Although they are often attached to the building by supports or rails, their size and mobility made them separate entities. The development of shed doors proceeded hand in hand with that of the sheds themselves. Sailcloth doors were often used during the first and second periods of shed construction. This simple solution proved impractical because storms often tore these doors off the buildings. A wind of 25 meters per second creates a stress of 70,000 kilograms on an average door of 900 square meters. Several sheds had cloth doors, for example, at Biesdorf, Bitterfeld, Brussels-Evere, Kiel, Leichlingen, München, Mannheim-Rheinau, and Wanne, while regular doors replaced cloth doors at such locations as Düsseldorf, Johannisthal, and Gotha. (Liegnitz temporarily used a sailcloth door and a section of a former tent shed so that LZ 19 could be part of the Kaiser maneuvers in 1913, but the shed was completed according to plan thereafter.) Most of the above-mentioned sheds were for small, nonrigid airships, and the large sheds replaced these cloth doors soon after completion.

Large, steel-door structures prevailed as entrance coverings for sheds, but with several variations in design. During the second, third, and fourth periods of shed construction, experiments were undertaken. The sheds at Allenstein, Baden Oos, and Frankfurt had hinged doors and functioned like any regular house door. Sliding doors that fit into the side of the shed replaced the cloth door on the Düsseldorf city shed. Folding doors were used in Köln and in the revolving shed at Nordholz. The practical solution was doors on rails, usually with side supports, which rolled open sideways. This solution may have been architecturally simple, but the doors created aerodynamic problems that hampered the safe operation of airships. Flat doors were moving structures with massive weights or side supports to prevent mishaps from strong winds, and they required strong electric motors to operate them. These doors caused wind turbulence in front of the shed, where tranquil conditions were desired to ensure the safe maneuvering of airships. [16]

Clamshell doors, the apparent answer, were used in Dresden, while Liegnitz and Posen had combination clamshell and sailcloth doors. Clamshell doors had the advantage, when open, of not causing wind turbulence, as did flat doors, making the handling of airships much easier. Clamshell doors were used exclusively during the fifth and final building period of airship sheds.

Wind screens were experimental attempts to decrease air turbulence in front of shed entrances. The first consideration of such screens can be found in the original plans for the Schütte-Lanz tent shed built in Mannheim-Rheinau, which envisioned four tents standing directly next to one another, with several wind screens forming a courtyard in front. These plans were never completed. One such wind screen, basically a large wall in front of the opening, was built at the Düsseldorf city shed and led to the destruction of LZ 8, *Deutschland,* on May 16, 1911. [17] A wind screen was also built onto the large double shed, Normann, in Nordholz, but no other information about it exists, and apparently it did not remain standing for long. As it resulted, these wind screens created more wind turbulence rather than less, and they were discontinued. The British used screens at most of their shed locations during World War I and also experienced extensive problems with them.

The walls of airship sheds were generally made of asbestos or sheets of thin concrete. Cement blocks covered the floors. Natural lighting was provided through wire-reinforced glass windows, tinted yellow on the roof to prevent ultraviolet light from overheating the gas cells. Clear glass was used on the sides of the sheds. Electric lighting was also provided, but there was no heating within the shed. A reasonably constant temperature was maintained inside a shed by using these building materials, which had some heat-insulating qualities.

Rigid-airship sheds, because of their huge size, naturally provided enemy aircraft with easy targets, and several attacks were made at various locations. The Germans stationed antiaircraft guns or fighter aircraft at shed locations to furnish some protection from attacks. Several interesting attempts were made at camouflaging these structures. In the case of Darmstadt, fake trees were erected and a forest painted on the sides of the building. In other cases, such as at Hannover and Mannheim, sheds were painted to make it appear as if roads or paths extended over the sheds. During World War II, the Friedrichshafen sheds were used for the V-1 and V-2 rocket programs, and they were painted so that they blended into the surrounding landscape. But the sheer size of rigid-airship sheds made any attempt at camouflaging useless.[18]

The German airship program encountered several logistical problems, which have been previously addressed. The demand for a proper number of sheds of the right size and located in the proper places was naturally the main concern. The logistical obstacle of transporting construction material to shed sites was generally solved by the nearby rail lines. The requirement of landing crews at a shed intended for use also brought forth certain problems in troop transport, housing, and supply.

The main logistical concern during World War I was supplying hydrogen gas, the demand for which reached monumental proportions. The dramatic increase in airship size, maximum altitude, and number of flights resulted in the need to

2.13. A road and trees were painted on the doors of the Darmstadt shed for camouflage. (Luftschiff Zeppelin Collection, John Provan)

augment the gas supply. In the period before World War I, several airship sheds were situated near hydrogen gas production plants. An underground pipeline from the nearby Griesheim-Elektron Chemical Company supplied gas to the Frankfurt Rebstock shed. Bitterfeld was also located next to a chemical factory. At the outbreak of World War I, the navy operated no hydrogen gas plants and obtained most of its hydrogen from the oil chemical company Germania, in Emmerich. Six naval plants producing a total of 160,000 cubic meters of hydrogen gas daily were operating by 1918. The naval headquarters at Hamburg had 2,000 gas bottles, capable of storing 5 cubic meters each, at the beginning of the conflict. At the point of greatest operation, early 1916, the military had 36,000 gas bottles with a total storage volume of 200,000 cubic meters and six gas storage facilities capable of holding 650,000 cubic meters of hydrogen.

In some cases, it was not only the production, but the storage compression, that presented the problems. In Ahlhorn, during 1916, gas production reached 30,000 cubic meters daily, and storage facilities could hold 125,000 cubic meters, but the compressors could only handle 12,000 cubic meters per day. Therefore, it required 10 days to fill all the high-pressure storage cylinders. After the raid on September 24–25, 1917, six airships returned to Ahlhorn and required over 170,000 cubic meters of gas, emptying the storage facility and 40 tank cars brought in from Staaken. Another raid would not have been possible for days, until the storage facilities could be replenished. Strasser informed Adm. Reinhardt Scheer that Operation Albion required all gas tank cars to supply gas for the six participating airships, warning him that it still might be impossible to send more than three airships on scouting missions over the North Sea on a single day. Due to the gas shortage, airship raids against England were out of the question.

The army usually built small gas plants, capable of producing 1,000 to 4,000 cubic meters daily. These small plants were not as cost effective as the larger plants.[19]

On June 28, 1912, while the airship *Schwaben* was being refueled, a fire broke out and destroyed it. The rubber material used for gas cells tended to create static electricity, which, when the flammable hydrogen leaked and a spark occurred, caused an explosion. A solution was found by using *Goldschläger-haut* (gold beaters' skin), the membrane covering part of the large intestines of cows, to produce the gas bags for rigid airships. Approximately 700,000 cow stomachs were required per airship. The membranes were cleaned, glued together, and reinforced by a thin cloth lining. These gas cells required constant repair and gas tended to escape. The amount of gas an airship lost daily depended on the condition of the gas cells, the functioning of gas valves, and the temperature inside the shed.[20] A 24,000-cubic-meter airship, flying 125 days each year (at only 320 meters altitude), required a minimum of 4 percent hydrogen refill per flight, and with temperature influences another 3 percent, or 210,000 cubic meters of hydrogen yearly. With a loss of 2 percent per day for another 125 days, such an airship consumed another 60,000 cubic meters annually. Each airship was repaired during the winter months and refilled thereafter, requiring another 24,000 cubic meters of hydrogen, bringing the total gas requirement for one airship to 294,000 cubic meters annually, not considering major raids on England and even larger airship designs.[21]

The Germans always filled their airships 99- to 100-percent full, reasoning that it was better to have gas escape rather than have air enter the gas bags and create the explosive mixture known as Knall gas. Maintaining the gas supply of airships at 100 percent required replenishing, or topping off, the gas cells on a daily basis.

The predicament with gas production was a problem not only of quantity but also of supplying the proper amounts to each location when required. There was often a great distance between the production location and a shed with a waiting airship. A steady supply of hydrogen for each airship was critical, and hydrogen loss occurred during regular operating flights, when supplying reconnaissance information, when securing shipping routes, and during the long raids against England.

An airship filled to its maximum capacity could carry a maximum bomb load. The combination of burned-off fuel, the release of bombs, and the race for altitude to elude enemy attack meant a massive loss of hydrogen gas. Because rigid airships have no ballonet to accommodate the expanding hydrogen gas, it had to be valved off. Therefore, we find a few instances of airships returning with half their gas valved.

The development of airships witnessed an increase not only in size, but also in gas loss. For example, LZ 41 (L 11) had a total volume of 31,900 cubic meters and lost 10,000 cubic meters of gas on a raid in June 1915, or one-third its volume. In October 1917, LZ 80 (L 35), which had a total volume of 55,200 cubic meters, lost 31,500 cubic meters during one raid against England. In other words, the size of the airships had doubled, but the gas loss per flight had tripled.

The so-called Feld Luftschiffer Trupps (Field Airship Detachments), later known as balloon sections, and Festungsluftschiffern (Fortification Observation Balloon Sections) created another dimension to the gas production dilemma. Hydrogen gas was required not only by the large rigids, and to a much smaller degree by the semirigid and nonrigid airships, but also by the Field Airship Detachments, which operated kite observation balloons during World War I. In August 1914, the army operated 10 Feld Luftschiffer Trupps; in 1915, 40; and in 1918, 56 *Trupps* and 184 balloon sections. Each balloon *Trupp* or section operated one (and at least one spare) kite balloon. These kite balloons required between 800 and 1,200 cubic meters of hydrogen gas for inflation, which occurred almost daily. Mobile field gas plants were built on railway cars and placed in operation by early 1918. These plants could produce between 1,200 and 1,500 cubic meters of gas daily, but that still meant that for the better part of the war, gas supplies had to be diverted from the rigid-airship program.

The transport of 132-pound compressed hydrogen cylinders was extremely laborious, so rail tank cars were built, which shipped the hydrogen gas in bulk under pressure to required locations. Four different types of rail cars were built during the war: 20 Type I rail tank cars with three cylinders were constructed, capable of carrying 1,550 cubic meters each; 151 Type II rail cars with two cylinders, capable of holding 1,920 cubic meters each; 10 Type III rail cars (with six cylinders each); and 60 Type IV rail cars (with fourteen cylinders each) ca-

2.14. *Hindenburg* (LZ 129) leaving the shed at Rhein-Main. The size of airships and their sheds presented engineering and construction problems that were never fully overcome. (Luftschiff Zeppelin Collection, John Provan)

pable of transporting 2,560 cubic meters each. These 241 railroad cars had a total capacity of 510,000 cubic meters and transported hydrogen from gas plants that had a surplus to distant locations. The gas plant at Seddin required 75 tank cars to ship hydrogen to bases at Seerappen and Wainoden. Forty tank cars brought gas from Staaken to the big Ahlhorn base, and another 50 tank cars brought gas from the closed-down base at Hage to Wittmund. A returning airship had to be directed to a location that could also refill the hydrogen gas, but if an airship was damaged or running low on fuel, the nearest shed location became a more important factor.[22]

After World War I, the sheds built in the fifth shed-construction period solved the hydrogen gas problem by providing gas facilities nearby. Rhein-Main received an underground pipeline from the Hoechst Chemical Company that provided hydrogen for passenger airships, and Friedrichshafen and Santa Cruz each had their own gas plants.

Tables 1–3 illustrate the extent of construction undertaken as part of the airship program.[23] According to Table 3, the army owned 36 percent of all sheds and the navy 31 percent, while only 13 percent were city owned, and 20 percent were used for construction of airships. An important fact is that of the 107 sheds built, only 14 were for nonrigid airships, and most of these were constructed before 1909–10.

As remarkable as it may seem, several German airship sheds remain standing. The Treaty of Versailles allowed German airship sheds to be rebuilt to a smaller size and converted for other proposes. The sheds that once stood in Wainoden are today the five market halls standing in Riga; part of one shed from Brussels is standing in Varel as a paper factory; portions of the Allenstein shed are standing in Darmstadt and used for storage; and part of the Baden Oos shed is used as a sawmill in Richtberg/Auggen. The shed in Seddin was spared destruction after World War I so it could be used by the Italian General Umberto Nobile for his attempted airship flight to the North Pole, and it exists today. The shed in Santa Cruz, built shortly before World War II, also remains standing and is used by the Brazilian air force as a hangar.[24]

It is interesting to note that the planning for rigid airship shed locations laid the foundation for many German airports that followed. Airplanes already played a role at Johannisthal, for example, but if we review the list of airship shed locations, we find many airports operating from the same grounds. Military air bases still operate at Ahlhorn, Lahr, Metz, Nordholz, Tegel, and Wittmund. Municipal airports can be found in Baden Oos, Löwenthal, and Leipzig; and Düsseldorf, Frankfurt, and Hamburg have emerged as large international

Table 1
German Airship Sheds Built in Germany

	Location	Year	Length (meters)	Width (meters)	Height (meters)	Construction Company
1	Ahlhorn I	1916	241	60	35	Güte-Hoffnungs-Huette
2	Ahlhorn II	1916	241	60	35	Güte-Hoffnungs-Huette
3	Ahlhorn III	1916	241	60	35	Hein-Lehmann Co.
4	Ahlhorn IV	1916	241	60	35	Zeppelin Hallen-bau Co.
5	Ahlhorn V	1917	260	75	36	Güte-Hoffnungs-Huette
6	Ahlhorn VI	1917	260	75	36	Güte-Hoffnungs-Huette
7	Allenstein	1914	191	35	28	
8	Baden Oos	1910	160	25	24	M.A.N.
9	Biesdorf (Berlin)	1910	135	25	25	Steffens & Noelle Co.
10	Bitterfeld I	1908	70	25	25	
11	Bitterfeld II	1910	160	35	25	Arthur Müller Co.
12	Darmstadt	1914	184	35	28	Seibert GmbH
13	Dresden (city)	1913	192	58	35	Zeppelin Hallen-bau Co.
14	Dresden II	1915	184	35	28	Zeppelin Hallen-bau Co.
15	Düren	1915	180	30	28	Ermus Co.
16	Düsseldorf (city)	1910	160	26	24	Stephan Elliesen Co.
17	Düsseldorf II	1914	184	35	28	Zeppelin Hallen-bau Co.
18	Düsseldorf III	1916	240	60	35	Zeppelin Hallen-bau Co.
19	Düsseldorf IV	—	232	40	35	M.A.N. (not completed)
20	Frankfurt (ILA)	1909	147	21	21	
21	Frankfurt (ILA)	1909	30	15	25	Arthur Müller Co.
22	Frankfurt (ILA)	1909	40	13	15	Arthur Müller Co.

(Continued)

Table 1 (*Continued*)

	Location	Year	Length (meters)	Width (meters)	Height (meters)	Construction Company
23	Frankfurt (ILA)	1909	62	45	20	Arthur Müller Co.
24	Frankfurt (Rebstock)	1910	160	30	25	Güte-Hoffnungs-Huette
25	Frankfurt (Rhein-Main)	1936	275	52	51	Seibert GmbH
26	Frankfurt (Rhein-Main)	1938	300	55	60	Seibert GmbH
27	Friedrichshafen I (Manzell)	1899	150	16	16	Hangleiter Co.
28	Friedrichshafen II	1905	140	26	25	
29	Friedrichshafen III	1907	150	25	23	Albert Buss & Cie Co.
30	Friedrichshafen (tent shed)	1909	141	20	19	L. Stromeyer & Co.
31	Friedrichshafen I	1909	178	46	25	Flender AG
32	Friedrichshafen II	1914	200	35	28	Zeppelin Hallen-bau Co.
33	Friedrichshafen III	1915	235	40	35	Zeppelin Hallen-bau Co.
34	Friedrichshafen IV	1930	250	50	46	Güte-Hoffnungs-Huette
35	Friedrichshafen (ring shed)	1936	270	50	—	Steel Works, Kaisers.
36	Friedrichshafen (Löwenthal)	1914	232	35	28	Zeppelin Hallen-bau Co.
37	Friedrichshafen (Löwenthal)	1931	270	46	49	Seibert GmbH
38	Gotha	1910	175	26	28	Stephan Elliesen Co.
39	Hage I	1915	180	34	28	Arthur Müller Co.
40	Hage II	1915	180	34	28	Arthur Müller Co.
41	Hage III	1915	180	34	28	Arthur Müller Co.
42	Hage IV	1915	180	34	28	Arthur Müller Co.
43	Hamburg	1911	160	45	26	H. C. E. Eggers & Co.

(*Continued*)

Table 1 (*Continued*)

Location	Year	Length (meters)	Width (meters)	Height (meters)	Construction Company
44 Hannover	1915	184	35	28	Zeppelin Hallen-bau Co.
45 Johannisthal I	1910	83	25	25	
46 Johannisthal II	1911	163	45	29	Arthur Müller Co.
47 Jüterbog I	1915	184	35	28	Zeppelin Hallen-bau Co.
48 Jüterbog II	1916	240	60	35	Seibert GmbH
49 Kiel	1911	170	25	25	Hans Luehmann & H. Co.
50 Köln-Bickendorf	1909	190	40	25	Gustavsburg Co.
51 Köln-Nippes	1909	40	16	13	
52 Königsberg	1912	180	40	25	Seibert GmbH
53 Lahr	1915	184	35	28	Seibert GmbH
54 Leichlingen	1909	80	23	24	
55 Leipzig	1913	184	60	29	Seibert GmbH
56 Liegnitz	1913	170	36	28	
57 Mannheim-Rheinau I	1909	137	26	25	v.May & Wer-kenthin Co.
58 Mannheim-Rheinau II	1914	200	35	28	M.A.N.
59 Mannheim-Sandhofen	1914	184	35	28	Zeppelin Hallen-bau Co.
60 Metz	1909	150	40	25	L. Bernhard Co.
61 München	1910	80	25	25	Ballonhallen GmbH
62 Nordholz I	1914	200	70	30	Steffens & Noelle
63 Nordholz II	1915	184	35	28	Zeppelin Hallen-bau Co.
64 Nordholz III	1915	184	35	28	Zeppelin Hallen-bau Co.
65 Nordholz IV	1916	244	60	35	M.A.N.
66 Nordholz V	1917	260	75	36	Güte-Hoffnungs-Huette
67 Nordholz VI	1917	260	75	36	Güte-Hoffnungs-Huette
68 Posen	1913	170	36	28	Arthur Müller Co.
69 Potsdam	1912	180	50	25	M.A.N.

(*Continued*)

Table 1 (*Continued*)

	Location	Year	Length (meters)	Width (meters)	Height (meters)	Construction Company
70	Reinickendorf I (Tegel)	1906	70	26	22	
71	Reinickendorf II	1907	70	16	25	v.May & Werkenthin Co.
72	Reinickendorf III	1909	100	25	25	L. Bernhard Co.
73	Schneidemuehl	1915	184	35	28	Zeppelin Hallenbau Co.
74	Seddin I	1915	184	35	28	Zeppelin Hallenbau Co.
75	Seddin II	1916	241	60	35	Güte-Hoffnungs-Huette
76	Seerappen	1916	240	60	35	Zeppelin Hallenbau Co.
77	Spich	1915	184	35	28	Zeppelin Hallenbau Co.
78	Staaken I	1916	240	40	35	Zeppelin Hallenbau Co.
79	Staaken II	1916	240	40	35	Zeppelin Hallenbau Co.
80	Strasbourg	1911	85	25	24	Seibert GmbH
81	Thorn	1911	101	25	23	J. Gollnow & Sohn
82	Tondern I	1915	180	34	28	Arthur Müller Co.
83	Tondern II	1915	180	34	28	Arthur Müller Co.
84	Tondern III	1916	244	60	35	M.A.N.
85	Trier	1914	180	35	28	Seibert GmbH
86	Wainoden I	1916	240	42	35	Seibert GmbH
87	Wainoden II	1916	240	42	35	Seibert GmbH
88	Wanne	1912	87	32	28	unknown
89	Wildeshausen	1916	240	40	35	M.A.N.
90	Wittmund I	1916	240	60	35	Zeppelin Hallenbau Co.
91	Wittmund II	1916	240	60	35	Seibert GmbH
92	Zeesen	1916	240	40	35	M.A.N.
93	Zülpich	1915	180	30	28	(not completed)

airports. The airship shed program provided Germany with 12 locations in all that are still associated with aviation.

The problems of airship shed location, construction, and operation led to many architectural and logistical dilemmas that were solved in numerous ways over the years. The solutions are important not only to a better understanding of the conditions under which rigid airships operated in the past, but also for future undertakings. Any rebirth of lighter-than-air flight, especially in Germany, which has no remaining large airship sheds, will encounter and have to resolve the same problems considered here.

Table 2
German Airship Sheds Built in Other Countries

	Location	Year	Length (meters)	Width (meters)	Height (meters)	Construction Company
94	Brussels-St. Agathe	1915	180	34	22	Arthur Müller Co.
95	Brussels-Etterbeck	1914	170	34	23	tent shed?
96	Brussels-Evere	1915	180	34	22	Arthur Müller Co.
97	Brussels-Gontrode	1915	180	34	22	Arthur Müller Co.
98	Jamboli (Bulgaria)	1916	240	42	35	Seibert GmbH
99	Kovno	1917	240	42	35	Seibert GmbH
100	Maubeuge (France)	1915	170	40	32	section added, M.A.N.
101	Namur I (France)	1915	180	28	30	Ermus Co.
102	Namur II (France)	1915	180	32	30	Ermus Co.
103	Namur III (France)	1915	180	32	30	Ermus Co.
104	Santa Cruz (Brazil)	1936	270	60	54	Güte Hoffnungs Huette
105	Schaulen (Lettland)	1917	180	30	30	Seibert GmbH[a]
106	Temesvar (Romania)	1915	180	30	30	Seibert GmbH
107	Warsaw (Poland)	1915	180	30	30	Seibert GmbH

[a] transportable shed, formerly standing in Warsaw, moved only once.

Table 3
Major Construction Companies of Sheds

	Number Sheds Built
Arthur Müller Ballonhallenbau, Charlottenburg, Berlin	15
Eggers & Co., Hamburg	1
Ermus, Deutsche Luftschiff-Hallenbau Ges., Berlin	4
Hein Lehmann & Co., Düsseldorf	1
Güte Hoffnungs Huette, Oberhausen, Werk Sterkerade	10
M.A.N., Maschinenfabrik Augsburg-Nürnberg, Werk Gustavburg	9
Steffen & Noelle, Berlin	2
Seibert GmbH, Saarbrücken	18
Stephan, Elliesen & Michaelis, Hamburg	2
Zeppelin Hallenbau Gesellschaft, Berlin	20
Other	13
Unknown	12
	Total 107

Army airship sheds: 7, 8, 9, 12, 13, 14, 17, 18, 19, 24, 30, 36, 38, 44, 46, 50, 52, 53, 55, 56, 58, 59, 60, 68, 69, 71, 72, 73, 77, 80, 81, 85, 93, 94, 95, 96, 97, 98, 99, 100, 105, 106, 107
   Note: Two of these sheds were not completed.
Navy airship sheds: 1, 2, 3, 4, 5, 6, 13, 15, 39, 40, 41, 42, 43, 47, 48, 49, 62, 63, 64, 65, 66, 67, 74, 75, 76, 82, 83, 84, 86, 87, 89, 90, 91, 98, 101, 102, 103
Private city sheds: 8, 13, 16, 24, 25, 26, 38, 43, 49, 50, 54, 55, 61, 68, 69
Construction company sheds: 9, 10, 11, 12, 24, 27, 28, 29, 31, 32, 33, 34, 35, 36, 51, 55, 57, 58, 59, 69, 70, 78, 79, 92

NOTES

1. Wolfgang Friebe, *Buildings of the World Exhibitions* (Magdeburg: Druckerei Volksstimme, 1985).

2. Friedrich Stahl, "Die Deutsche Luftschiffhallen," *Luftfahrt* 24: 375–77 and 2: 21–24.

3. W. J. Watson, "Airship Factory and Dock of the Goodyear Zeppelin Corp.," *Aeronautical Engineering* 4 (Oct./Dec. 1932): 191–201.

4. G. Christians, *Anlage und Betrieb von Luftschiffhäfen* (Berlin: Verlag von R. Oldenbourg, 1914), 28–29.

5. Ibid., 27–28.

6. Emil Eli, *Inden Gaerten pranen Kaiserblumen* (Moritz Schavenburg: GmbH Lahr, 1980), 43–52.

7. Christians, *Anlage,* 15–26.

8. O. Leitholf, *In Der Bauingenieur* (Berlin, 1923), 581–83; Günter Schmitt, *Luftschiffe über Biesdorf* (Marzahn: Holga Wenda Druckerei, 1990).

9. Kurt Puzicha, *Marine Luftschiffer Kameradschaft,* Heft 3 (1981).

10. O. Krell, "Zeitschrift für Flugtechnik: Motorluftschiffahrt," Sept. 28, 1928, as mentioned in Douglas H. Robinson, *Giants in the Sky: A History of the Rigid Airship* (Seattle: University of Washington Press, 1971), 121. Although Robinson also mentions Graudenz and Dresden as proposed sites for revolving sheds, I have never located information on these.

11. Puzicha, *Marine Luftschiffer Kameradschaft,* Heft 1 (1988); Dr. Gebauer, "Der Marineluftschiffhafen Ahlhorn und sein Untergang am 5. Januar 1918," *Luftfahrt* 4 (1928): 50–52.

12. *Jahrbuch des Deutschen Luftfahrer Verband,* 1912.

13. Seibert Company, "Gutachten über den Einsturz der Leipziger Luftschiffhalle." N.d. Located in the private collection of Edmund Sedelmayer.

14. Gustave Eiffel, *Neue Untersuchungen über den Luftwiederstand und den Flug,* 1914.

15. R. Sonntag, "Windsaugwirkungen am Dach der Luftschiffhalle 'Nord' in Staaken" (publisher and date of article unknown).

16. Christians, *Anlage,* 118–24.

17. Robinson, *Giants,* 58.

18. This information was taken from photos in my collection, which demonstrate the attempts of camouflaging airship sheds.

19. Douglas H. Robinson, *The Zeppelin in Combat: A History of the German Naval Airship Division, 1912–1918* (London: G. T. Foulis, 1962), 256–59; and Douglas H. Robinson, "Hydrogen for German Airships in World War I," n.d.

20. Robinson, *Giants,* 355–56.

21. Christians, *Anlage,* 11–14.

22. Ibid., 19.

23. Information in these tables is from Stahl, "Die Deutsche Luftschiffhallen," *Luftfahrt* 24: 375–77 and 2: 21–24; and my collections.

24. Puzicha, *Marine Luftschiffer Kameradschaft,* Heft 3 (1981).

 Alexandre Herlea

The First Transcontinental Airline

Franco-Roumaine, 1920–1925

This chapter deals with the Compagnie Franco-Roumaine de Navigation Aérienne (CFRNA), known more commonly by its abbreviated name, Franco-Roumaine. Created in April 1920, the airline remained in operation until January 1, 1925. Tracing the history of this important French company, which opened the first transcontinental air route in Europe and the world, makes an interesting case study of the creation and development of early European air carriers. This exposition will deal with the general and specific characteristics of Franco-Roumaine, notably how technical, economic, political, and legal factors affected the company and its achievements. This is not meant to be an extended analytical treatment of the company and its history; rather it is intended only as a brief factual survey.

The opening of an air route following World War I reflected the prevailing attitude of sporty achievement and risk-taking that characterized the beginning of aviation. The level of technology in the early 1920s was such that it was almost impossible to establish an air transport operation as a profitable activity. Franco-Roumaine overcame this problem by making subsidy agreements with the French government and the different countries it planned to serve. From the beginning, Franco-Roumaine distinguished itself from other early carriers by

(1) A substantial amount of capital, a large portion of which was of foreign origin. This gave the company operating reserves and gave it a multinational character. In some ways, Franco-Roumaine can be thought of as one of the world's first multinational companies. (2) The acquisition of the best equipment, in which quality was the only consideration. Frequently, early air carriers obtained their equipment from their own airplane factories, and their airplanes did not always meet the highest standards. Such was not the case with Franco-Roumaine. (3) The introduction of the world's first scheduled night flights. (4) Ensuring that countries served by Franco-Roumaine were active participants in the company by using native technicians and local facilities.

At the same time, Franco-Roumaine, like other airlines, was dependent on the development of aeronautical technology (airplanes, engines, navigation and communication instruments, ground installations, runway lights, and so forth), on the economic situation facing the aeronautical industry following the war, on political decisions, and on changing national and international airline and aviation legislation.

At the end of World War I, the former belligerent countries possessed not only an important air industry, but also large numbers of surplus airplanes suitable for future conversion to commercial air transportation. The opening of the first airlines and the organization of the first national and international companies dates from this period.

France was actively involved in the nascent industry. She was the first to try to put into action an effective aeronautical policy oriented toward boosting the development of commercial aviation. The key early figure was Pierre-Etienne Flandin, who, while assistant secretary of state for aeronautics from January 1920 to February 1921, initiated a policy of aviation development that was oriented as much to commercial aviation as it was to the military. Flowing from his office was a steady stream of public orders and technical decisions that affected commercial and military aviation. By carefully managing credit arrangements, he laid the foundation for the postwar rebirth of markets and firms. In addition, Flandin initiated the liquidation of aircraft manufacturing stocks, extended his authority to the army, and subsidized manufacturing companies that were developing new aircraft especially adapted for commercial transport. Flandin also played an important part in drawing up the Convention Internationale de la Navigation Aérienne (CINA).

To get an idea of the French aeronautical industry's situation and the level of subsidy, one should note that the purchasing credit of the industry went from 160 million francs in 1921 to 300 million francs in 1925, while subsidies increased from 28 million francs in 1921 to 48 million francs in 1925. Numerous prototypes of commercial transport aircraft appeared between 1920 and 1923, and orders for mass production came afterward (more than 3,000 airplanes and engines were delivered from 1921 to 1923). France viewed aviation as an important part of economic development and a means of extending its political and diplomatic influence in the new postwar world. National policy considered it imperative to support such new countries as Poland, Czechoslovakia, and Romania, created after the dismemberment of Austria-Hungary and now menaced by Soviet Bolshevism.

Against this background, Franco-Roumaine, the eighth airline company in France, was created through the initiative of the Romanian minister of foreign affairs, Nicolas Titulescu, who presented the idea at the Trianon Peace Conference on June 4, 1920, the signing of the peace treaty with Romania. Most notably, Titulescu affirmed that aviation, which was an instrument of war, ought to transform itself into an instrument of peace and become a new and highly profitable means of transportation and communication.

The idea coalesced as the result of the work of the director of the Romanian Banque Marmorosh, Aristide Blank, who accompanied Titulescu to the peace conference, and a young French lieutenant, Pierre de Fleurieu, who, after serving in aviation during the war, was demobilized and hired by Banque Marmorosh's Parisian subsidiary. At the end of 1919, Fleurieu received an assignment from Blank to study the possibility of creating an airline linking Paris and Bucharest. This route had considerable political interest because it would help connect France to Romania and to the countries of the Petite Entente. Therefore, the diplomatic and military dimensions were as important as the economic possibilities of such an airline.

Aristide Blank committed himself to the project as it was set forth in March 1920 by providing 2.5 million francs. At the same time, Flandin, as assistant secretary of state for aeronautics, promised to have subsidies cover the line's deficit (thereby following traditional policy). As an interim measure, he facilitated the acquisition of airplanes from the army for starting the service while arrangements were made for the delivery of aircraft better adapted for passenger transport.

The Compagnie Franco-Roumaine de Navigation Aérienne was chartered on April 23, 1920. Fleurieu was the director-general of the company; General Maurice Duval (former chief of military aeronautics) was president of the administrative council; Paul Hermant became the commercial director; and Albert Deullin was the chief pilot. The first survey flight, which provided experimental verification of the project, took place that same month with a Potez 7 piloted by Deullin. Fleurieu accompanied him as a passenger.

The inaugural route was to be Paris-Strasbourg-Prague-Warsaw. Negotiations opened in Prague for the acquisition of landing rights, the organization of local administrative services and airplane maintenance and repair, and establishing the legal formalities covering the entry and exit of air cargo. These negotiations resulted in a 10-year monopoly granted by the Czech government and an annual subsidy of five million crowns. Poland granted ground installations and a subsidy in the form of supplying free fuel equal to an annual sum of one million francs. The French government had an additional stake in the new line, because it wanted official mail to reach Prague and Warsaw without running the risk of its being intercepted and read by German dispatchers.

On September 20, the Paris-Strasbourg stretch was officially opened. Flights were on a daily basis; the time of departure was 2:30 P.M.; and the price for a round-trip ticket was 2,400 francs. On October 4, the Strasbourg-Prague route was inaugurated with three flights weekly, followed later by daily departures. Because of generally poor winter weather conditions, flights were to be reduced in November and suspended in December.

In 1920, Franco-Roumaine transported 70 passengers, more than 500 kilograms of freight, and 70 kilograms of mail. Although the volume was low, the line's viability was sufficiently demonstrated.

At the end of November, the company had acquired 31 airplanes (out of 185 in the French airline fleet). The first airplanes were Salmson 2A2s equipped with 260-horsepower nine-cylinder Salmson Caton-Unne Z 9 engines. They had a cruising speed of 130 kilometers per hour at 2,000 meters altitude. The airplane carried 258 kilograms of cargo and had a maximum flying time of three hours. The Potez 7 airplanes were ready for service in July. They were equipped with twelve-cylinder V-type Lorraine-Dietrich 12 Da engines producing 370 horsepower and had a cruising speed of 180 kilometers per hour, a range of 500 kilometers, and a cargo capacity of 330 kilograms. The Potez was a much more comfortable airplane than the Salmson, which continued to serve the less-traveled Strasbourg-Prague leg of the route. About half the airplanes were converted from military specifications. Franco-Roumaine recruited 15 pilots between May and November 1920. Until January 1, 1921, the military aviator's certificate was still recognized, and the pilots did not have to obtain special commercial licenses.

The company's financial situation at this time was poor. It survived only by subsidies and grants from the state. These handouts to support airline companies were divided into those covering wear and upkeep (the value of aircraft depreciated and maintenance costs increased after 200 hours of flight), equipment (a function of distance traveled and the power of the engine), transport (a function of cargo and speed at 2,000 meters altitude), and the military (the company recognized that it might have to provide airlift for the army). In 1920, Franco-Roumaine's income was 366,000 francs, of which 347,800 francs were subsidies. The company's debt ran at about 30 percent of its total assets.

The company's financial position improved in January of the following year. On the eleventh, for instance, grants earmarked for the acquisition of new aircraft were modified, and changes were made to certain subsidies, making them retroactive. In addition, the government provided grants for flying over foreign territories. Also in January, the airline hoped to attract additional clientele by setting new, reduced fares: 150 francs from Paris to Strasbourg, 500 francs from Paris to Prague, and 800 francs from Paris to Warsaw. In February, largely as a result of the Franco-Polish treaty of alliance, signed on January 19, the airline opened its Prague-Warsaw line with flights three times weekly. In July, the airline added daily flights to Warsaw. September marked the highest number of kilometers flown (92,800), but that same month the airline suffered its first fatal accident.

Franco-Roumaine also acquired new airplanes, notably the Blériot Spad 33, the Potez 9, and the Blériot Spad 46. The latter two used the same engine, a 370-horsepower Lorraine-Dietrich. In July, the total number of aircraft in the inventory came to 47. These airplanes were expensive, costing from 100,000 to 130,000 francs each, and thus placed a further financial burden on the company. The shareholders covered this with commitments totaling 8,250,000 francs, which brought the company's capitalization to more than 10 million francs. During the year, the company organized maintenance and repair operations at the Paris-Le Bourget, Strasbourg, Prague, and Warsaw airports. Because it was set up to handle the fitting of different types of motors to different airframes, the shop at Le Bourget was particularly important. From both an operational and a financial point of view, Franco-Roumaine became a sounder company in 1921.

Attempts at opening a new leg to Bucharest were another important development in 1921. Despite German competition, agreements were negotiated with Austria (valid for 10 years) and Hungary (valid for 20 years). These understandings provided for a working monopoly and an obligation for these countries to furnish ground installations. Romania, which had already awarded Franco-Roumaine a 20-year concession, also committed itself to planning and maintaining airports and establishing air navigation aids throughout the country. One of the highlights of the year was a flight from Paris to Constantinople by Deullin in a Spad 46 and De Marnier in a Potez 9. During the stopover in Bucharest, an enthusiastic crowd met the two pilots. The level of interest was such that King Ferdinand held an official reception for the aviators on their return flight.

In December, Franco-Roumaine suspended flight operations for the year.

The company at that point had 71 airplanes and 21 pilots. It had flown 607,433 kilometers and transported 2,136 passengers, 43,932 kilograms of air freight, and 2,039 kilograms of mail. For the year, Franco-Roumaine, which theoretically was able to transport 212,601 ton-kilometers, actually carried only 122,463 ton-kilometers, thereby resulting in a meager commercial yield of .57. The company's principal competition was the railroads, rather than foreign airlines.

A by-product of Franco-Roumaine's operations was the creation of a successful commercial aircraft market in eastern Europe. For example, the Czech Skoda works and the Industria Aeronautica Romana (IAR) factories of Brasov, Romania, acquired licenses to manufacture Lorraine-Dietrich engines. These arrangements effectively thwarted British, German, and Italian efforts to establish aviation footholds in these countries and led to a peculiar mission for Franco-Roumaine. The company now represented the interests of the French aviation industry outside France. Fleurieu understood the material and political responsibilities of this situation and created an organization (which still exists today) named the Office General de l'Air to represent of the French aeronautical industry abroad.

The flights resumed in February 1922. On April 14 of that year, Fleurieu signed an agreement regarding the airline's service from Paris to Warsaw. It superseded the previous operating agreement and introduced a new set of requirements. The pact also fixed the minimum number of aircraft in the Franco-Roumaine fleet at 63. But 1922 was, above all, characterized by the establishment of the Constantinople leg of the airline's route structure. The Prague-Vienna-Budapest line opened on May 1, the Budapest-Arad-Bucharest leg on September 15, and the Bucharest-Constantinople route on October 3. Pilot Claude Beauregard in a Spad 46 opened the section to Bucharest, and Louis Guidon carried through with the extension of the route to Constantinople. The entire transcontinental route covered 3,150 kilometers, and four new airports were opened. The Paris, Prague, and Bucharest workshops were equipped and organized for carrying out major overhauls of airplanes and engines. Camille Lepianquais, a mining engineer working for the Spad company, studied and executed the opening of the Bucharest-Constantinople line and organized the Bucharest-Baneasa repair shops.

But the line to Constantinople remained unprofitable, with a low capacity margin and commercial yield of only .27. On the Prague-Warsaw leg, the statistics for 1922 show that Franco-Roumaine aircraft covered 673,000 kilometers and carried 942 passengers, 32,000 kilograms of cargo, and 2,300 kilograms of mail. From May to December, aircraft on the Prague-Constantinople connection flew 163,000 kilometers and carried 232 passengers, 11,700 kilograms of cargo, and 700 kilograms of mail. By the end of the year, Franco-Roumaine had 84 airplanes and 139 engines, and it employed 25 pilots.

For Franco-Roumaine, 1922 was also characterized by numerous failures, adding to the firm's chronic deficit. Financial losses were symptomatic of all airline companies at the time, but Franco-Roumaine's were especially acute because the French government had as much prestige at stake in the firm as it had money. One should also stress the irregular passenger demand on the new routes and the relative lack of air cargo. The used capacity margin or commercial yield on the Bucharest-Constantinople leg was half that of the Paris-Prague line.

The company underwent additional changes in 1923. Despite losses and excess capacity, Franco-Roumaine added a new route from Budapest to Bucharest via Belgrade. There was also a shift in corporate personnel. On May 29, Albert Deullin died and was replaced by Maurice Nogues as chief pilot. On September 20, Jules Bétrand replaced Pierre de Fleurieu as director-general. The company's administrative council brought in new members, as well. Nogues introduced night flights starting with the Paris-Strasbourg connection (trial flight on July 27–28) and then the Bucharest-Belgrade run, which he flew with Guidon on September 20. These night flights involved the acquisition of new airplanes, notably the Caudron C 61, a trimotor equipped with radio and night-flying instruments. The Caudron carried seven passengers and 220 kilograms of baggage, and flew at 166 kilometers per hour. The engines were 180-horsepower Hispano-Suizas. Some Spad 56s were also tried out on night flights. They were equipped with nine-cylinder air-cooled Gnome et Rhone Jupiter engines. The airplanes were paid for in large part by state subsidies. On any flight beyond 200 kilometers, the airline was required to have its aircraft carry navigators.

Night flights brought additional demands. Barbier-Bernard-type acetylene beacons were used for airport runway and en route navigation lights. The construction of nighttime emergency landing strips was necessary. Night flights also involved a change in schedule to make possible a combination train and air connection. Bucharest could be reached from Paris in one day by first taking the night train to Strasbourg and then flying on to Bucharest.

Backing this up was a major technical organization. The airline's principal shops in Paris-Le Bourget, Prague, and Bucharest-Baneasa were set up for major maintenance and repairs of airplanes, engines, flight instruments, electrical and radio equipment; and for the assembly of the most complex aircraft components, such as fuselages, wings, empennage, and landing gear. In 1925, the Le Bourget repair shop, which had not undergone appreciable modifications in two years, occupied an area of 600 square meters and employed 180 people.

The year 1923 also marked the beginning of competition for Franco-Roumaine on the Vienna-Budapest route by a German company, Trans-Europa

Union. Germany changed its aviation policy in other ways, too, creating great difficulty for Franco-Roumaine. For example, Germany confiscated aircraft that, because of breakdowns, had to land in Germany. During the year the airline recorded six fatal accidents.

The airline's fleet and personnel stayed at about the same level, employing 22 pilots and having 80 airplanes, of which 8 were Salmsons, 5 Potez 7s, 12 Potez 9s, 14 Spad 33s, 38 Spad 46s, and 3 Caudron C 61s. In 1924, Franco-Roumaine acquired new aircraft, including additional Caudron C 61s and one Caudron C 81, a luxurious trimotor with a 400-horsepower Lorraine-Dietrich middle engine.

From 1922 to 1925, Franco-Roumaine was one of the world's most important airline companies, both in terms of numbers of passengers (12,305 in 1923) and in the size of its route network (increased to 3,717 kilometers in November 1924 with the opening of a route to Ankara, Turkey). The company terminated night flights on the Paris-Strasbourg stretch to fly from Paris to Bucharest and inaugurate flights from Paris to Moscow. Nogues made the first flight to Moscow on November 14 in a Caudron C 81. In 1924 Franco-Roumaine flew daily to Budapest (Bucharest in the summer) and Warsaw, and biweekly from Budapest to Constantinople via Bucharest.

Despite its success, Franco-Roumaine's financial situation continued to deteriorate. In 1924, 80 percent of the company's income was in the form of subsidies. These amounted to about 11.5 million francs from the French government and 2.5 million francs from other countries (Czechoslovakia, Romania, Poland, and Yugoslavia). For the 1924 financial year, the French Parliament voted against providing Franco-Roumaine with the subsidies asked for by the assistant secretary of state for aeronautics, and on January 26 a new outline of economic stipulations was drafted. On May 31, other national regulations were drawn up, aimed at reducing subsidies. On June 26, the company's stockholders held a general meeting, where they decided to enlarge the administrative council with four new administrators and change Franco-Roumaine's corporate name to CIDNA (Compagnie Internationale de Navigation Aérienne) starting on January 1, 1925. The shared capital was reduced to 8,250,000 francs; henceforth, the company was 50 percent French, 20 percent Czech, 19 percent Romanian, and 11 percent other nations.

As the heir to CFRNA, CIDNA continued to represent French diplomatic interests in eastern Europe, and it carried on with the improvement and renewal of its aircraft and ground installations and the extension of its routes.

The following information about the company is an epilogue to the story of this pioneering transcontinental airline.

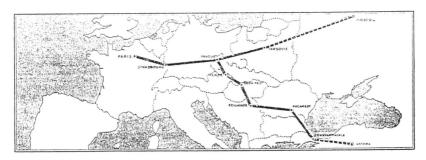

Bulletin de Renseignements N° 3

MARS 1924 ————— ——— MARS 1924

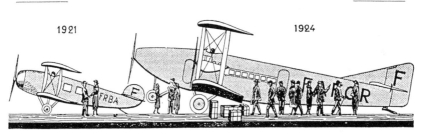

1921   1924

Progrès technique du matériel de la Compagnie

| Avion SALMSON 1921 | | Avion CAUDRON C 81 1924 | |
Modèle de guerre transformé		Aérobus commercial	
Envergure	11ᵐ75	Envergure	26ᵐ30
Longueur	8ᵐ50	Longueur	17ᵐ·
Surface.	37ᵐᵉ	Surface	145ᵐᵉ
Puissance du moteur	260 Cv.	Puissance des 3 moteurs . . .	900 Cv.
Poids enlevé	180 Kg.	Poids enlevé	1·000 Kg·
Poids total en vol	1·380 Kg.	Poids total en vol ·	6·370 Kg·

3.1. This newsletter from Franco-Roumaine, March 1924, shows the route from Paris to Constantinople and proposed extensions to Moscow and Ankara, as well as the equipment changes between 1921 and 1924.

Over the next decade the airline acquired Caudron C 61s, Caudron 92s, Spad 56s, Farman-Jabirus, Potez 32s, Fokker F VIIs, and Fokker VIIbs. Airfields and repair shops were enlarged and modernized. The earliest and most important was the one at Le Bourget, the network's starting point, followed by those in Prague, Budapest, Bucharest, and Constantinople.

In 1931, the network consisted of the Paris-Strasbourg-Nuremberg-Prague-Vienna-Budapest-Belgrade-Bucharest line, with daily service (the Paris-

3.2. This cartoon of a Farman trimotor appeared in the Franco-Roumaine newsletter from July 1924.

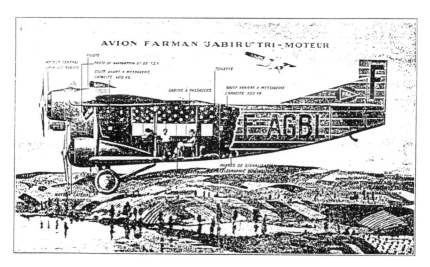

3.3. The company newsletter from April 1925 featured a cutaway drawing of a Farman trimotor.

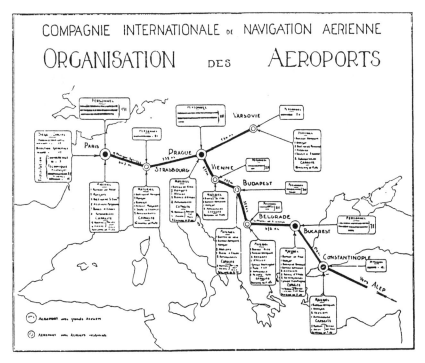

3.4. The November 1925 newsletter showed the airline's routes and airports, with principal repair and maintenance depots in Paris, Prague, and Bucharest.

Strasbourg and Belgrade-Bucharest lines were flown at night); and the Prague-Breslau-Warsaw, Belgrade-Sofia-Istanbul, and Vienna-Graz-Zagreb-Belgrade routes being operated by an Austrian and Yugoslavian company, respectively.

From its formation to October 1, 1932, Franco-Roumaine's aircraft flew 18.5 million kilometers (16.5 million with passengers) and carried 105 ton-kilometers of mail and 2,890 ton-kilometers of freight.

Of the 20 companies that once existed in France, only 5—Air Union, Lignes Farman, Air Orient, Cie Generale Aeropostale, and CIDNA—remained in operation in 1932, partially as a result of the French government's policy encouraging mergers. The gloomy financial condition of these companies, financed 80 percent by the government, motivated CIDNA to reconsider the organization of air transport.

On December 11, 1932, a law regulating the aviation market was voted on. Although the law laid down the principle of competition among numbers of

airlines, the minister of air, after appealing to the five airlines to combine existing routes (and eventually merge), opted for only one national company. On
May 31, 1933, CIDNA, Air Orient, Air Union, and SGTA formed SGELA
(Société General pour l'Exploitation des Lignes Aériennes). From their union
and the repurchasing of Aeropostale, Air France, a mixed concessionary public
service company, was born on August 30, 1933.

Thus ended not only CIDNA, heir of CFRNA, but its route network as well,
because Air France did not resume the Paris-Constantinople line.

SOURCES

Chadeau, Emmanuel. *L'Industrie aeronautique en France, 1900–1950*. Paris: Fayard,
1987 (especially chapter 5, 150–70).
Compagnie Franco-Roumaine de Navigation Aérienne. *Bulletin de Renseignements*,
Oct. 1923–Dec. 1925.
Danielopol, A. Dossier on Compagnie Franco-Roumaine de Navigation Aérienne. Among
other documents, the dossier contains testimonies and accounts related to Franco-
Roumaine's principal Romanian initiators and promoters, whom Danielopol knew
very well. Among them are Nicolas Titulescu, Aristide Blank, Savel Radulescu, Jean
Bastaky, and Radu Tabacovici.
——"Histoire de la Cie. Franco-Roumaine de Navigation Aérienne." Conference a
l'Ambassade de France a Bucarest, 1972. Manuscript.
Davies, R. E. G. "CFRNA." *Air Pictorial* 28 (May 1966): 174–75.
——"Chronology of CFRNA-CIDNA, 1920–1933." Manuscript.
Dollfus, C., and H. Bouche. *Histoire de l'aeronautique*. Paris: L'Illustration, 1932.
Gibbs-Smith, Charles H. *Aviation: An Historical Survey from Its Origins to the End of
World War II*. London: H. M. Stationery Office, 1970.
Guidon, L. "Souvenir de la Franco-Romaine." *Icare: Revue de l'Aviation Française*, 73
(1975).
Herlea, Alexandre. "Les moteurs d'aviation: naissance et evolution en France jusqu'a la
fin de la 2eme Guerre Mondiale." *L'archeologie industrielle en France* 15 (1987):
113–39.
Istoria Aviatiei Romane. Bucharest: Stiintifica si Enciclopedia, 1984 (especially chapter
7, 232–44).
Musée de l'Air. Centre de Documentation. *Dossier Cie. Franco-Roumaine*. Among the
items in this collection are CFRNA and CIDNA leaflets with schedules and fares and
numerous photographs and other illustrative material.

 **PART TWO**

Flight and Society

■■■■■■
■■■■■■ Dominick A. Pisano
■■■■■■

Introduction

In 1946, William F. Ogburn, along with two collaborators, published a book titled *The Social Effects of Aviation*. Ogburn's work, although little noticed at the time, represented a breakthrough in the ways people thought and wrote about aviation. Ogburn made a number of insightful predictions based on sociological research on the influence of aviation on American society. His primary contribution, however, was as a voice of reason and restraint in a period of intense and often misdirected optimism about the future of aviation in the United States. Ogburn's sober views on aviation's prospects were based on what ordinary people were thinking and feeling rather than what industry moguls and promoters foolishly believed possible.

Thirty-seven years later, another innovative book appeared that forced historians to reconsider their thinking and writing about the history of aviation. Joseph Corn's *The Winged Gospel: America's Romance with Aviation, 1900–1950*, departed from the standard approach to writing the history of aviation. Corn's own hopes for the book were to move away from chronicling the history of aviation in the "tradition of aviation enthusiasm" for enthusiasm's sake and to analyze "the feelings, attitudes, and behavior which characterize the phenomenon" and thus "illuminate one such instance of technological enthusiasm in American history."

Unfortunately, in the decade since the publication of *The Winged Gospel*, little work has been done that follows the path that Corn and Ogburn outlined so well. That aviation has to a large degree escaped the scrutiny of sociologists and social and cultural historians is somewhat surprising given the dramatic changes in the way in which historians have thought and written about history over the last two decades. While standards for scholarship in the area have risen dramatically, even now the bulk of writing about aviation consists of hagiographic biography and memoirs, insubstantial journalistic accounts, and examples of enthusiast literature, very little of which gives any indication of aviation's effects on people and cultures. A quick review of almost any aviation book catalog will bear me out.

That is why I was so pleased to be invited to chair the "Flight and Society" session of the International Conference on the History of Civil and Commercial Aviation in August 1992 at the Swiss Transport Museum in Lucerne. This session came at a perfect time in the proceedings, that is, midweek: after discussions about the history of airports, technical development in civil and commercial aviation, development of commercial aircraft, and logistics and routes; and before discussions of military and commercial aviation, the pioneers, and new frontiers in the history of civil and commercial aviation. Hence, the discussion of flight and society bridged the gap between two traditional methods of looking at the history of aviation.

Why is this aspect of the history of aviation or of any technological endeavor important? First, and most important, without it we cannot understand the story in all its complexity. Second, historians of technology are paying increasing attention to the importance of the social nature of technological development as a way of increasing our understanding of technology. Without doubt, the integration of technology with social and cultural concerns is an important trend in the history of technology; witness works like Eugene S. Ferguson's *Engineering and the Mind's Eye* (1992) and Wiebe E. Bjker, Thomas P. Hughes, and Trevor Pinch's *The Social Construction of Technological Systems* (1987). Third, related to the social ramifications of technology are its cultural underpinnings—the assumptions, attitudes, behaviors, myths, and ideologies that underlie it. With the exception of *The Winged Gospel,* this is an area that remains relatively untouched.

The studies presented in Part Two reflect the ways in which commercial and civil aviation have had an effect on society in four specific areas: aerospace medicine, the air-traveling public, gender in commercial aviation, and the airplane and mass transportation via the private airplane. While these areas are not apparently interrelated, when one stops to consider them, they are tied together by themes of illusion and reality and the way the aviation industry exploited perception to convince people of the necessity for commercial and private aviation.

In his article, "Aviation Medicine: Its Past, Present, and Future," Rudolf von Baumgarten, M.D., discusses what he calls the "economy-class syndrome"— long, overnight flights to Europe that leave the traveler exhausted and jet-lagged. This is only one of the unpleasant realities of traveling by air that are masked by appeals to its romance and adventure. Roger Bilstein, in "Air Travel and the Traveling Public: The American Experience, 1920–1970," looks at the airline industry's attempt through advertising to attract passengers by promoting service and comfort and to overcome some of the less favorable aspects of flying commercially. Lee Kolm, in "Stewardesses' 'Psychological Punch': Gender and Commercial Aviation in the United States, 1930–1978," analyzes the exploitation of women in the airline industry's marketing strategies to attract customers and give them the illusion that flying commercially is like sitting in the comfort of your home or in a fine restaurant. Finally, William F. Trimble, in "The Collapse of a Dream: Lightplane Ownership and General Aviation in the United States after World War II," sees through the illusionary nature of an idea that failed—the mass use of lightplanes for commuting and recreation.

Although neither a social nor cultural history of aviation in the United States exploring these themes and others has yet been written, I am optimistic that as areas of society and culture in which the airplane has played a role come to light, the social dimension of aviation will be recorded, analyzed, and recognized as an important aspect of the history of technology. Historians of European aviation are fortunate to have Michael Fritzsche's *A Nation of Fliers:*

German Aviation and the Popular Imagination, recently published by Harvard University Press, and Robert Wohl's forthcoming book on aviation and the Western imagination. Meanwhile, the papers given at the session of the International Conference on the History of Civil and Commercial Aviation were an important step in recognizing the historical importance of flight in its relationship to society. My hope is that they will spur historians of aviation to investigate further the ideas presented here and other relevant themes.

Rudolf von Baumgarten

Aviation Medicine

Its Past, Present, and Future

The development of aviation medicine from its origins to the present paralleled step by step the technical developments of aviation and the development of medical sciences. Aviation was initiated about two centuries ago in France, when the Montgolfier brothers flew their famous hot-air balloon in September 1783 in Versailles. This was also the beginning of experimental aviation medicine. Because the physiological effects of ascent in a balloon were not yet known, a sheep, a duck, and a rooster were chosen as passengers—the first animal experiment in aviation medicine. The balloon landed eight minutes later in a forest with its occupants unharmed. It apparently was safe for humans to fly.

Only two months later, two French noblemen, Pilatre de Rozier and the Marquis d'Arlandes, volunteered for a manned flight in the "Montgolfière." Stating that the honor to be the first flying men could not go to criminals, they changed places with a condemned man who had been tentatively selected for the flight. The two men took off on November 21, 1783, from the Bois de Boulogne near Paris and landed safely in a farm field after 25 minutes in the air. They folded and packed the balloon and went home in a horse-drawn carriage.

It is little known that at the time of the flight Pilatre de Rozier was already a

4.1. A sheep, a duck, and a
rooster were the only passengers
on board the Montgolfier
brothers' hot-air balloon for its
flight over Versailles in September 1783. (Courtesy of Johann
Ambrosius Barth Press,
Heidelberg)

distinguished medical doctor and the superintendent of the Royal Museum of
Natural History. He noted after the flight that flying had no unfavorable effects
on the human physical system.[1] Thus, it can be said that aviation medicine accompanied human efforts to fly right from the beginning.

Only a few days later, on December 1, 1783, J. A. C. Charles and Charles
Robert, competitors of the Montgolfiers, took off in Paris with a hydrogen-
filled balloon designed by Charles, a physicist from the French Academy of
Science. On this flight the two passengers flew in a strong wind for about
27 miles, from Paris to Nesle, reaching an altitude of almost 9,000 feet. Robert
experienced a sharp pain in one of his ears, which he attributed to the cold temperature.[2] He was probably reporting the first case of what we call today bar-
otitis, a painful syndrome occurring during fast ascent but more often during
quick descent, in the latter case due to air trapped in the middle ear. Otherwise
the passengers were unharmed, and many more flights with "Montgolfières" or
"Charlières" followed during the rest of the eighteenth century.

Curiously enough, it was J. A. C. Charles, the inventor of the hydrogen balloon, who first identified the physical laws describing the interrelationship of
temperature, volume, and pressure of gases (the "Charles Law"), explaining the
lift of hot-air balloons. The Mongolfiers at this time still believed that smoke
was a special gas, lighter than air. The first fatalities in aviation occurred when
Pilatre de Rozier tried to cross the English Channel in a combination hydrogen
and hot-air balloon. This idea proved to be disastrous, because—as could be
expected—sparks from the hot-air balloon rose and set fire to the hydrogen balloon, and the whole combination crashed into the sea. De Rozier and his passenger lost their lives in this first fatal aviation accident. In the same year, Jean
Pierre Blanchard successfully crossed the English Channel in a hydrogen balloon. Dr. John Jeffries, an American physician who was interested in the effects
of flying on man, accompanied him for a fee of 700 pounds sterling.

  With ascents of balloons to higher reaches of the atmosphere, the principal
dangers of high-altitude flight were discovered: extreme cold and hypoxia (the
lack of oxygen in the blood). In October 1804, Count Francesco Zambeccari,
Pascal Andreoli, and a third man named Grasetti took off from Bologna in a
balloon that later had to be rescued by a ship in the Mediterranean Sea. The crew
suffered from frostbite on their hands and feet, and Zambeccari had all his fin-
gers amputated afterwards. They also reported that they had vomited and lost
consciousness at high altitude. Two physiologists, Paul Bert[3] in Paris and
Nathan Zuntz[4] in Berlin, systematically studied the effects of simulated high
altitude on humans in hypobaric chambers on the ground in the nineteenth century. They concluded that it was not the ambient atmospheric pressure but the
diminished partial pressure of oxygen that causes hypoxia. In an actual flight in
a gas balloon with two passengers, Gaston Tissandier reached an altitude of
28,000 feet, when all three man fell unconscious. Tissandier survived, but his
two passengers, the scientists Joseph Crocé-Spinelli and Theodore Sivel, died
of hypoxia. James Glaisher and Henry Coxwell later experienced symptoms of
hypoxia during a balloon flight to 32,960 feet. There Glaisher suddenly fell
unconscious while Coxwell pulled the valve line with his teeth, his hands already immobilized by the severe cold.[5]

  It is surprising that human beings (in contrast to most animals) have very few
subjective symptoms of hypoxia, so they often are not aware of the danger.
Some subjects during high-altitude flight even report the feeling of euphoria
(elated mood, or *Höhenrausch*) in the early stages of hypoxia. Today, soaring
pilots in the mountains can reach altitudes of 30,000 feet and more in un-
pressurized cockpits. The danger of hypoxia when flying at these altitudes with
inappropriate oxygen-supply systems cannot be overestimated.

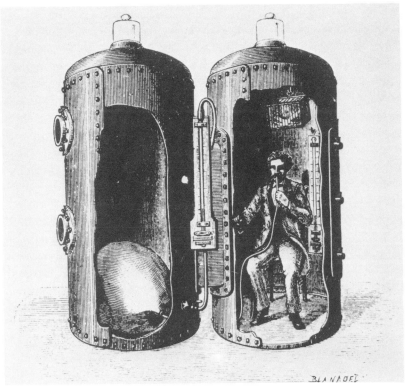

4.2. Hypobaric chambers, designed by Paul Bert in Paris in 1874, were used to study the effects of high-altitude flight on humans. (Courtesy of Johann Ambrosius Barth Press, Heidelberg)

Two more dangers of flying were discovered later. During rapid ascent, nitrogen bubbles can form in the human blood and tissue, causing cardiovascular and neurological symptoms. This is similar to the dangerous "divers' sickness" (the "bends") experienced after fast ascents from the bottom of the sea. Today a combination of these problems sometimes occurs when sport divers board a commercial airplane shortly after their last ascent from diving. Once in the air, symptoms of decompression sickness can then result when latent divers' sickness is compounded by the diminished cabin pressure in the airliner. Furthermore, as with Charles Robert, trapped air in the sinus cavities and middle ear can cause painful symptoms of disbarism from changes of the outside air pressure. Also, after unprotected exposure to extreme high altitude (above 36,000 feet), the water content of the body can start to vaporize (boil), but this event is more relevant to space crews than aviators.

The physiologists Bert and Zuntz, after their systematic studies in aviation medicine in the nineteenth century, developed the first oxygen-supply systems for fliers. In addition, their hypobaric and hyperbaric chambers on the ground were used not only in aviation medicine but also for the treatment of tuberculosis, which at that time was one of the most common and life-threatening diseases.

It is safe to say that the most important discoveries in aviation physiology were made when only lighter-than-air flight was possible. Pressurized cabins, which we have now in most airliners and all spacecraft, were first used in high-altitude balloon flights such as the one by the Swiss scientist August Piccard. In 1931, he reached a recorded altitude of 51,961 feet in his pressurized gondola over southern Germany. All later high-altitude flights in balloons were made in pressurized capsules.

Aviation medicine also has close links to the early years of heavier-than-air flight. One of the first men to fly successfully in a hang glider was a tailor, Albrecht Ludwig Berblinger.[6] Most historians know the famous story of the

4.3. Paul Bert and Nathan Zuntz developed the first oxygen-supply system for fliers of high-altitude balloons. (Courtesy of Freie Universitat Berlin)

"tailor of Ulm," who splashed into the Danube during his unsuccessful flight demonstration in 1811. Count Zeppelin, grandfather of the famous airship builder, had ordered Berblinger to demonstrate a flight across the Danube to allow the visiting King of Württemberg to watch this sensation conveniently from his boat. Even 150 years later, during a competition of 35 well-trained pilots in modern, high-performance hang gliders, only one of them was able to cross the Danube at this unsuitable place, and he broke a collarbone when he crashed on the embankment on the other side of the river.

Few recall that before his attempted crossing of the Danube, Berblinger had already performed successful flights on the Michelsberg, a hill north of Ulm. Not only a successful aviator, he was also a famous maker of arm and leg prostheses for amputees. Some principles of his artificial knee joints are still in use in modern prosthesis design. He also constructed phantom-models for instruction in obstetrics and developed new kinds of trusses to support hernias. In recognition of his accomplishments in aviation and medicine, the German Aerospace Medical Society created the Albrecht Ludwig Berblinger Prize, awarded annually to young scientists who have excelled in scientific work in aviation medicine.

Otto Lilienthal, 100 years ago, was the first to study the flight of birds systematically, using scientific methods with the aim of building manned aircraft. He had already used a wind tunnel to test airfoil shapes and constructed and sold

4.4. Albrecht Ludwig Berblinger unsuccessfully tried to cross the Danube River with a hang glider in 1811. (Courtesy of Stadtarchiv Ulm)

many hang gliders with which he and others succeeded in long downhill flights from natural and artificial hills. On his last flight, however, his craft stalled in a sudden gust, turned to the left, and crashed. Lilienthal broke his neck and died one day later. His last words were reported to be "Opfer müssen gebracht werden": "Sacrifices have to be made."

In the early days of heavier-than-air flight, a high percentage of flights unfortunately ended in crashes. After their first engine-powered flights, the Wright brothers crashed more than once during landing maneuvers. The activity of flight surgeons at this time consisted more in treating injured aviators than in accident prevention or medical examinations. The main problem was the low air speed of the early airplanes and the narrow margin between flight speed and stall speed. A strong gust from behind or any loss of engine power could lead to an immediate stall, rendering the aircraft unmaneuverable unless the pilot went into an immediate dive in the hope of picking up sufficient air speed to recover the airplane before hitting the ground. The rapid development of airplane and engine technology in World War I mostly took care of such stall problems, especially when the early pusher-type airplanes, with the engine in the rear, were replaced by tractor airplanes, with the engine in front.

As the engine power and speed of aircraft increased considerably during World War I, a new and unexpected medical problem emerged: Disorientation occurred during aerobatic maneuvers and sharp turns. Moreover, when flying in conditions of restricted visibility in fog, in clouds, or at night, all pilots completely lost their sense of orientation and not infrequently crashed to the ground. It was discovered that the human organ of equilibrium, the so-called vestibular system, is good for orientation only on the ground, not in the air. Humans are distinctly terrestrial animals. In evolution humans have not developed fins for swimming or wings and feathers for flying, nor have they a vestibular system fit for compounded angular and linear accelerations. Humans have mastered the ability to move at sea, in the air, and lately in space only by having developed suitable devices and instruments with their hands, their language, and most of all their superior brains.

The vestibular system was perfected during the phylogenetic development of human beings, but only for use on the ground. The system shows us precisely where is up and where is down and so permits us an upright stance and gait, even with closed eyes or in the dark. But the vestibular organ is not fit for use on any moving platform, such as a car, boat, airplane, or spacecraft, and we can become carsick, seasick, airsick, or even spacesick. Moreover, any pilot who loses sight of the horizon must also lose sense of the aircraft's attitude if not guided by instruments. The reason is that the so-called otolith organ in the inner

4.5. Orville Wright's accident at Fort Myer in 1908 resulted in the death of
Lt. Thomas Selfridge. (Courtesy of United States Air Force Museum)

ear cannot distinguish between pure gravitational and combined gravito-inertial forces, the latter occurring during changes of direction (turns). Pilots then are misled about their real spatial attitude. Even today one of the leading causes of accidents in general aviation is flying into bad weather without proper instrumentation, the necessary training, or recent practice in instrument flying.

As early as 1917, the American inventor Elmer Sperry constructed a gyrocompass, which he later perfected into turn indicators, artificial horizons, and autopilots. These instruments were introduced in most larger civil and military aircraft in the early 1930s. The artificial horizon, with a small aircraft silhouette on its face, constantly indicates to the pilot the attitude of the airplane: whether it is pitched up or down, whether the wings are level or banked, and whether the aircraft is turning left or right. Such instruments allow pilots to recognize the position of the real horizon even without any outside visibility. This invention alone permitted man to fly on instruments at night or in the clouds. It still takes much training and practice to make a pilot always believe what these instruments indicate, especially if the aviator's subjective sensation tells him or her otherwise.

A related problem occurred recently when military airplanes and airliners made in the former USSR were flown by West German pilots after the reunification of Germany. In some of the Russian gyroscopes the small aircraft silhouette was the moving part, and the horizontal line was kept steady on the glass in front of the instrument. In the gyroscopes of Western aircraft, the aircraft symbol is printed on the glass, while the line representing the horizon is the moving part. This made extensive retraining of the pilots or a reinstrumentation of the airplanes necessary. [7]

It was first recognized during World War I that air crews should be selected according to their health and abilities and medical doctors trained in aviation medicine should be allocated as "flight surgeons" to aircraft squadrons. Air medical examinations were relatively simple then compared to now. The medical section of the German air force in 1915 performed flight medical examinations in which the candidates for flight training had only to be found free of organic diseases and able to pass several psycho-physiological tasks, such as recognizing targets on a quickly rolling panorama of a landscape. They also had to react to different colored lights which were flashed on or around their central field of vision. [8]

At the same time in Britain, six examining stations were established for the medical evaluation of all pilot candidates. Good cardiovascular conditioning was required. Most important was the ability of candidates to tolerate the effects of simulated altitude by breathing air in the laboratory for a few minutes with gradually reduced partial pressure of oxygen. Amazingly, 61 percent of the men were found fit to tolerate breathing air equivalent to that at 20,000 feet, 25 percent passed out at 15,000 feet, and 14 percent could not tolerate an altitude greater than 8,000 feet.[9] The main reason for these tests was that at this time German airships were bombing London from great altitude. Fighter aircraft had to be developed and men found who were able to fight the airships at high altitude. Few of the Allied airplanes in World War I were equipped with oxygen-supply systems, whereas German Zeppelins already used them. The breathing tests conducted in Britain, however, were found later to be of little value, because they did not reflect the circumstances in real flight, when the pilots would be exposed to the thin air for much longer periods of time. Practical experience soon made it clear that 12,000 feet altitude was the limit a man could generally tolerate in flight without being affected by some symptoms of hypoxia.

As early as 1917, 67 medical examining units were established in large American cities by order of Lt. Col. Theodore C. Lyster, Medical Corps, to screen the many applicants, from which approximately 20,000 men were accepted for wartime aviation. The tests included full visual acuity in both eyes, normal color vision, full hearing in both ears, and perfect functioning of the vestibular apparatus. It was later argued that some of the flying aces of World War I would not have been able to pass all these tests.[10] Bill Thaw of the Lafayette Escadrille had only one functioning eye. Georges Guynemer had severe tuberculosis. Alfred A. Leitch, a very successful Canadian World War I ace, had a severely deformed foot. Six other outstanding pilots had pathological nystagmus (flicker of the eyes) and would have been classified as "not fit to fly."

Psychological factors were also regarded as important. The French authority Dr. L. Guibert wrote in 1917, "the first thing that would be necessary (for an aviator) is a great liberty of spirit. He should avoid family attachments and other liaisons too absorbing. He should accustom himself to react against anxieties and unpleasant conditions of all sorts. How can the pilot be a complete master of his apparatus, if he is distracted in his mind and his thought is elsewhere?"[11]

The United States Army Air Service in Europe during World War I was the first to attach special flight surgeons to the squadrons. Their duty was the monitoring of the health and efficiency of the air crew. Pilots in most air forces were advised to restrict the intake of alcohol, coffee, and nicotine, and to limit their sex lives.

Military airplanes in World War II were nearly all equipped with well-functioning oxygen systems and parachutes, but they still lacked pressurization and sometimes did not even provide adequate heating. Frostbite was a common injury among British and American bomber pilots, especially of the waist gunners, who stood near open windows, exposed to the slipstream and bitter cold of high altitude. Large doses of vitamin A were given to British night-fighter and night-bomber crews to increase their night vision. Dive-bomber pilots complained about the temporary loss of vision (blackout) on recovering from fast dives or in sharp turns at high speed. Because of that, aviation physiologists began to study the effect of positive Z-axis acceleration on the cardiovascular system.

The first flight surgeons had been military physicians, and aviation medicine was a part of the armed services. For civilian fliers, no federal regulations existed until 1926. Civilian aircraft were not registered, and pilots were not examined for their physical qualifications. The growing number of civilian aircraft, however, as well as the number of aircraft accidents in which the health of the pilots played a role, made federal regulations in aviation medicine necessary. In the United States, the Air Commerce Act of 1926 provided the first regulations calling for the licensing of aircraft, medical examinations, and the rating of airmen and aircraft. That year the Aeronautics Branch of the Department of Commerce appointed Dr. Louis Hopewell Bauer as the first medical director of aeronautics. Rightly regarded as the founder of civil aviation medicine in the United States, he drew up the physical standards for airmen with progressively strict requirements for the three classes, namely private, industrial, and transport pilots. This classification, with some minor changes, is still used.

In 1939, the first civilian air medical examiners (AMEs) were designated in different cities. Many of them were not only interested in aviation medicine but were pilots themselves or had been trained as flight surgeons during World War I. The AMEs had to send copies of their medical reports for review to Dr. Bauer's office. The rapid growth of aviation, with the growing number of aircraft and pilots, soon made the appointment of more AMEs necessary. In 1940, as many as 43,902 pilot physical examinations took place in the United States, and the number of appointed AMEs grew to 816. Following Dr. Bauer's system, similar licensing systems were introduced in most European countries. Pilots and other flying personnel had to be medically relicensed for flying at regular periods varying between six months and two years, according to the kind of flying they performed.

Pilots and medical doctors of any specialization soon complained that the medical criteria for flying and the red tape connected with it were too rigid. They argued that all physicians should generally be allowed to perform air medical examinations without any special training. This was understandable from the viewpoint of pilots, especially the young ones, who did not want to have to pay the examination fee repeatedly or travel, often long distances, to a designated AME or who wanted to fly in spite of some physical deficiencies. Among pilots the opinion was common that many of the physical standards for pilots were unnecessary and that a private doctor or even the flight instructor would be better able to detect any disqualifying medical defects than an appointed AME. Even today such opinions are voiced, in spite of statistics showing that it was not unusual for aircraft accidents to be caused by physical deficiencies of the pilots. In a recent report concerning 4,227 accidents on file, it was shown that pilots with physical defects were involved in 45 percent more accidents than pilots with normal health.

The system of aviation medical examinations almost broke down in the United States shortly after the end of World War II. At this time there arose the economic problem of how to convert the huge American aircraft industry to civilian demands. Theodore P. Wright, President Franklin D. Roosevelt's civil aeronautics administrator, predicted an enormous growth in private flying, believing that thousands of families would own private airplanes, much as they did private cars. He predicted that by 1956 about 400,000 such lightplanes would exist, costing only about $2,500 or less each. Because only about 50,000 civil aircraft existed in the United States in 1944, this would be an almost tenfold increase in the number of aircraft within 10 years. More than 1,000 Army Air Forces flight instructors were jobless in the United States after World War II, and they hoped to earn a living teaching civilians how to fly. It was not recognized at this time that buying, maintaining, and servicing an airplane, as well as the availability of an airport and often restricting weather conditions, seriously limited such expected growth.

In any case, at this time the red tape and the rigidity of flight medical examinations were regarded as the primary handicaps to substantial growth of civilian aviation in the United States. Therefore, the existing private pilot examiner system was abolished in June 1945.[12] Physical examinations for student and private pilots, including medical certificates, could now be performed by any "competent licensed physician." Only commercial and airline transport pilots would still be required to be examined by a designated AME. The air medical examinations performed by private doctors consisted only of a set of questions that could be answered yes or no by any licensed physician. This was regarded as sufficient to determine whether the pilot had a physical defect that might interfere with his safe operation of an airplane. Dr. Bauer, the editor of the *Journal of Aviation Medicine,* in June 1945 called this "the most backward step" taken by civil aviation since its beginning in the federal government.[13] In protest, he resigned his post as a medical adviser to the Civil Aeronautics Administration in 1945.

As it resulted in following years, the former rigid licensing regulations were not the obstacle to the development of civil aviation. The production of private airplanes fell to less than 3,400 units in 1949 in spite of the relaxed medical regulations. In view of the growing number of civilian aircraft accidents, the former system of air medical examinations performed by specially trained designated physicians was reintroduced. In 1949, more than 5,000 physical examination reports on student and private pilots were reexamined to compare the performance of the 1,142 nondesignated examiners with that of the 48 designated examiners.[14] It turned out that 116 administrative errors had been committed by nondesignated examiners per 100 examinations as compared to 14.7 errors by the designated examiners. A review of the reports of the nondesignated examiners also found that 1,800 certificates were issued that should have been denied. Another 2,700 issued certificates should have had a restricted notation (such as wearing eyeglasses while flying). Finally, 1,500 certificates were denied that should have been granted, and 10,000 certificates were issued with restricted notations that should have been issued without any restriction. It was concluded that "errors resulting in the certification of unfit applicants may endanger the public safety, while those which result in the denial to fly of qualified individuals will have an adverse effect on the promotion of civil aviation."

In 1966, as a result of the Transportation Act, the Federal Aviation Administration (FAA), including its responsibilities for aviation medicine, came under the control of the Department of Transportation. The medical branch of the FAA, located in Oklahoma City, now has about 420 employees working in a variety of medical, research, education, and safety programs.

In the years between the two world wars it was recognized that aviation medicine was not only a service to the community but also a special science needing its own scientific institutes as well as journals specializing in air medical research. To mention only a few, in the United States, the *Journal of Aviation Medicine* was founded in 1930; today it appears under the name of *Aviation, Space and Environmental Medicine*. In Germany the periodical *Luftfahrtmedizin* appeared first in 1936. Two years later the *Revista Medicina Aeronautica* appeared in Italy.

Research depends on able scientists who promote the knowledge in their special field by scientific work and discoveries. In the United States, Gen. Harry George Armstrong, M.D., was director of research at Wright Field (now Wright-Patterson Air Force Base). In 1939, he published the first comprehensive book on aviation medicine, which soon found general recognition around the world.[15] He also was one of the first to perform toxicological studies about the danger of carbon monoxide in the exhaust of aircraft engines. The large

American Air Force Institute of Aviation Medicine in San Antonio, Texas, was named a few years ago after General Armstrong.

In Germany, the government strongly supported aviation medicine before and during World War II. At the Flugmedizinische Institut (Institute of Aviation Medicine) in Berlin-Buch, such well-known scientists as Hubertus Strughold, Siegfried Ruff, Otto Gauer, Heinz von Diringshofen, Harald von Bekh, Bruno Müller, and others worked on aviation medicine. The quantitative data on the effect of positive and negative C-axis acceleration on the cardiovascular system was studied by experiments using animals in large centrifuges.

Unfortunately, a few German SS physicians in the Nazi concentration camp of Dachau during World War II performed studies on hypoxia and undercooling by using the inmates as subjects for their cruel experiments.[16] It was determined after the war that the Institute of Aviation Medicine did not participate in or order any of these experiments. The physicians who initiated and performed concentration camp experiments and who were apprehended after the war were severely punished.

In an operation code-named "Paper Clip," some scientists of the Institute of Aviation Medicine came to the United States shortly after the war, and they continued their scientific and applied work. Professor Hubertus Strughold, already recognized for his research and books on aviation medicine,[17] in particular, became well known again in the United States by initiating the first space medical activities in the Air Force Institute of Aviation Medicine. The Hubertus Strughold awards for achievement in aviation medicine are still given annually in the United States and Germany to scientists who do outstanding work in this field.

A special field of aviation medicine is aviation psychology. Special institutes are responsible for basic research and applied work in this field. It is well known from statistical studies that the so-called human factor is one of the leading causes of aircraft accidents. In 1942 the German Supreme Command suddenly ordered the end of psychological testing in the military. It was reported after the war that this was done for two reasons: Too many combat-fatigued pilots were declared unfit for flying, and the son of General Wilhelm Keitel and the nephew of Field Marshal Hermann Göring were found unsuited in these tests to become officers.[18]

Today, all student pilots training for a professional career in aviation in Germany are screened according to their psychological ability and emotional stability. This is necessary for reasons of safety but also has an economic factor. Airline and military flying schools must eliminate many students because of poor progress at a stage when considerable money and effort has already been

4.6. Hubertus Strughold, a German national, was responsible for the introduction of space medicine in the United States. (Courtesy of H. Fuchs)

spent in vain by the airline and the student for the training. In Hamburg, the psychological section of the Institute of Aviation Medicine is testing candidates for pilot training for Lufthansa and some other airlines. About 40 percent of the applicants are rejected after these tests, far more than for any medical reason. On the other hand, statistics show that significantly fewer pilots who took these tests drop out of training later, compared to the time before these tests were introduced.

In modern aviation medicine, accident research and accident prevention are important priorities. Prevention begins with the counseling of engineers in aircraft factories concerning the safe and ergonomic construction of aircraft. For instance, sturdy attachment of the passenger seats to the floor of the aircraft is important. Not long ago shoulder belts became mandatory for light aircraft, as had long been the case for automobiles. Many head and face injuries could have been avoided during forced landings if shoulder belts had been introduced earlier. However, the "weak links" found in old light aircraft in front of and behind the cockpit provided "crush space" and helped to prevent or diminish serious injury of the crew during crash landings. Unfortunately, these weak links have been eliminated from most modern light aircraft.

Attention to better ergonomics in cockpit design can help to avoid typical professional diseases of aircrew. After the introduction of more ergonomically correct cockpit seats some years ago in most airliners, the percentage of back ailments of professional pilots decreased. Excessive noise in the cockpit can come from the engine or airflow on the skin of the airplane. In some modern airliners the noise coming from the ventilation system for cooling cockpit instruments exceeds the tolerances recommended by industrial medicine. Improvements are necessary here to avoid hearing loss of cockpit crew, especially the older pilots. Quicker aircraft evacuation in case of fire on the ground must be provided. Evacuation slides should be improved so that the users cannot be hurt when reaching the ground. The use of ejection seats in military airplanes has already helped to save the lives of thousands of pilots. With the present ejection systems, however, spinal injuries caused by the high initial acceleration are not uncommon.

Mass transportation of passengers in modern airliners over long distances creates new problems for aviation medicine. Sleeping berths for passengers during extended night flights hardly exist any more. Most flights between the United States and Europe are night flights, although flights starting early in the day would be less stressful. The few hours of darkness are not very restful for the passengers, who are presented with sumptuous meals, coffee, alcohol, passive smoking, and movies. It is not easy to achieve sufficient rest in an economy-class seat that cannot be adequately reclined and in which the legs cannot be fully stretched. Even healthy elderly passengers—and especially those with some latent cardiovascular or renal condition—have problems with swollen legs. They also can become short of breath, restless, and prone to thrombosis of the legs. In aviation medicine this is called the "economy-class syndrome." Long-distance jet aircraft such as the Boeing 747-400 or the Airbus 340 can fly halfway around the globe with only one refueling stop. Nonstop flying times of sixteen hours and more are achievable. Although the two-man cockpit was introduced in recent years to reduce the numbers of crew members, now an extra cockpit crew has to be carried on board for such long-duration flights. One crew takes over the controls while the other shift can rest in a special crew compartment.

Higher speeds and long-duration flights aggravate the problem of diurnal time shift ("jet lag") during transmeridional flight. Aviation medicine has recently been trying to find suitable ways to prevent jet lag by special diets or medicines. After westbound flights, important meetings should best take place in the morning, when people are at the peak of their performance. After eastbound flights, the evening hours are better. For some professionals, such as musicians, it is not possible to give performances in the morning after westbound flights. In such instances, only readaptation over the course of several days is helpful. It is worth mentioning, too, that prolonged waiting periods on the ground; time-consuming transport to and from airports; and standing in long lines when checking in or, in some places, while passing through security checkpoints, immigration, and customs further impair the well-being of long-distance passengers.

Modern long-range airliners have to fly at greater altitude for reasons of fuel economy. Passengers as well as the crew are exposed to higher levels of radiation. They also have to breathe the dry cabin air, which is contaminated by a relatively high ozone content and the expired breath of the passengers, to say nothing of cigarette smoke. Irritation of the eyes, respiratory distress, and frequent colds can result. What may be just tolerable for the passengers, who encounter these conditions infrequently, exceeds the tolerance limits of the crew, who are exposed to them more often. On the other hand, humidification of the cabin air and ozone filters add to the aircraft's load. This in turn restricts the number of passengers and cargo and adversely affects the economy of the airlines.

The professional image of airline pilots has changed considerably during the last decade. Formerly the technical skills—how to take off, fly, navigate, and land an airplane—were considered paramount. In the cockpit of modern giant airliners, complex electronic equipment has to be programmed and interpreted in flight. The job of an airline captain today requires many more management and computer skills than before.

When manned spaceflight began, aviation medicine extended seamlessly into space medicine. Experts in aviation medicine such as Hubertus Strughold, Ashton Graybiel, and Charles Berry now expanded their field into what was then called "aerospace medicine." NASA built large space centers at Cape Canaveral, Florida; Houston, Texas; Huntsville, Alabama; and Mountain View, California, each having a department of space medicine. Also in Europe, institutes formerly restricted to aviation medicine and several universities engaged in space medicine. In the early days of manned spaceflight, space medical activities were dedicated mostly to such applied studies as working on life-support systems, food, and hygienic systems for astronauts. The maximum time a human can tolerate weightless conditions was determined by step-by-step increases in the duration of space missions. Russian cosmonauts demon-strated that space missions of one year and possibly more can be tolerated by humans with only temporary impairment of health after return to earth.

The conditions of orbital weightlessness also provide an opportunity for im-portant basic research in medical sciences by experiments in space that cannot be done on earth. Experimental space medicine today encompasses almost all branches of medicine, including neurophysiology, ophthalmology, immu-nology, radiology, and cardiovascular medicine. Several experts in aerospace medicine have already been permitted to participate as astronauts in spaceflight and perform their own medical experiments there. The American astronaut Bill Thornton, M.D., provided the first anthropometric measurements of the fluid shift in space from the lower to the upper parts of the body.

The limits of manned spaceflight are not known yet. Still unsolved problems

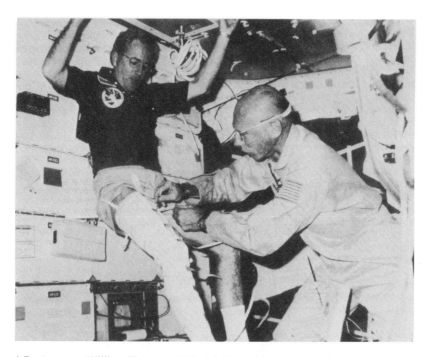

4.7. Astronaut William Thornton, M.D. (right), making an in-flight anthropometric experiment on Richard Truly during space shuttle mission STS 8. (From *Aviation, Space and Environmental Medicine* 58 [1987]; courtesy of Aerospace Medical Association)

are connected with the flight of humans to other planets of our solar system, because such missions would take several years. Radiation occurring during unpredictable solar flares, changes of mineral balance (especially calcium), and muscular and cardiovascular deconditioning are some of the problems yet to be solved. Artificial centrifugal gravity, achieved by rotation of a large spacecraft, could help to prevent such deconditioning of space crew during long flights in the future.

In view of the many urgent problems of humans on earth, the question has been posed whether the enormous costs and efforts involved in aviation and spaceflight are justified. Herman Oberth, one of the fathers of spaceflight, who died only a few years ago, answered this question as follows: "There is no real purpose of space flight. Space flight is simply the expression of the human urge to explore distant regions. So the seas, all the continents and finally air and now space were explored. This is a natural phenomenon and we have to try to make the best of it."

This statement is also valid for physicians working in aerospace medicine. Wherever and for whatever reasons humans determine to travel, the task of the physician is to protect their health on the journey.

NOTES

1. Eloise Katherine Engle, *Man in Flight: Biomedical Achievements in Aerospace* (Annapolis, Md.: Leeward Publications, 1979), 5.

2. Douglas H. Robinson, *The Dangerous Sky: A History of Aviation Medicine* (Seattle: University of Washington Press, 1973).

3. P. Bert, *La pression barométrique: Recherches de physiology expérimentale* (Paris: Masson et Cie., 1878).

4. H. Gunga, *Leben und Werk des Berliner Physiologen Nathan Zuntz (1847–1920)* (Husum: Matthiesen-Verlag, 1989).

5. H. Coxwell, *My Life and Balloon Experiences*, vol. 2 (London: W. H. Allen, 1889), 138.

6. J. Kriebel, A. Kornhuber, and W. Scherb, *Berblinger: Jahrbuch der Deutschen Gesellschaft für Luft- und Raumfahrtmedizin*, vol. 1 (1991), 629–33.

7. H. Pongratz, H. Vaic, and M. Reinicke, "Inside-out, Outside-in: Probleme beim Einsatz unterschiedlicher Fluglageanzeige," in *Proceedings, Congress of the German Aerospace Medical Society in Potsdam*, Oct. 1992 (Hamburg: Mitteilungen der DGLRM, 1993).

8. Robinson, *Dangerous Sky*.

9. Ibid.

10. A. Mitscherlich and F. Mielke, *Medizin ohne Mensch- lichkeit* (Frankfurt: Verlag Fischer, 1962).

11. L. Guibert, "Hygiene of the Aviator," in *Report of Inspection: Générale,* vol. 1, no. 32 (Paris, 1918).

12. CAA news release, Apr. 6, 1945.

13. L. H. Bauer, *Journal of Aviation Medicine* 16 (1945): 47.

14. Biometrics Branch, Medical Division Office of Aviation Safety, "Examiner Performance on Class III. Reports of Physical Examination for Student and Private Pilots." Mimeograph, C.A.A., July 15, 1949.

15. Harry G. Armstrong, *Principles and Practice of Aviation Medicine* (Baltimore: Williams and Wilkins, 1939), 28.

16. Mitscherlich and Mielke, *Medizin ohne Mensch- lichkeit;* T. Reimer, *Die Entwicklung der Flugmedizin in Deutschland: Arbeiten aus der Forschungsstelle des Institutes für Geschichte der Medizin der Universität* (Köln: F. Hansen, 1979).

17. Pongratz, Vaic, and Reinicke, "Inside-out, Outside-in"; Reimer, *Die Entwicklung der Flugmedizin in Deutschland.*

18. G. Flik, *Zur Geschichte der Wehrpsychologie.* Untersuchungen des psychologischen Dienstes der Bundeswehr (Bonn: Bundesministerium für Verteidigung, 1988), 23.

Roger E. Bilstein

Air Travel and the Traveling Public

The American Experience, 1920–1970

The classic film, *Casablanca,* appeared in 1942. In the film's final moments, Humphrey Bogart and Ingrid Bergman say a dramatic farewell at a fog-shrouded Moroccan airfield. The ambience of the scene was similar to many stock cinematic departures at railway terminals and seaports. But this leave-taking was notably updated—it occurred at an airfield, not a train station or ship wharf. Rather than the receding wail of a train whistle or the melancholy groan of a ship's horn, audiences heard the drone of airplane engines as the Air France Lockheed Electra carried the heroine away from her lover. Even for nonfliers in the audience, the airplane symbolized new standards of travel in a modern world.

During the half-century between 1920 and 1970, air travel changed from the novel to the norm. During the 1920s and 1930s, the airlines struggled to overcome concerns about air travel safety and build a market, particularly in competition with railway Pullman services. World War II engendered a broader awareness of a new "air-age world." In the postwar era, significant advances in aircraft technology revolutionized coast-to-coast schedules and ushered in global air travel, with attendant changes in the marketing of airline transportation.

In the United States, the government's airmail service in 1918 marked the beginning of continuous, regularly scheduled aviation operations. By 1925, basic routes stretched from coast to coast, a network of beacons provided navigational aid, and operational procedures were in place. Increasing numbers of Americans relied on airmail delivery for personal as well as business correspondence, and aviation received broad recognition as a factor of modern life. All this helped set the stage for passenger air travel.

During the early 1920s, one of the most important efforts to establish passenger lines was made by Aeromarine Airways, which carried several thousand patrons, almost exclusively tourists. Aeromarine's converted World War I–era flying boats operated over the Great Lakes region in summer, shifting to Florida's coastline in winter. A scheduled run to Havana often carried thirsty Americans trying to escape the rigors of Prohibition. But Aeromarine and other hopefuls lacked a consistent source of year-round income, an essential benefit supplied by federal mail contracts in the Air Mail Act of 1925. This legislation triggered the formation of commercial airlines, leading to major companies like American, United, Eastern, and others. The evolution of these early contract carriers created a demand for new aircraft, large enough to carry passengers.[1]

For travelers with a yen for aerial adventure, it became possible to patch together a coast-to-coast trip. In 1927, such a trip took 32 hours, cost $400, and usually meant cramped seats in the spartan, four-place passenger compartment of a single-engine Boeing Model 40 biplane. There were other inconveniences. Airlines still made more money carrying mail than carrying passengers. Anywhere along the trip, if a more profitable sack of mail turned up, the passenger got out. Waiting for the next flight in Peoria, Omaha, or elsewhere might take several hours to a day or so. Passenger complaints were not uncommon.[2]

On shorter routes with heavier traffic, 12-passenger airliners like the Ford Tri-Motor offered such creature comforts as stewards, apples, sandwiches, lukewarm coffee from a thermos, and aspirin. The latter was no joke, because the Fords had little soundproofing, primitive ventilation, and pitiful heating. On winter flights, the cabin temperature hovered around a crisp 50 degrees Fahrenheit. Weather delays en route, forcing unscheduled overnight stops, happened consistently. Writing in *World's Work,* a traveler who endured all these hardships during a trip in 1929 remained optimistic. "You will save a lot of time," he reported, "and come down safely."[3]

Saving time became a recurring theme in airline advertising. Two other catchwords were also frequently repeated: comfort and safety. But as late as 1941, fear of flying led the list of reasons travelers preferred trains or buses. Moreover, as one authoritative text noted, "One of the most serious problems still faced by air transportation is the opposition of women to their husbands' or other relatives' traveling by air."[4] Airline executives had begun to recognize these problems during the 1930s, and new styles in advertising began to emerge.

One market analysis, made for a major airline in 1930, included a profile of the year's passengers: a total of 2,500 fares. The travelers represented a surprising diversity of origin, representing 407 different cities in 34 states. Still, only 7 large cities furnished 47.72 percent of the passengers, while 400 other cities supplied 52.28 percent. Eighty-five percent of the passengers came from major businesses and high-income residential areas. The lesson here seemed to be that airline advertising held interest for a small group of people. Thousands of prospective air travelers simply did not care to board an airplane. Those who flew did so despite subtle but real social pressures. A former World War I pilot remembered the opposition to air travel from friends and family in the 1930s. "Some of us kept it a secret, not only from wives, but from creditors as well," he

5.1. Through the 1930s and early 1940s, passengers came from upper-income groups and received deferential treatment. With a DC-3 looming in the background, a Cadillac limousine picks up passengers for transfer to connecting flights or to provide service to the terminal at New York's La Guardia Airport. (Courtesy of American Airlines; 2083 B)

recalled. "But every one of us was proud to make a business appointment in a distant city, saying that we would fly to keep it. It gave us prestige."[5]

True, many did not fly out of fear. A variety of other reasons, however, surfaced in market surveys, explaining the reluctance of those who had flown only once or twice. Many arrived at the airport to discover canceled flights and then had no time to make a good train connection. Some complained of limits on luggage. Fares were too high. There were many secondary complaints about lack of insurance, noise and vibration, lack of comfort in the airplane cabin, and so on. The biggest problem seemed to be a basic lack of familiarity with airline travel and its value in daily business matters.[6] And that was what American Airlines addressed in its sales campaigns.

Some aviation executives recognized that the inability of airlines to carry passengers comfortably at night meant that they could not compete with the Pullman. Ralph Damon, president of Curtiss Aeroplane and Motor Company, pressed the idea with the development of the Curtiss Condor in the early 1930s. American introduced Condor sleeper service on May 5, 1934. To boost the new service, American took out a two-page spread in *Time* (June 25, 1934) to extol its virtues: "As you sleep, your lungs gratefully drink in cool, fresh, uncontaminated air. You are in a realm removed from smoke and cinders; soot and dirt; far away from dust." There was no direct mention of trains and Pullman service, but the inference was clear. Readers were asked to send in a coupon to receive literature about sleeper plane service and timetables.[7]

Some ads backfired. American ran a full-page ad in the *Saturday Evening Post* (October 1935), asking, "Shall we serve cocktails to passengers?" The ad said that many passengers were accustomed to cocktails aboard ocean liners and "fine trains" and requested them in flight. Hostile responses shot down the whole idea.[8]

During the winter and spring of 1936–37, a rash of airline accidents occurred, generating glaring headlines. A series of debates engaged American's executives as they brainstormed ways to combat all the nasty publicity. Finally, a strategy began to emerge. Given the intense news coverage, a statement from a leading airline official would certainly get attention—if anyone was willing to make such a statement. C. R. Smith decided to make the plunge, and a full-page commentary appeared in major coast-to-coast papers on April 19, 1937. "Afraid to Fly?" the ad queried. The text admitted that travel and fatalities often went together. But air travel had rapidly achieved high safety standards. Theoretically, a passenger might make 14,165 trips between New York and Chicago before running the risk of an accident, the ad advised. All travel had risks, the Smith commentary stated, but air travel was the quickest, most efficient, and most modern way of travel. Nervous travelers had only to become acquainted with flying to dispel their fears and be convinced of the inherent advantages of air travel.

The ad was a big hit. Most newspapers gave it a special break in position, and many ran supportive editorials. One national news commentator read almost all of the text during a regular broadcast. Several competing airlines had it reprinted for broader distribution. American succeeded in turning adverse attention into a positive event.[9]

Advances in the design of airliners, making them faster, more reliable, and more comfortable, clearly helped in marketing air travel. In 1934, airlines began operating the 14-passenger DC-2; in 1936, the 21-passenger DC-3 went into service. Both airplanes could cruise at nearly 200 miles per hour, and their operating costs helped airlines realize meaningful profits.[10]

Still, air travel continued to be something of an adventure. The well-known writer (and former DC-2 pilot) E. K. Gann recalled that many of his flights through turbulent summer weather in the Midwest caused acute passenger discomfort:

> The . . . air is annoyingly potted with a number of minor vertical disturbances
> which sicken the passengers and keep us captives of our seat belts. We sweat in
> the cockpit, though much of the time we fly with the side windows open. The
> airplanes smell of hot oil and simmering aluminum, disinfectant, feces, and
> leather, and puke. . . . The stewardesses, short-tempered and reeking of
> vomit, come forward as often as they can for what is a breath of comparatively
> fresh air.[11]

In the face of such experiences, vigorous marketing was certainly required.

The persistent difficulties of persuading people to fly in the 1930s often prompted publicity campaigns featuring movie stars and other well-known personalities. Shirley Temple, the popular child star, posed in a series of photos for American Airlines. Most of these endorsements came after 1935 because film stars were invariably prohibited by contract from risking their lives aboard airplanes. Deletion of such restrictive clauses represented a valuable commercial boost to the airlines. Later endorsements came from Eleanor Roosevelt and a variety of nationally prominent business leaders and their wives, because airlines realized that wives consistently discouraged air travel by their spouses.[12]

During the 1930s, airlines occasionally experimented with discounted fares, but no consistent program evolved until 1935, when American Airlines established its Air Travel Card system. A deposit of $425 allowed travelers to use their cards to charge trips at a 15-percent discount. By the end of the decade, all

5.2. Early marketing often relied on photos of well-known public figures for publicity and to promote the image of safety and respectability. Here, Shirley Temple, child star of the 1930s, helps load copies of her film aboard an American Airlines transport. (Courtesy of American Airlines; A00-122)

the major domestic lines offered similar cards, which travelers could use on any of 17 different airlines. In 1941, the major carriers began selling tickets on a credit plan, launching the "fly now—pay later" phenomenon.[13]

The airlines tried a variety of approaches to keep passengers happy and encourage them to return as customers. During the late 1930s, American Airlines recognized special patrons, celebrities, and politicians with an Admiral's Club certificate, a nice complement to the Flagship theme of American's airliners. When the company moved into new quarters at La Guardia Field, New York, in 1938, the mayor of the city jokingly remarked that he might make some money by renting his sumptuous VIP suite at the airport. American Airlines actually liked the idea, and Fiorello La Guardia's suite became the first Admiral's Club facility. The company reproduced these club suites at major hubs around the country, and other airlines eventually followed suit.[14]

Some of the best publicity came accidently as a result of destructive weather. At a time when so few people flew, comprehensive news stories about the dramatic use of aviation in emergencies represented invaluable public relations copy. A catastrophic flood in the Louisville area in January 1937 required fast action by relief officials. Eastern Airlines and American Airlines responded by adding dozens of trips to carry medical teams, clothing, and food. A grateful city later presented a special bronze plaque of thanks to the airlines.

In September 1938, an even more severe emergency occurred. A massive hurricane roared across the New England coast, devastating the entire region from Long Island through Vermont and New Hampshire. Telephone and telegraph lines were down everywhere. With bridges washed out, railroad tracks under water, and trees blocking miles of roads, the situation was chaotic and remained so for many days. Aviation was the only means of travel into and out of the area. Thousands of people who had never gone anywhere by air now besieged the reservation desks of American, the prime carrier between New York and Boston. American's schedules rose from 10 flights per day to more than 40. Doctors, nurses, and specialists flew into New England, along with 60,000 tons of food, clothing, and medical supplies. Other airlines pitched in; Eastern, TWA, and United detached airplanes to join the task. During one eight-day period, the airlines carried more than 8,000 passengers and 317,000 pounds of mail. The emergency airlift proved a godsend to beleaguered disaster officials. More than that, the dramatic emergency airline operations carried hundreds of new airline passengers and gave air transport a huge boost in public esteem.[15]

Still, the number of flying travelers trailed far behind the number of those who used Pullman schedules. In 1938, 15,539,847 travelers chose Pullman, compared to 1,176,858 airline patrons, or just 7.6 percent of the Pullman market. But the airlines were building momentum. The ad campaign launched by American Airlines not only won new business—it also won awards. The Chicago Advertising Club honored the line in 1939 for an illustration of an obviously contented businessman leaning back in his airline seat with the cut line: "Here I am—the fellow who said he would never fly!" Shortly after, American slashed the word "fly" from its advertising because the company was selling transportation, not flying. A country-wide journal of the advertising industry, *National Ad-Views,* gave American a special award in 1939, largely because the company underplayed commercialism in favor of selling a transportation service and generally building public confidence in a new form of travel against considerable popular resistance.[16]

In fact, the decline of popular resistance was evident not only in rising numbers of passengers, but also in the frequency with which airline travel appeared as a positive icon in support of other consumer items. During 1939 and 1940, the pages of the *Saturday Evening Post* carried a variety of ads for cigarettes, automotive lubricants, typewriters, shirts, and raincoats in which airline themes were used to bolster the reputation and quality of the product. One of the most substantial examples of this new respectability appeared in ads sponsored by the Air Transport Association during November 1940. The Equitable Life Assurance Society determined that air travel had reached a level of safety and reliability that justified a reduction in rates and across-the-board availability to all air travelers. Trip insurance had cost one dollar per unit of $5,000 coverage; now the rate was 25 cents per unit, the same as for rail travel. For the airline industry, this represented a true benchmark of progress.[17]

The experience of World War II whittled away considerable resistance and created a new awareness of air transport. For Americans, the dramatic, long-distance aerial blow against Pearl Harbor in 1941 revealed the ways in which air power had restructured geographical relationships. Aviation could deliver bombs, and it could also deliver cargo and passengers. The capacity to move people, especially, evoked a new sense of global proximity.

The catalyst for this new awareness was the Air Transport Command (ATC). Civilian airliners, pilots, ground personnel, and executives were literally drafted overnight to support military transportation needs. By June 1942, the ATC network touched all six continents; no spot on the globe was more than 60 hours away. At the peak of wartime operations, ATC transports took off across the Atlantic about once every 13 minutes; across the Pacific, about once every 90 minutes. All this represented a remarkable lesson for pilots and executives alike: air travel had suddenly reached global maturity.[18] The problem lay in convincing the public.

Early in the war, the assistant secretary of commerce for air, Robert Hinckley, joined with the Institute of Aeronautical Sciences to launch a list of appropriate titles on aviation for use by teachers. Called the Air Age Education Series and published by Macmillan in 1943, the list ran to some 20 books covering everything from technical aspects to biology, literature, and geography.

One of the authors, Professor N. L. Engelhardt, from Teachers College of Columbia University, wrote *Education for the Air Age,* a title that captured the flavor of this didactic set of books. Another book by Engelhardt—*Toward New Frontiers of Our Global World*—published the same year, caught the spirit of the era and represented the approach used by aviation organizations to promote postwar air travel. The book targeted junior and senior high school students. "In this Air World," Engelhardt emphasized, "distances are measured in time rather than in miles." A pair of illustrations graphically made the point. A train required 18 hours to make the 617-mile trip from El Paso to San Antonio, Texas. The distance from New York to London was nearly six times as far (3,460 miles), but it actually took less time to travel.[19] The time factor figured in much prewar airline advertising for domestic flights in the United States. Postwar ads repeated the theme and expanded it worldwide.

During the war, thousands of service personnel became accustomed to rapid transit in aircraft. They developed a new awareness of the unique ability of aviation to diminish age-old barriers of time and distance. Even for the huge majority of civilians who did not fly, the drama of wartime aerial operations sharpened an awareness of aviation and air power that carried over into the postwar era.[20]

During World War II, the Air Age Education movement also ventured into didactic magazine ads. American Airlines ran a full-page layout in magazines during 1943. Against a scenic background of active commercial retail activities, a father and his son, in military uniform, gaze skyward at an American DC-3 transport. The father obviously lags behind the younger generation in understanding aviation; the son explains to him the role of aviation in speedy transportation, which saves time in a modern world. A boxed statement within the advertisement offered a didactic analysis of the anticipated impact of the war on air travel. Many who had never traveled by airline before Pearl Harbor had become aware of the airline's significance during the domestic war effort. People learned not only from military communiqués about the value of air transportation, but also from personal experience, that "use of air is indispensable today."[21]

In the postwar years, manufacturers joined their airline customers in a combined effort to lure Americans into air travel. As the major travel periodical of the era, *Holiday* magazine presents a visual history of changing styles in advertising campaigns, and both airframe and power-plant manufacturers bought space there. Eager to break into the airline industry, the Glenn L. Martin Company became one such advertiser, and the wording of its ad copy characterized much of the postwar era. Martin's advertisement in *Holiday*'s August 1947 issue featured a sorority girl with a party invitation in hand from the Delta Sigma Omega fraternity. The full-page spread depicted her on the telephone with a friend and featured a rhetorical question in bold lettering: "I'd love to go . . . but have I enough time?" The copy stressed that airlines were indeed in the business of selling time. At airports and travel agencies, the ad claimed, "alert Americans [are] buying an hour, a day, a week." The time gained enhanced the enjoyment of a weekend, permitted a longer vacation, or benefited business. "High above the plodding earth, away from dirt, noise, and crowds, you gain time, time, time!" In case the gentle reader had forgotten, a list of airlines equipped with Martin 2-0-2 and 3-0-3 airliners was included, with the reminder that Martin products helped the airlines make such opportunities available. Curious readers could learn more about this new travel phenomenon by writing the Martin Company for a free book, *How to Travel by Air.*[22]

The pages of *Holiday* became a logical place to snare new travelers, especially those with leisure and money for specialized vacations. United Aircraft, the engine manufacturer, went angling for sport-fishing types with an ad picturing unique spots in Chile, Mexico, and Florida. "Thanks to modern air travel," the message declared, "thousands of sportsmen each season visit the world's great fishing regions." Anglers in search of the ultimate fishing hole could send for a free booklet, *100 of the World's Best Fishing Spots,* and also receive a convenient list of air fares to these locations.[23]

The airlines themselves weighed in with travel ads for an escape from the rigors of winter weather. Lacking international routes, American Airlines encouraged people to board its "Sun Country" routes to the Gulf and the Southwest United States. Operators with foreign connections offered opportunities to visit Latin America. Panagra and Pan Am took a two-page spread to entice vacationers on a grand tour of "Eight Colorful Cities" spread around the east and west coasts of South America. Travelers were also encouraged to book December flights to enjoy the novelty of "Summer!" in South America. And TWA made the most of "The Flight before Christmas" on its December connections across the United States or overseas to Europe.[24]

These faraway places had become much more accessible as the result of rapid development of four-engine intercontinental airliners like the Lockheed Constellation, capable of reliable schedules across long stretches of ocean, over high mountain ranges, and above turbulent weather. The Douglas DC-6, for example, could carry from 68 to more than 100 passengers in pressurized comfort at speeds of 300 miles per hour.

The increasingly familiar phenomenon of airline travel elicited comment from seasoned travelers. Bernard de Voto, essayist and social critic for *Harper's,* made a transcontinental flight in 1952 and analyzed his experience for the magazine's readers. The airplane was a DC-6, and the flight included a stopover in Denver, Colorado, midway across the continent. De Voto groused about the way patrons were herded about in the terminals and waiting lines. Although the meals turned out to be discouraging affairs (the old box lunches were better, grumbled de Voto), and there were no cocktails to be had, everything else was a marvel. While airborne, he reported, "you are surrounded with luxury above your station and treated with a deference elsewhere reserved for movie actors."

With delight, de Voto rediscovered the broad, open spaces of America; the checkerboard pattern of section-line roads bequeathed by the Northwest Ordinances; the passes and river crossings used by pioneers of past centuries. He reveled in the quiet and smoothness of the flight, allowing him to read notes and correct galleys, an impossible task on a train. De Voto admitted that he liked to travel by car because it never allowed for boredom. "But it is the slowest way,"

5.3. Post–World War II airliners included the graceful Lockheed Constellation. With such new equipment, the airlines began regular nonstop, coast-to-coast flights and launched new routes across the Atlantic and Pacific. Global travel had become a reality. (Author's collection)

he wrote, "and there is no answer to the speed of a plane." As a chronicler of the nation's westward movement, he expressed amazement at the incredible shrinkage of time in modern air travel. The airplane arrived in Denver in slightly less than five hours, and de Voto planned to have dinner that night with friends in Palo Alto, California. "Logic dissolves away when you summon up the other schedules," he wrote, "five or six months by ox team, seven or eight weeks by steamboat and stage coach, forty-two hours by streamliner and the East's lesser trains." He seemed to feel that high-speed travel was changing things too fast. "I hope they never compress it further with jets," he wrote.[25]

As more and more Americans took to the airways, issues of etiquette began to emerge. *McCall's* magazine addressed the subject in 1957 as part of its booklet on modern family manners. The booklet's author was Carolyn Hagner Shaw, a syndicated columnist and protocol expert from Washington, D.C., where she was touted as the doyenne of arbiters on social graces. Among other things,

she reminded passengers to recheck luggage weight (to exceed one's established poundage was certainly considered raffish) and to make sure that advance tickets were in hand, because "space is limited." On entering the airplane, "choose any available seat you prefer," except on overseas flights, where
seats were reserved.[26]

These aspects of seating etiquette remind us that air travel was primarily a
first-class phenomenon in the 1950s. Airlines competed with railways for an
upscale clientele that had the money for what was still a comparatively expensive mode of travel. Airline passenger cabins had no distinctions between first
class and economy, for example, because first class was the only standard available. In this respect, the airlines made a good effort to provide the sort of food
service expected by travelers accustomed to attractive cuisine aboard steam-
ships and good trains. Even if airline kitchens failed to offer high-quality meals
on a consistent basis from the cramped, cold confines of airliner galleys,
meals at airline terminal restaurants were generally of high levels of excellence.
Patrons at airline terminals were likely to be well-heeled and expected good
service and good cuisine. In many cities, terminal restaurants continued to
rank as better eating spots into the early 1960s. As remembered by one Hous-
tonian, the Cloud Room at Hobby Airport was a "swank place to eat" in the
1960s, and—compared to Houston's railway station—the people encountered
at Hobby were better dressed and better mannered, and the atmosphere was
more cosmopolitan.[27]

Although in-flight food services left something to be desired, liquor services
were common on domestic trunk routes by 1957, a practice that international
carriers had followed for some years. In fact, certain concoctions had already
acquired the status of hallowed tradition. When postwar flights across the Atlantic became more regular during the late 1940s, many passengers began to
appreciate the pleasures of "Irish Coffee." Compounded of strong coffee and
thick cream, laced with a liberal dose of Irish whiskey, this recipe emerged as a
traditional libation of postwar transatlantic fliers, who needed a special mixture
of something hot to revive them after a long, chilly flight and something to
soothe the tensions induced by the hours of listening to droning engines. The
drink originated in 1942, when a chef at the flying boat terminus of Foynes,
Ireland, was attempting to perk up some damp, recently arrived wartime passengers. He added some local whiskey to the coffee. An appreciative passenger
asked if he had been drinking Brazilian coffee. No, the chef replied, it was Irish
coffee. A legend was born.[28]

De Voto's desire for cocktails represented one of several changing social and
cultural features of air travel. Many Americans retained a puritanical outlook

regarding liquor, and the association of booze with flying seemed especially obnoxious. Liquor services were still frowned on by Delta Air Lines, a position reinforced by the Deep South, Bible-belt market of Delta's home territory. Religious periodicals in the region carried editorials praising Delta for its opposition to Demon Rum. But Delta's aerial prohibition was bad for business. Free corsages to women and expensive cigars to male passengers failed to overcome the lure of martinis and manhattans offered by others. Airline rivals whose flights began in the South and ended up in the North began to cut deeply into Delta's competing routes. In the spring of 1958, Delta succumbed to the inevitable, although it sold liquor rather than dispensing free drinks, as some airlines did. The religious press urged boycotts, and many Delta employees protested, but liquor prevailed. After 1958, alcoholic beverages became standard on airlines throughout the United States.[29]

Social and cultural changes were also evident in matters of race. During the 1930s, the airlines unquestionably discriminated against black passengers. At reservations desks, if a caller sounded like a black person, or if the call came from a black neighborhood, reservations personnel said that there were no seats available. One wealthy black businessman in Chicago evaded these barriers by sending his white chauffeur to buy tickets. On DC-3 transports, black passengers found that they were herded into one of the single-row seats on the right side of the plane. Before World War II, air terminals in the South rarely had segregated facilities because black citizens seldom flew. During the war, as black military personnel began to fly, passengers who could get tickets were seated on a first-come-first-served basis. During the 1950s, separate black and white accommodations appeared in southern terminals, but Atlanta's new Hartsfield Airport, opened in 1961, had no segregated facilities.[30] Along with civil rights legislation in 1960s, equality in terminals and airline seating became the norm.

Increasingly, the motion picture industry used the theme of air travel as a box-office draw. In 1951, an MGM film called *Three Guys Named Mike* appeared, featuring Jane Wyman, Howard Keel, and Van Johnson. Among the promotional materials for the film was a pamphlet featuring Jane Wyman's testimony about learning the work requirements of stewardesses with American Air Lines, praising their poise and sophistication. The pamphlet was an overt blurb for American Airlines, as well as for the movie—an intriguing example of the use by the motion-picture industry of the concept of airline operations. Even if the majority of Americans had not flown in an airliner, the idea itself was obviously judged to have positive appeal for movie audiences. The image of the air travel industry was obviously improving.[31]

The continued appearance of aeronautical themes in recognized icons of popular culture underscored its acceptance and maturity. Airline toys had been available since the 1930s, and another symbolic event occurred in 1964, when the makers of Barbie dolls introduced boyfriend Ken as an airline pilot, complete with flight bag.[32]

Off the movie screen, real-life airline crews began to receive additional training to make passengers feel more comfortable. To allay fears of flying, in the early 1950s the airlines turned to motivational research—consumer psychology. A leading practitioner of that emerging discipline was Dr. Ernest Dichter, a Viennese analyst who had migrated to the United States after World War II and set up the Institute for Motivational Research. Dichter was asked to find a way to bypass the fear of flying. His first recommendation was to get more female spouses into the air to build family support for flying, so that both husband and wife felt less anxious about flying on business trips. Next, Dichter stressed the need for a "psychologically calm environment" in flight. Stewardesses received special instructions about demeanor to reassure nervous travelers; pilots received elocution lessons so that their spoken messages to the passenger cabin reflected just the right "voice of authority from the flight deck."[33]

Intensified competition for market share led to a variety of strategies. Continental Airlines sponsored some of the most flamboyant marketing events. In 1956, the company began operations on its Los Angeles-Denver-Chicago route, a highly competitive market. Continental lavished attention on this run with what it called Gold Carpet Service. Arriving DC-7B transports were met by uniformed, gold-helmeted ground crews who trotted out to the airplane in military unison. Around airports and at travel agencies, Continental also stationed a phalanx of midgets, rigged out in finned helmets, gold spacesuits, and a miniature rocket backpack that emitted outer-space beeps. Harding Lawrence, a senior executive at Continental, had a hand in these shenanigans. In the 1960s, as head of Braniff International, Lawrence won publicity by having stewardesses wear high-fashion clothes and painting his airline fleet in a rainbow of pastel colors. Some airplanes featured distinctive, abstract designs by the avant-garde artist, Alexander Calder.[34]

For frequent air travelers, longer flights at higher altitudes often meant longer hours of boredom. When Bernard de Voto crossed America in a pressurized DC-6, the time spent above overcast made "flying the dullest mode of travel."[35] Marketing departments apparently had been worrying about this drawback and accepted the notion of in-flight movies. The idea had been tried in Europe by British and German lines in the mid-1920s, although these early experiments seem to have been exactly that. In the United States, Universal Air Lines tried this diversion on its Chicago-Minneapolis route in 1929, but this, too, seems to have been a short-lived effort.[36] In 1959, an American entrepreneur perfected a lightweight, 16-millimeter film projection system, established a company called Inflight Motion Pictures, and began looking for a customer. TWA, fighting Pan Am for passengers and trying to lure more patrons into first-class seats, decided to screen airborne films. The scheme began on coast-to-coast flights in 1961, when Lana Turner appeared in a film titled *By Love Possessed*. The film itself faded into obscurity, but airline movies became customary.[37]

As business traffic climbed and business executives junketed long distances across the United States and off to unusual, appealing global destinations, spouses also wanted to make the trip. Especially in the postwar era, executive travelers realized that the family treasury could reasonably allow spouses to come along, so that additional days were often earmarked for strictly recreational time together. A greater appreciation of world cultures and international relations began to evolve as a result of foreign travel.[38]

Competition from nonscheduled airlines in the late 1940s and early 1950s finally pushed the major trunk lines into modifying their universal one-class service and establishing coach fares. Mixed-class service on the North Atlantic routes began in 1953. Improved, four-engine airliners like Super Constellations, DC-7s, and Stratocruisers provided additional seats, and airline travel became a transportation phenomenon. In 1951, airline passengers exceeded Pullman travelers for the first time. By 1957, airlines had surpassed both trains and intercity buses in passenger miles, making airlines the nation's leading intercity passenger carrier. In 1956, more travelers between America and Europe went by air than by sea.[39] For international travel, a variety of inland cities like Chicago and Houston joined such traditional gateways as New York and San Francisco, creating new travel markets for the airlines and exciting travel prospects for business and pleasure passengers.

Technology brought further changes in airliner capabilities and patterns of air travel. Introduction of the Boeing 707 in 1958 gave the airlines a 600-mile-per-hour jet able to carry over 190 passengers. When it entered service in 1970, Boeing's 747 jumbo jet, with a capacity of more than 400 passengers, made front-page headlines around the world. The passenger capacities of postwar airliners and their increasing speeds kept passenger fares at affordable levels, and fast trips made air travel even more appealing to broader segments of the traveling public.

Historian and cultural critic Daniel Boorstin expressed misgivings about the new mode of air travel as it had evolved by the early 1960s. In his 1964 book, *The Image: A Guide to Pseudo-Events in America,* Boorstin acknowledged the

5.4. During the 1960s, the speed of jet travel and the passenger capacity of jet airliners marked a new plateau in the evolution of air travel. The public introduction of the mammoth Boeing 747 in the late 1960s generated strong popular interest. (Courtesy of Boeing Company; P 43711)

remarkable facility of jet-propelled, long-range air travel. At the same time, jet travel at 33,000 feet robbed travelers of the stimulating landscape en route, one of the greatest joys of travel. "The tourist," Boorstin complained, "gets there without having gone." Having arrived, the tourist was further insulated in an "American style" hotel, though shrewd managers might include a sampling of "local atmosphere" somewhere in the decor. As Conrad Hilton remarked of his globe-girdling string of hotels, "Each of our hotels is a 'little America.'"[40]

Some Americans simply refused to travel by air, considering it unsafe. A *Holiday* article in 1969 turned up an interesting list of confirmed nonfliers, including comedians Jimmy Durante and Bob Newhart, and composer-conductor Andre Previn. Pianist Glenn Gould was pathologically afraid to fly and arranged his concert tours to be compatible with train schedules. Stanley Kubrick, director of the space-age film *2001: A Space Odyssey,* and science fiction

5.5. With more seats, efficient schedules, and declining ticket costs, postwar airliners attracted a much more diverse cross section of the traveling public. The democratization of air travel also contributed to the possibility of family travel. (Courtesy of American Airlines; 23473)

guru Ray Bradbury refused to travel by airline. Baseball star Jackie Jensen confessed, "I gave up playing baseball so I wouldn't have to fly." In the opinion of television star Jackie Gleason, "The best way to fly is by train." Actress Joanne Woodward traveled by air, but did so reluctantly. "You travel by train but you are sent like a package by plane," she said.[41]

Nonetheless, air travel seemed to grow unchecked. Business activities and the relatively low costs of economy air fares drew thousands of Americans to domestic and foreign airline travel. The internationally acclaimed social critic, Max Lerner, referred to the new phenomenon in his book, *America as a Civilization*, published in 1957. "The new Air Age, whose impact is just beginning to be felt, has further heightened the mobility of Americans," Lerner wrote. The sprawling new airports suggested an epoch when distances would lose all meaning. Airplanes would not replace cars, Lerner said, but they would certainly change travel patterns and create a greater democratization of travel: "What the Air Age has done has been to make the faraway vacation possible for the boss's secretary as well as for the boss."[42]

Democratization occurred on domestic as well as international routes, but it was the latter that produced some of the more striking patterns. Before the war, transoceanic leisure travel by steamship consumed many days of time. Only the wealthy elite could afford the expense or the several weeks required to arrive in Europe, see the sights, and venture home again. Postwar transatlantic flights permitted an astonishing cross-section of travelers to take a 10-day vacation they could afford. Conrad Hilton put it succinctly. "What used to be a month-long vacation trip is now almost a week-end possibility. . . . The airplane is here to stay."[43] Economy fares, package tours, and resort hotels run by American companies offered white-collar and blue-collar travelers affordable and reassuringly modern American conveniences.

The arrival of jets during the 1960s enlarged the range of affluent, footloose Yankees. Midwestern couples who might have summered in the Black Hills of South Dakota now jetted off to snorkel around the Seychelles in the Indian Ocean. By 1970, five million Americans made annual treks somewhere abroad, and only 3 percent went by sea. Historian Daniel Boorstin wrote, "The United States was the first nation in history so many of whose citizens could go so far simply in quest of fun and culture. The size of this phenomenon made international travel, for the first time, a major element in world trade."[44]

The scheduled inaugural of the Boeing 747 prompted an editorial in *Holiday* to the effect that such jumbo jets would stimulate far more people to travel, ranking such airplanes with the auto as a contribution to mobility.[45] The 747 itself appeared on the cover of *Holiday*'s issue for July 1969, and the entire magazine focused on the various ramifications of air transportation. "The heroic days of air travel," the editors proclaimed, "are over."[46]

NOTES

1. Roger E. Bilstein, *Flight Patterns: Trends of Aeronautical Development in the United States, 1918–1929* (Athens: University of Georgia Press, 1983), 48–49; William Leary, "At the Dawn of Commercial Aviation: Inglis M. Uppercu and Aeromarine Airways," *Business History Review* 53 (summer 1979): 180–93.

2. Civil Aeronautics Board, *Handbook of Airline Statistics* (Washington, D.C.: Government Printing Office, 1964), 445.

3. Myron M. Stearns, "All Aboard by Air: Transcontinental Passenger Service," *World's Work* 58 (Apr. 1929): 39–41. For a definitive overview of airline companies and the development of their routes in the United States, see R. E. G. Davies, *Airlines of the United States since 1914* (New York: McGraw-Hill, 1962). Social and economic trends are addressed in Carl Solberg, *Conquest of the Skies: A History of Commercial Aviation in America* (Boston: Little, Brown, 1979).

4. John H. Frederick, *Commercial Air Transportation* (Chicago: Richard D. Irwin, 1942), 325–26.

5. Paul Peter Willis, *Your Future in the Air* (New York: Prentice-Hall, 1940), 33–34. Willis was a marketing and public relations executive for American Airlines during the 1930s.

6. Ibid., 37–39; Frederick, *Commercial Air Transportation,* 299–305. Until 1934, American Airlines was called American Airways. In this paper, the more recent corporate name is used for consistency.

7. Willis, *Your Future,* 59–61; Robert Serling, *Eagle: The Story of American Airlines* (New York: St. Martin's, 1985), 55–59. For a convenient reference on airliners, covering entry in service, performance, seating, and other miscellany, see Kenneth Munson, *Airliners between the Wars, 1919–1939* (New York: Macmillan, 1972).

8. Willis, *Your Future,* 67.

9. Ibid., 66–67, 73–82; Serling, *Eagle,* 103–4.

10. Munson, *Airliners between the Wars,* 162–65.

11. Ernest K. Gann, *Fate Is the Hunter* (New York: Simon and Schuster, 1961), 57.

12. Kenneth Hudson, *This Was Air Travel: A Social History* (Totowa, N.J.: Rowan and Littlefield, 1972), 61; Robert Atwan, *Edsels, Luckies, and Frigidaires* (New York: Dell, 1979), 305. The latter, an illustrated study of advertising, has several aviation examples.

13. Frederick, *Commercial Air Transportation,* 328–29.

14. Serling, *Eagle,* 100, 144–49.

15. Willis, *Your Future,* 107–9; Serling, *Eagle,* 107–8; Federal Writer's Project, *New England Hurricane* (Boston: Hale, Cushman, and Flint, 1938), 7, 41, 58. Various issues of the *New York Times* (Sept. 21–Oct. 1, 1938) also described the extensive devastation of this storm.

16. Willis, *Your Future,* 125–26, 140–41.

17. See, for example, various issues of the *Saturday Evening Post,* vols. 211–13. The endorsement by Equitable appeared in vol. 212 (Nov. 16, 1940), 83.

18. For comments about effects of the ATC experience on airline personnel, see Serling, *Eagle,* 153–80. For insights on the global reach of the ATC, see Oliver La Farge, *The Eagle in the Egg* (Boston: Houghton Mifflin, 1949).

19. N. L. Engelhardt, *Education for the Air Age* (New York: Macmillan, 1943); N. L. Engelhardt, *Toward New Frontiers of Our Global World* (New York: Noble and Noble, 1943), 7, 33.

20. This awareness is implicit in much of the commentary offered by William Field-

ing Ogburn, *The Social Effects of Aviation* (Boston: Houghton Mifflin, 1946). The concept was further enlivened for me by Professor Robin Higham, a well-traveled transport pilot during World War II (telephone interview with the author, July 2, 1992).

21. Reprinted in Atwan, *Edsels*, 135.

22. *Holiday* 7 (Aug. 1947): 79.

23. Ibid. 12 (Oct. 1952): 2.

24. Ibid. 12 (Nov. 1952): 1, 25, 92–93, 149; Ibid. 12 (Dec. 1952): 40, 164.

25. Bernard de Voto, "Transcontinental Flight," *Harper's* 205 (July 1952): 47–50.

26. Carolyn Hagner Shaw, "*McCall's* Family Manners," bound in *McCall's* (Apr. 1957): 1, 10. Details of postwar equipment and seating are covered in Kenneth Munson, *Airliners since 1946* (New York: Macmillan, 1975).

27. The cultural flavor of air travel over several decades is implicit in Hudson, *This Was Air Travel*. Interview with Gay Carter, Houston, Texas (July 2, 1992).

28. From a brochure of the Foynes Flying Boat Museum, supplied by R. E. G. Davies, National Air and Space Museum.

29. W. David Lewis and Wesley Phillips Newton, *Delta: The History of an Airline* (Athens: University of Georgia Press, 1979), 310–15.

30. Serling, *Eagle*, 228; Betsy Braden and Paul Hogan, *A Dream Takes Flight: Hartsfield Atlanta International Airport* (Athens: University of Georgia Press, 1989), 129–30.

31. Author's notes from MGM promotional brochure, *Three Guys Named Mike* (1951), in a private collection. See also Serling, *Eagle*, 250–52.

32. Paris and Susan Manos, *The World of Barbie Dolls* (Paducah, Ky.: Collector Books, 1990).

33. Vance Packard, *The Hidden Persuaders* (New York: McKay, 1957), 24–25, 31–33, 64–66.

34. Robert Serling, *Maverick: The Story of Robert Six and Continental Airlines* (Garden City, N.Y.: Doubleday, 1974), 118–19; John J. Nance, *Splash of Colors: The Self-Destruction of Braniff International* (New York: Morrow, 1984), 33–36.

35. De Voto, "Transcontinental Flight," 48.

36. Tom Huntington, "That's Entertainment," *Air and Space* (June/July 1992): 58–62; *New York Times* (Feb. 18, 1929).

37. Irving Kolodin, "Headphone Hunting at 30,000 Feet," *Saturday Review* 4 (Apr. 16, 1977): 20–24.

38. Interview with Robin Higham. This is also implicit in various advertisements of the 1950s in such magazines as *Holiday,* cited above.

39. Civil Aeronautics Board, *Handbook,* 452–55, 461, 530.

40. Daniel Boorstin, *The Image: A Guide to Pseudo-Events in America* (New York: Harper, 1964), 94–98.

41. "Is It Safe to Fly?" *Holiday* 46 (July 1969): 52–53.

42. Max Lerner, *America as a Civilization* (New York: Simon and Schuster, 1957), 97.

43. Quoted in Boorstin, *Image*, 97.

44. Caskie Stinnett, "How Mombasa Became the New Place," *Saturday Review* 4 (Apr. 16, 1977): 11–14; Daniel Boorstin, *The Americans: The Democratic Experience* (New York: Vintage, 1974), 517–18.

45. Caskie Stinnett, "Editorial," *Holiday* 46 (July 1969): 27.

46. Ibid., cover note, 3. By the 1970s, air travel for Americans was no longer the novelty it had been. In the late 1940s, it was estimated that only 10 percent of the nation's adult population had taken a commercial flight, and the figure in 1962 was 33 percent. By 1972, about one-half (54 percent) of the population had taken an airline trip, and 63 percent had done so by 1977. During the 1930s, about 90 percent of airline trips involved business; during the 1970s, about 50 percent of passengers were vacation and leisure travelers. Robert Serling, *Wrights to Wide Bodies* (New York: Air Transport Association, 1978), a brochure issued on the seventy-fifth anniversary of the Wright brothers' first flight, contains miscellaneous passenger statistics. See also ATA News Release, "Gallup Poll Finds 63 Per Cent of American Adults Have Flown" (Nov. 21, 1977). Both copies are in the author's files.

 Lee Kolm

Stewardesses' "Psychological Punch"

Gender and Commercial Aviation in the United States, 1930–1978

When Western Air Express displayed its new Fokker 32 to the admiring crowd gathered at the Alhambra, California, airport in 1930, the gala festivities included a line of chorus girls dancing across the wings. The sight of white female bodies adorning technological apparatus was not unusual in the aviation business. A year later, a trade journal suggested that airport administrators could "Draw Crowds to the Port with a Beauty Contest." Under a photograph of white women draped on the struts, wings, and propeller of a Travel Air 6000, the article explained that "beauty lends charm to anything."

Lending charm to air travel was what Boeing Air Transport envisioned when it devised a similar place for white women in 1930. The company decided that "there would be a great psychological punch to having young women stewardesses."[1] Stewardesses did more than lend charm, however. Like the chorus girls and beauty contestants, they provided a feminine presence that highlighted, by contrast, the masculinity of technological mastery and aeronautical achievement. This gender arrangement, soon standard among airline companies, created a "psychological punch" that reverberated through the decades.

Gender is integral to the history of commercial aviation, and analyzing gender issues contributes to the "wider view" apparent in recent scholarship in aviation history. The wider view looks beyond aircraft technology to the people and organizations that have shaped aviation history, and wider yet, to the historical cultures of which these people and organizations have been a part.[2] Analyzing airline history in the wider view shows that gender has been as important in shaping the history of commercial aviation as the factors historians more usually analyze, such as aircraft designs and route structures. "Gender" refers not to biological sex, but to the dichotomous cultural images and hierarchical social relations that have made sexual differences historically significant in peoples' experiences and identities.[3] Gender influenced airlines' marketing strategies, their management techniques, and flight attendants' occupational identities in the three periods of in-flight service: the formative years of the industry, from 1930 to 1942; the war and postwar era, from 1942 to 1958; and the jet age, from 1958 to government deregulation in 1978.

The first period began in 1930, when Boeing Air Transport Company hired the first stewardesses as an experiment to serve the few passengers who braved this new form of transport. Companies had previously asked the copilot to attend to the passengers, and a few had assigned the task to male attendants, who were also responsible for baggage, ticketing, or other ground duties. Boeing's novel choice for cabin service was white female nurses, and gradually through the decade most of the other companies in the United States followed their lead, including American Airlines in 1933 and TWA in 1935.[4]

In this formative period, the expansion of passenger service rested upon convincing the public of the safety of air travel. Airlines hired women in part to draw upon wider cultural conventions, which equated femininity with domesticity, nurturance, and civility; women helped them tame the image of flight. A stewardess in 1932 explained why airlines hired women for the job by pointing out that passengers felt "in their element" in surface vehicles, but aloft they felt "distinctly out of it." "Here's where we girls step into the scheme," she continued. "By taking our home-making instincts into the cabins of the commercial airliners, we can lend familiar aspects to which travelers may cling."[5]

To reinforce the familiar and reassuring images of stewardesses, most airlines hired only young women who were graduate nurses. Airlines preferred nurses for their discipline, responsibility, and good sense. "Institutionally trained girls are schooled to serve the public," explained one executive, and another praised their "devotion to duty."[6] The medical qualification gave airline managements confidence that nurses would exercise their "home-making instincts" even when thousands of feet above the nearest supervisors.

These strategies worked. Popular descriptions of commercial flight praised the feminine presence as a source of solace to the uneasy traveler. An account from a popular magazine in 1933 of a flight over the Rocky Mountains described the stewardess as a comfort, buffering passengers from both the savagery of the wilderness and the rationality of the cockpit:

> Black overhead, queer lights reflected from the snow beneath; the dark, savage rock masses washed by intermittent swirls of snow. The stewardess knows that up front in the cockpit the pilots are doing their stuff, steady and imperturbable as ever. It's up to them, that end of it. But the other end, back here in the cabin, facing these anxious eyes, this is her domain, this is the human side. Smile— and make it convincing.[7]

The steady, imperturbable, masculine cockpit contrasts with the human, feminine cabin, the site of smiles. Such contrasts depicted the safety of the enterprise, not only by bringing warmth and nurturance aloft, but also by creating a contrast that highlighted the manly aeronautical prowess of the cockpit. Such contrasts were typical in descriptions of commercial flight in the first years of air travel.

The contrasts that highlighted masculinity were essential to marketing air travel because the feminine influence threatened to make aviation appear too soft and easy to be credible as a serious business. Amelia Earhart acknowledged this danger in a radio address titled "Women's Influence on Air Transport Luxury." Earhart extolled the comfort and safety that women brought to modern air travel, making it suitable even for her grandmother, but, she hastened to clarify, "I do not wish to imply that air travel is an effeminate sort of thing." Pilots initially worried that the presence of stewardesses implied flying was, at least in part, an effeminate occupation. Longtime United Airlines stewardess Mary O'Connor recalled that when she began flying in 1933, "pilots really held a very dim view of having their hitherto all-male realm in the sky invaded by women." Another early stewardess met similar reactions among pilots who feared that the sight of women would wither their manliness. At a fuel stop on her first flight, the pilots told her, "Don't get out of the plane. Don't let anybody see you."[8]

The feminine threat was contained by the social relations of flight, which separated and distinguished the cockpit from the cabin, the masculine from the feminine. The division of labor that distanced pilots from duties that seemed demeaning or servile by assigning passenger service to females preserved the image of the rational, steady, imperturbable cockpit. An aviation reporter explained why airlines hired women by pointing to the perceived incongruity between masculine dignity and feminine caretaking: "Instead of a friendly but frequently clumsy co-pilot secretly annoyed at having to turn himself out of the dignity of his cockpit every so often and merge himself into the roles of waiter, guide and occasional head-holder, if the skies got rough, here was a clever young woman." The threat of women's invasion was also mitigated by the hierarchy that distanced the flight deck from the cabin. While this hierarchy was necessary for the safe and orderly operation of the aircraft, pilots reinforced it with rituals of hazing, pranks, and teasing that served, in the words of an observer, to "keep air hostesses in their place."[9] The masculinity of flight was also preserved by airlines' portrayal of the meaning of air travel to their male passengers. The advertisement reproduced here appealed to men's imaginations of wives pining at home for their return. The fantasy of a waiting wife helped distinguish the gender of the male passengers who conducted business by air.

Race as well as gender influenced whom airlines hired to serve their passengers. Until state courts forced airlines to integrate their cabin crews in the late 1950s, all stewardesses were white. Airlines might have turned to the most comparable vocation, Pullman service, and employed black men, especially because trade journals, career guides, and popular accounts often likened in-flight service to Pullman service. But only one airline hired Pullman porters: New England and Western Airways, which operated in the summer of 1930 from New York to eastern cities. One aviation reporter praised the choice for the same reasons others endorsed female nurses, pointing out that the porters "had the necessary training and background to render the right sort of service." Further, the presence of porters provided reassurance, "for it supplied the familiar atmosphere of the Pullman car and made flying seem a lot less strange."[10] As this description makes clear, airlines did not discriminate on the basis of race in deference to white passengers' preferences.

Most airlines, however, hired only people with white skin because skin color, like sex, was a cultural point of distinction that helped airlines sell seats. In the first years of air travel, selling seats meant luring passengers away from the rival railroads, and part of the lure was a promise that airline cabin service was superior to Pullman service. To distinguish airline cabin service and signal its superiority, companies hired those with white skin. This ranking was explicit in some sources from the early years of air travel. For example, a vocational guide praised the stewardess for making air transport "an exceedingly pleasant mode of travel" and continued with an unmistakable reference to Pullman service: "She hasn't accomplished this success by holding a whisk broom in one hand and holding the other, Gypsy like, waiting to be crossed with silver." Other accounts bragged outright about the racial superiority of the airline cabin crew. One claimed of a particular stewardess: "You know the first instant you see

6.1. Airline advertisements from the 1930s stressed family values. This advertisement from 1938 encouraged wives to permit their husbands to fly and indicated that, while women waited at home, breadwinning by air was a particularly masculine occupation. (D'Arcy Collection of the Communications Library, University of Illinois at Urbana-Champaign, courtesy of American Airlines)

Olette Hasle that she has path-breaking blood; that she is of the Nordic breed which conquered the great Mid-Northwest."[11]

From the early stewardesses' point of view, the gender and racial distinctions in the airline enterprise and in popular depictions were acceptable. The job's exclusivity not only helped sell air travel to the white public, it made the white stewardesses feel elite among women. "Here I am," one stewardess crowed, "one of the very first in what is the newest occupation for women in the whole world." To protect their positions, stewardesses emphasized gender differences to argue for what they, as white women, could add to the enterprise, even though this emphasis kept them in the cabin and away from the controls. The stewardess who claimed women had "home-making instincts" accepted that "there aren't going to be any girl air-mail or passenger flyers." She clarified that "capability has nothing to do with it"; but if a woman were in the cockpit, "every passenger, man or woman, would quit the ship at the next fuel stop."[12] Stewardesses' emphasis on women's uniqueness put them at odds with such women as Amelia Earhart, who sometimes minimized gender differences to argue for women's equal access to the cockpits of commercial airliners. But this appeal to gender differences, to "home-making instincts," did win white women a permanent, if limited, place in aviation.

The second era in the history of American in-flight service began in 1942, when the wartime need for nurses forced airlines to drop the medical qualification and hire women who had spent a year or two in college. The war was also a turning point because it created demand for airlines to transport military personnel, which combined with larger aircraft and the public's increased acceptance of air travel to swell the quantity of customers and the size of companies.[13]

In the context of this growth, airlines forged a meaning of gender that was different from that of the earlier years. The contrasts defining gender no longer communicated safety; they now stood for service. Service had become an increasingly important area of competition among airlines since the late 1930s because many other areas of competition had been restricted by government regulation.

Airline managements in this second period valued having women aloft to offer personal service and friendliness in the midst of the growing anonymity of air travel. TWA defined a stewardess as "a diplomat in skirts." The airline called stewardesses "diplomats" because they mediated between the companies and the customers and added the "skirts" to indicate that this mediation was congenial and caring. United Airlines created a fictional stewardess character named "Mary Mainliner," who described in their ads the attention she lavished on the company's passengers. "My job is making people happy," she said in one ad.

American Airlines also embodied the caring side of its corporate image in their cabin crew. Ads for the company claimed, "The Flagship stewardess personifies the friendly service for which American Airlines, Inc. is known." This campaign elaborated on the feminine qualities that made for good service: "Her gracious manner and thoughtful attention to her passengers add immeasurably to the comfort and the pleasure of their trip."[14]

To ensure that stewardesses displayed the desired version of femininity, airlines devised special management techniques, especially important now that companies could no longer rely on the discipline associated with a nursing degree. Training programs that lasted several weeks and included classroom instruction, practice flights, and grooming courses were a first step. Replacing the "old independent procedure, the learn-as-you-go method" of the early 1930s, these programs taught the techniques of handling passengers. In addition, rules and regulations helped create the corporate brand of friendly femininity. Some airlines required women to quit when they reached age 32 or 35, when their enthusiasm might dwindle, and some forbade marriage after finding it made stewardesses, in the words of one supervisor, "too independent in attitude."[15]

"Gracious manners" and "thoughtful attention" did not alone sell airlines' services. While stewardesses' femininity in the corporate view centered on diplomacy, friendliness, and charm, the pilots' masculinity stood for the contrasting component of superior airline services: on-time reliability. Pilots in the second era were portrayed as intelligent, stable, professional, and dependable. In the same campaign that claimed an American Airlines stewardess "adds friendship to the Flagships," the company asserted that the captain "commands your Flagship and your confidence." One ad showed the stern, serious face of the captain looking out of the cockpit and listed his commanding qualities: "He represents a highly selective group, chosen by virtue of intelligence, stability and judgement. . . . He is a serious-minded, efficient professional flyer who defines his responsibility in terms of regular and dependable operation." Even the aircraft interior was imbued with difference, as a vocational guidebook described: "Leaving the flight deck, with its air of quiet authority, the door is closed. We return to the comfort and serenity of the passenger cabin."[16]

Reinforcing the distinctions of gender was the hierarchical relationship between the dignified cockpit and the serene cabin. One stewardess recalled of her relationship to the captain: "He was the king. . . . The captain came first, then the copilot, and *then* the passengers." Male passengers in this era, however, did not enjoy this status over the stewardesses. Their masculinity continued to be established by their superior standings in their families and communities. An advertisement from American Airlines pictured a businessman ascending the steps of an airplane while his wife and son waved good-bye. The copy read: "There are some very personal reasons for favoring travel by air. Not the least of these is the open admiration that air travelers receive from family, from neighbors, even from the crowd at the airport. A boy likes to look up to his father— and fathers would be less than human if they did not enjoy it."[17] In this scene, the father's standing as an admired man derived from his position, different from that of his earthbound wife and son. With the distinctions of gender resting on the exclusion of women from the flight deck and the image of a businessman's wife waiting at home, gender arrangements were not threatened by the presence of female passengers. Airlines in this second era were attentive to expanding the female market and responded to the perceived needs and concerns of women travelers.

Stewardesses in this second period continued to endorse the rigid division of labor and the airline's ideals. They embraced their positions as feminine mediators between the companies and the customers, despite being subordinate to the captain-kings, in part because they considered friendly service a practiced proficiency that they took pride in achieving. One former stewardess from this era dubbed herself and her colleagues "professional people pleasers." In addition to pride, airline training gave these women the interpersonal skills they needed to secure livings as wives in postwar middle-class marriages that were to center on intimacy, togetherness, and family harmony. Tommie Heck, whose picture represented Continental Airlines' friendly service from 1941 to 1946, testified that her "association with Continental can be best remembered by the awareness of other people's needs and how important it is to show that in all we do."[18] In addition, airline work gave women uniforms and a paycheck for practicing the interpersonal skills that in other settings, such as the family, were less visible.

Airline work offered another reward. Like their counterparts in the 1930s, the white women who filled this position benefited from its continued exclusivity, summed up in this second period by the word "glamor." In airline publicity and popular materials, stewardesses were called the "glamor girls of the air," their grooming routines were "glamorizing," and an aircraft was "the glamorous setting for their glamorous jobs."[19] Like "safety" and "service," "glamor" was defined through contrasts. The worldly stewardess contrasted with the naive first-time flier, the exotic acquisitions adorning her abode contrasted to the drab flat of the average clerk typist, and the technological sophistication of her daily life opposed the "primitive" and "savage"[20] peoples she visited. At-

6.2. In advertisements from the postwar years, the gender image of male passengers continued to derive from contrasts with their earthbound families. In this 1951 advertisement, business flying distinguished the man from his wife and son. (D'Arcy Collection of the Communications Library, University of Illinois at Urbana-Champaign, courtesy of American Airlines)

tracted to these flattering racial and class contrasts, stewardesses accepted corporate versions of femininity and affirmed their place in aviation on the basis of gender differences.

The third period began with jet service in 1958. Jets further expanded the industry by opening up markets to smaller cities, as well as eventually decreasing flight times and increasing passenger loads. Most important, jet service offered an irresistible time savings to business commuters, making air travel routine for jet-age businessmen. Airlines had always responded most to the lucrative business market, and their response to businessmen in the jet age created a new place for gender in commercial aviation.

Sexual adventure was the gender motif of the jet age because air travel began to threaten, rather than affirm, white middle-class masculinity. Jet-age expansions in the 1960s made air travel into just one more part of the "rat race" that many of these men lamented. It had transformed them from admired fathers into "organization men" whose intelligence, stability, efficiency, and dependability had left them bowed under the weight of corporate bureaucracy and dulled by the drone of suburban banality. Airline managements empathized. In an advertisement, Braniff Airlines addressed the problem: "You've made the trip to Dallas in the same airplane so many times, you feel you could fly it yourself. (At least you'd like to try. *Anything* to break the monotony)."[21] What did masculinity mean if breadwinning meant monotony? The generation of businessmen who flew by jet from sales offices in New York to business meetings in Cleveland felt their sons had little to admire in how they made a living.

In the mid-1960s, companies promised to restore masculinity through sexual adventure. Braniff Airlines was the most overt. In 1965 it offered to break the monotony with what it called "The Air Strip," stewardesses who removed successive layers of clothing during the flight. Continental Airlines ran an ad in the same year showing a stewardess's backside as one of the many attractions aboard, and in 1968 TWA offered on domestic flights "gorgeous creatures" who created exotic atmospheres with foreign costumes and foreign meals. At the sacrifice of previous efforts to attract women aloft, these adventurous and titillating advertisements and atmospheres restored businessmen's masculinity by offering stewardesses' sexuality as a feminine contrast. They also affirmed businessmen's masculinity by placing the male passengers above stewardesses in the in-flight hierarchy. Delta Airlines claimed in its ads that when served by the hostess, "you get to feel like a leading man."[22] By creating "leading men," airlines offered male travelers a version of the masculinity that pilots had enjoyed since the 1930s. Now every male passenger was king.

Imagine the trauma these cultural portrayals underwent when a sex-

Our first run movies
are so interesting
we hope you're not
missing the other
attractions aboard

Our Golden Marquee Theater, which features movies and two kinds of
stereo music, is so interesting that some passengers might miss the other
niceties of Gold Carpet® service. • For example, in First Class and Club
Coach a gourmet meal prepared by Lucien Dekeyser. (Truly a delicious,
delightful experience.) • Or the services of our extra man on board... the
Director of Passenger Services. No other airline provides this extra man
who's aboard every Golden Jet to serve all three classes. • Entertainment,
yes. We have the best. But don't miss all the rest of the services that
make Continental "the one for fun." Reserve a seat through your
Travel Agent, or by calling Continental at AN 3-4240.

Only Continental offers three classes of service on every Golden Jet.

	JET GOLDEN	CLUB COACH	FIRST CLASS
Chicago to Los Angeles	$90.95	$105.45	$114.55
Chicago to Denver	47.25	55.40	76.10
Chicago to Kansas City	23.15	27.15	32.95

(All fares plus tax)

**CONTINENTAL
AIRLINES** 🦅

Charge the flight on American Express Card, Carte Blanche,
Diners' Club, Air Travel Card or Continental's own Credit Plan.

Golden Marquee Theater is on 5 non-stop flights
to Los Angeles.

6.3. In the 1960s and 1970s, breadwinning seemed more monotonous than masculine.
Advertisements such as this from 1965 presented the stewardess as the feminine foil
that distinguished a businessman's gender. (D'Arcy Collection of the Communications
Library, University of Illinois at Urbana-Champaign, courtesy of American Airlines)

discrimination suit in 1971 forced airlines to hire men as stewards. The perceived contradictions between masculinity and subordination ultimately changed the very definition of the occupation as airlines and the public alike responded to the sight of men in the cabin. Airlines scrambled to adjust; TWA, for example, searched for a uniform design that would communicate a steward's subordination to the flight deck and the senior cabin crew, yet, in the words of a trade journal, "project the proper image by allowing a man his dignity." Some passengers were equally troubled. One told the *New York Times* that it "wasn't until I saw my first steward . . . that I began to take seriously the fact that these people are there for public safety and not just for drinks and decoration." And he added, "I'm still hesitant about asking a steward for something when there's a stewardess around."[23] Pressured by cultural contradictions, and pressured as well by the federal government's intensified interest in cabin safety procedures, in-flight service workers became safety professionals.

Another pressure for change came from the female cabin crew. Women in the generation of flight attendants that brought in the jets initially joined the previous generations in esteeming and defending women's uniqueness; many chose the job as an expression or confirmation of their womanhood. One recalled that when she joined the airlines in the mid-1960s she had preferred women's jobs, "jobs with uniforms: first a nurse, then a stewardess." She chose to wear uniforms, she said, "so that I would know I was a woman, so that everyone could see I was playing a woman's role." But as she watched the role of stewardess change from path-breakers and "professional people pleasers" to what she called "flying geisha girls," "sex objects in the sky," and "wind-up Barbie dolls," she felt alienated from the jet-age portrayal of womanhood. Like many flight attendants in this era, she felt that this image reduced her status, especially in relation to passengers. Her colleague put it in just these terms, complaining that passengers seemed to think, "Why should I listen to you? You're nothing but a girl!"[24]

In addition, color exclusivity began to erode in the late 1950s when airlines were forced to consider all applicants regardless of race. The *New York Times* recognized the stakes by reporting that companies feared the pool of "white stewardesses would dwindle fast if the 'glamor' of the job were 'down-graded' by employment of Negro girls."[25] To preserve racial distinction and protect the job's elite status, some white women used racial metaphors, such as "geisha girls," to distance themselves from the sexy and subservient images of airline service. As airline work lost its elite racial associations, white women were less willing to identify with a job built on gender differences.

Partly in response to cultural demotions, many stewardesses in the early 1970s distanced themselves from the airlines' renditions of gender by calling themselves "flight attendants" and insisting on the importance of their safety functions. A Pan Am employee, for example, told a reporter that she did not think of herself as "a sex symbol or a servant." Instead, she asserted, "I think of myself as somebody who knows how to open the door of a 747 in the dark, upside down, and under water."[26] In short, she thought of herself as a "safety professional," a necessary employee with an expertise that had nothing to do with gender. Identifying themselves as safety professionals was a tempting, perhaps necessary, strategy for flight attendants; it bolstered their more active and independent unions, which flourished in these years, and it helped inspire their many successful legal challenges to the airlines' policies on marriage and age.[27]

This strategy also allowed flight attendants to recoup their authority over passengers. As one said about her duties in the early 1980s, "I'm in charge, and I'm the one who's running the show, and I'll always be a step ahead of you. It's my moment of victory or power." But this strategy was also dangerous. By distancing themselves from preconceptions of womanhood, by seeing womanhood as only a liability, these women left themselves open to the problem summed up by the flight attendant who enjoyed her power aloft, but she admitted, "Back down on the ground I'm just a little nothing again."[28]

"Just a little nothing again"—this poignant admission points to the conclusion that the history of gender in commercial aviation is neither a history of progress nor regress, but a history of changing dilemmas inherent in societies that categorize people by sexual differences and make these differences determinants of lives and livelihoods. In the first two periods, from 1930 to the jet era, when stewardesses were relatively elite, subject only to the captain-king, they articulated their contribution to aviation on the basis of what they believed was special about white women, considering themselves homemakers in the sky. While theirs was a positive evaluation of white womanhood, this position reinforced cultural stereotypes and segregated these women to limited positions in the industry. When white stewardesses were demoted in the jet age, subject to all of the passenger-kings, they sought to escape gender and called themselves safety professionals. While this position won them union strength and civil rights, they no longer supported or defended gender differences and risked instead feeling that women were "nothing."

For airlines, gender in the history of commercial aviation was equally ambiguous. In the 1930s, employing white women to provide a domestic atmosphere helped sell air travel by taming the image of flight, but it locked airlines into hiring practices that in the jet age brought them to court for race and sex discrimination. In the postwar years, white femininity helped solve the public relations problems that mass transport made pressing, but by portraying the job of stewardess as a prelude to homemaking rather than as a professional career, the airlines spent a great deal of money training a transitory labor force. And in the jet age, the use of sexual images to transform the beleaguered business customer into a "leading man" ultimately resulted in a disaffected labor force and helped determine which few airlines survived deregulation.

NOTES

1. Oliver E. Allen, *The Airline Builders* (Alexandria, Va.: Time-Life Books, 1981), 102–3; Russell J. Brinkley, "Draw Crowds to the Port with a Beauty Contest," *Airports* 7 (Sept. 1931): 23. The memo from Boeing Air Transport was reprinted by Horace Sutton in "Isle-Hoppers, Aisle-Walkers," *Saturday Review,* May 15, 1965, 37–38.

2. James R. Hansen, "Aviation History in the Wider View," *Technology and Culture* 30 (July 1989): 643–56; Joseph Corn, review of *Flight in America 1900–1983: From the Wrights to the Astronauts,* by Roger E. Bilstein, *Technology and Culture* 26 (Oct. 1985): 871–73.

3. Sherry B. Ortner, "Is Female to Male as Nature Is to Culture?" in *Woman, Culture, and Society,* ed. Michelle Zimbalist Rosaldo and Louise Lamphere (Stanford: Stanford University Press, 1974), 67–87; Joan Kelly, "The Social Relations of the Sexes: Methodological Implications for Women's History," *Signs* 1 (summer 1976): 809–24.

4. Western Air and Pan American hired male "couriers" in 1928, and TAT hired them in 1929. Eastern Air Transport had hired a few nurses in the early 1930s but removed all cabin attendants when the mail contracts were canceled in 1934. When this company filled the position again it employed white men until the wartime shortages of men forced it to hire women in 1944. Carl Solberg, *Conquest of the Skies: A History of Commercial Aviation in America* (Boston: Little, Brown, 1979), 110, 215.

5. Olette Hasle, quoted in W. B. Courtney, "High-Flying Ladies," *Colliers,* Aug. 20, 1932, 30. Joseph Corn first pointed out this use of gender in *The Winged Gospel: America's Romance with Aviation* (New York: Oxford University Press, 1983).

6. Anonymous executives quoted by Robert W. Hambrook in "Airline Hostesses," *Air Commerce Bulletin* 11 (Aug. 15, 1939): 33.

7. Francis Vivian Drake, "Air Stewardess," *Atlantic Monthly,* Feb. 1933, 190.

8. Amelia Earhart, "Women's Influence on Air Transport Luxury," *Aeronautic Review* 8 (Mar. 1930): 32; Mary O'Connor, *Flying Mary O'Connor* (New York: Rand McNally, 1961), 25; Harriet Fry Iden, quoted in George Vecsey and George C. Dade, *Getting Off the Ground* (New York: E. P. Dutton, 1975), 271.

9. Alice Rogers Hager, "Romance and Valor Add Glamour to Routine of Flying

Hostesses," *New York Times,* Dec. 5, 1937; Leo Freedman, "The Duties of an Air Hostess," *Popular Aviation* 12 (Feb. 1933): 124.

10. C. B. Allen, "The Airline Attendant's Job," *Aviation* 30 (Apr. 1931): 245.

11. Ben B. Follett, *Careers in Aviation* (Boston: Waverly House, 1940), 101; Courtney, "High-Flying Ladies," 30.

12. Harriet Hefron Gleeson, quoted in Helen McLaughlin, *Walking on Air: An Informal History of Inflight Service of Seven U.S. Airlines* (Denver: State of the Art, 1986), 11; Olette Hasle quoted in Courtney, "High-Flying Ladies," 30.

13. "Between 1943 and 1946 inclusive," R. E. G. Davies found, "the number of passengers carried by the domestic scheduled airlines increased four-fold, a rate of growth never exceeded before or since." Although this growth did taper off immediately after the war, the postwar trend toward mass transport continued. R. E. G. Davies, *Airlines of the United States since 1914* (Washington, D.C.: Smithsonian Institution Press, 1972), 325.

14. Morris B. Baker, *Airline Traffic and Operations* (New York: McGraw-Hill, 1947), 141; *Time,* March 21, 1949, 47; *Life,* Oct. 10, 1949, n.p. The advertisements are from the D'Arcy Collection of the Communications Library of the University of Illinois at Urbana-Champaign.

15. O'Connor, *Flying Mary O'Connor,* 59. A memo from 1937 from a supervisor at TWA complaining about the effects of marriage was reprinted in Gwen Mahler, et al., eds., *Wings of Pride: TWA Cabin Attendants, A Pictorial History, 1935–1985* (Marceline, Mo.: Walsworth Publishing, 1985), 41. TWA began terminating hostesses upon marriage in 1941.

16. *Life,* Oct. 10, 1949, n.p., from the D'Arcy Collection; Mary Murray, *Skygirl: A Career Handbook for the Airline Stewardess* (New York: Duell, Sloan and Pearce, 1951), 21.

17. The former flight attendant was quoted in Roger Rawlings, *The Last Airmen: Exploring My Father's World* (New York: Harper & Row, 1989), 92 (emphasis in Rawlings); *Time,* Dec. 17, 1951, n.p., from the D'Arcy Collection.

18. McLaughlin, *Walking on Air,* 55, 171.

19. "Glamour Girls of the Air," *Life,* Aug. 25, 1958, 68–77; Betty Peckham, *Sky Hostess* (New York: T. Nelson & Sons, 1941), 35. The last phrase appeared in the following two sources in the same month, suggesting it may have derived from an airline press release: "Air Stewardesses Mark Anniversary," *Western Flying* 25 (May 1945): 84; and Maxine Finley, "Flight Veterans," *Douglas Airview* 12 (May 1945): 37.

20. Elisabeth Lansing, *Nancy Naylor Flies South* (New York: Thomas Y. Crowell, 1943), 108, 140. For another example of contrasting representations, see Murray, *Skygirl.*

21. *New York Herald Tribune,* Jan. 7, 1966, from the D'Arcy Collection.

22. *Dallas Times,* Dec. 12, 1965; *Chicago Tribune,* Jan. 11, 1965; *Chicago Tribune,* Apr. 3, 1968, from the D'Arcy Collection; *American Aviation* 32 (Mar. 3, 1969): back cover.

23. T. J. Wright, "Haute Couture Lines Vie in the Competitive Skies," *Airline Management* 4 (Oct. 1972): 19; passenger quoted in Anna Quindlin, "Flight Attendants: An Old Stereotype Is Given the Air," *New York Times*, Apr. 24, 1978, quoted in Roberta Lessor, "Unanticipated Longevity in Women's Work: The Career Development of Airline Flight Attendants," Ph.D. diss., University of California, San Francisco, 1982, 152.

24. Paula Kane with Christopher Chandler, *Sex Objects in the Sky: A Personal Account of the Stewardess Rebellion* (Chicago: Follett Publishing, 1974), 154, 19, title page, and 63; Elizabeth Rich quoted by Letty Cottin Pogrebin in "The Working Woman," *Ladies Home Journal*, Nov. 1976, 86.

25. "Stewardess," *New York Times*, Dec. 29, 1957.

26. Anonymous stewardess, quoted by Lindsy Van Gelder, "Coffee, Tea or Fly Me," *MS*, Jan. 1973, 87.

27. Flight attendants' union history is analyzed by Frieda S. Rozen, "Technological Advances and Increasing Militance: Flight Attendant Unions in the Jet Age," in *Women, Work and Technology: Transformations*, ed. Barbara Drygulski Wright (Ann Arbor: University of Michigan Press, 1987), 220–37; Georgia Panter Nielsen, *From Sky Girl to Flight Attendant: Women and the Making of a Union* (Ithaca: ILR Press, 1982); and Deborah G. Douglas, *United States Women in Aviation, 1940–1985* (Washington, D.C.: Smithsonian Institution Press, 1991).

28. Anonymous stewardess, quoted in Lessor, "Unanticipated Longevity," 208.

William F. Trimble

The Collapse of a Dream

Lightplane Ownership and General Aviation in the United States after World War II

Few industries have been as volatile as aircraft manufacturing. Heavily dependent on the military as an outlet for its products and vulnerable to both short-term and long-term economic cycles, the industry has undergone severe periodic contractions. Intense as these dislocations have been, few can compare with the one afflicting the lightplane industry between 1947 and 1951. From a total of more than 33,000 aircraft manufactured in 1946, output declined by half in 1947, bottoming out at only 2,300 in 1951. That year, production amounted to less than 7 percent of what it had been in 1946.[1]

Never robust to start with, the lightplane industry had by the late 1930s achieved a measure of stability that promised steady if not spectacular growth. Led by the Piper Aircraft Corporation, which manufactured more than 1,800 airplanes in 1939, the industry received a boost with the establishment of the Civilian Pilot Training Program (CPTP) that year. Administered through colleges and universities, the CPTP created an increasing demand for lightplanes as trainers and significantly added to the number of Americans who received flight instruction.[2]

But the legacy of the 1930s was mixed. Lightplane technology had changed little in nearly two decades, and manufacturers were suspicious, if not downright hostile, to such government agencies as the Civil Aeronautics Administration (CAA) and the National Advisory Committee for Aeronautics (NACA). The industry's skepticism arose in part from the abortive efforts of the CAA in the 1930s to create the $700 "airplane for everyman," which most manufacturers considered detrimental because they thought it would cause potential customers to defer buying current models priced far higher. Nor did CAA airport development programs, which funneled money toward big-city airports served by the airlines, offer much help. For private flying to expand, many more small fields were needed in suburban and rural areas. As for the NACA, most of its research work was oriented toward assisting the military and manufacturers of commercial aircraft, not the lightplane business.[3]

Prewar efforts aimed at developing "spinproof" and simplified-control aircraft were not generally well received by the lightplane community. Fred E. Weick, a former NACA engineer, joined the Engineering and Research Corporation (ERCO) in Washington, D.C., where he designed a two-place, all-metal, low-wing monoplane with controls linking the ailerons and rudders. Produced as the Ercoupe, the airplane was easy to fly and virtually impossible to spin. Although touted as a boon for the novice flier, the Ercoupe worried veteran pilots, who argued that such an airplane would lend a false sense of security to inexperienced aviators and therefore compromise rather than enhance flight safety. ERCO produced only a few more than 100 Ercoupes before the war.[4]

World War II brought prosperity to the industry but did little to change its structure. Lightplane manufacturers produced military observation, liaison, and utility aircraft, in addition to fabricating components for larger aircraft companies. But the emphasis on production meant that virtually nothing could be done to develop new and more efficient aircraft types or take advantage of some of the advances being made in engine and airframe technology. To make matters worse, wartime expansion presented the lightplane industry with an overcapacity problem as it entered the postwar era.

Nevertheless, lightplane manufacturers hoped to reap profits from a rich harvest of fliers trained during the war. Admiral John H. Towers, one of the navy's pioneer aviators, whose wife, son, and daughter had taken up flying, commented in 1944 that once the war was over the major contention in his household was likely to be, "Who's going to fly the family airplane today?" Piper published a booklet that same year claiming that lightplanes will "dominate the air just as popular-priced automobiles dominate the road. . . . We can look forward to a great air age after the war."[5]

John Paul Andrews reflected some of the same optimism in a book, *Your Personal Plane,* published in 1945. Dismissing wild speculation that one in four

7.1. Fred E. Weick and his innovative Ercoupe. With its novel control system, the airplane was easy and safe to fly. (Courtesy of the National Air and Space Museum; 83-12597)

individuals with pilot training would buy a personal plane (leading to guesses that the postwar market for lightplanes might top one million), Andrews estimated that as many people who owned pleasure boats might own airplanes. He reckoned that by the end of the 1940s, the market might reach 350,000 lightplanes per year, worth $200 million and creating a "big industry in little planes." Volume output, reduced manufacturing costs, improved designs, enhanced safety, and the widespread financing and construction of community landing fields, or "airparks," entered into Andrews's equation.[6]

Unwarranted as they may have been, such optimistic visions of personal flying carried over and were even enhanced in the postwar era. Nonaviation magazines, among them *Business Week* and such unlikely periodicals as *Better Homes and Gardens*, featured glowing articles on the pleasures of the family airplane. Most significant was a piece in *Fortune*'s February 1946 issue covering the latest offerings of lightplane manufacturers and declaring that "the trend is in the right direction—toward cheaper, safer airplanes. . . . The outlook is good." There was also the expectation that returning veterans, who had been exposed to the practicality of the airplane and flying during the war, would take advantage of the flight training program offered to them under the Servicemen's Readjustment Act (more commonly known as the G.I. Bill). In an editorial in *Aviation News* in March 1946, Robert H. Wood wondered how the lightplane industry would have enough volume to cope with the anticipated deluge of new aviators.[7]

The growth of the industry in 1946 fueled optimism about the long-term prospects of lightplane manufacturing. The 14 leaders in the lightplane industry delivered 31,500 aircraft worth more than $88 million. Piper led the numbers race with nearly 7,800 airplanes, challenged by Aeronca with 7,500. Cessna was third with nearly 4,000, and Taylorcraft fourth with 3,100. In dollar value, Beech was the leader, manufacturing $18.7 million worth of airplanes, after which came Aeronca and Piper at $13.5 million each. Backlogs were high, reaching nearly 21,000 two-place and 16,000 three- and four-place aircraft in

7.2. Piper hoped the PA-12 Super Cruiser, larger and more comfortable than the famous Cub, would appeal to the family man who wanted to keep flying in the postwar years. (Piper Aircraft, courtesy of the National Air and Space Museum)

October. Piper opened a new plant in Ponca City, Oklahoma, to which it transferred production of J-3 Cubs in 1946.[8]

Not only did manufacturers meet the demand with stepped-up production
of existing offerings, they also introduced attractive new models. Cessna's
120/140 series, the superb Beechcraft Bonanza, the Aeronca Chief, and the
Stinson Voyager appeared. ERCO began producing an improved version of the
simplified-control, Fred Weick-designed Ercoupe, and Luscombe resumed
sales of its prewar all-metal Silvaire. New competitors also entered the market:
North American Aviation, traditionally manufacturers of military aircraft,
came in with the four-place Navion; Republic offered the Seabee amphibian;
Globe Aircraft Corporation began production of its sleek bonded-plywood
Swift; and Culver introduced the Model V, with its "Simpli-fly" control system
and antispin characteristics.

A possible omen, however, was the decision by the Bendix Aviation Corporation, a major supplier of parts to the industry, to give up its plans to enter the
lightplane field.[9] Bendix's decision came after a market survey showed that all
was not as it seemed in the booming lightplane business. One of the problems
faced by all manufacturers was the delivery of materials. For a while manufac-

7.3. The all-metal Cessna 140 was one of many new models offered by the industry
immediately after World War II. (Cessna Aircraft, courtesy of the National Air and
Space Museum)

7.4. Republic's Seabee amphibian was displayed at the 1947 New York Aviation
Show. (*Aviation Magazine,* courtesy of the National Air and Space Museum)

turers had been able to get by using surplus stocks of fabric, plywood, and aluminum, but by early 1946, those supplies were critically depleted. The 1946
steel strike led to a shortage of steel tubing at Piper, which in February had to lay
off 1,900 workers at its Lock Haven, Pennsylvania, factory. In July, Taylor-
craft, which had recently completed a $1-million expansion of its plant in Alli-
ance, Ohio, had to cut back production due to lack of engines.[10]

Another cloud on the horizon in 1946 was the marginal financial position of
most lightplane manufacturers. Despite turning out unprecedented numbers of
aircraft, Piper saw its profits decline in the fiscal year ending September 30,
1945. In March 1946, Piper announced a new stock offering, hoping to use the
proceeds to retire some of its outstanding debts, and other firms followed suit.
Unfortunately, the value of lightplane stocks severely declined in the second
half of the year. Piper's common fell from $15 a share to less than $4 in early
1947. Aeronca's and Cessna's securities fared better, but they, too, suffered
during the crash. Globe Aircraft marketed 150,000 shares of common and pre-

7.5. Sleek, safe, and easy to fly, the Culver Model V came out in anticipation of a huge market for personal aircraft. (McCormick-Armstrong Co., courtesy of the National Air and Space Museum)

ferred stock in early 1946. Although the company paid a dividend on the pre-ferred shares in July, it proved to be the last payment made by the firm. By the end of the year, its common stock was considered worthless, and its preferred was trading in the penny range.[11]

As lightplane sales climbed through the first half of 1946, some observers counseled caution. William A. M. Burden, assistant secretary of commerce for air, commented in January, "Two factors will make or break the private flying boom": safer and easier-to-fly airplanes, and a "drastic improvement" in the nation's airport system, which had not undergone significant expansion since before the war. *Aviation News* reported the possible "softening" of the light-plane market, based on census figures in August showing an increase in sales but a marked decline in the backlog of orders. In an article in the March 1946 issue of *Flying* magazine, John H. Geisse, assistant administrator for private flying in the Civil Aeronautics Administration, wrote that manufacturers had to do much more than wait for orders to flow in. Of critical importance was safety. Before the war, studies had shown lightplanes to be unusually vulnerable to damage or loss in accidents, not all of which were attributable to the pilot.

Geisse urged manufacturers to make improvements in prewar designs aimed at augmenting safety. Like Burden, Geisse identified airports as another major concern. Without a significant increase in the number of airports and attention to their location and accessibility, there was little chance the industry would continue to expand.[12]

The public statements of Burden and Geisse revealed the ambiguous role of the Civil Aeronautics Administration in stimulating change in the postwar light-plane industry. In 1944, Theodore P. Wright, CAA administrator, had joined the chorus of those predicting a huge market for personal airplanes in the years after the war. The next year, Wright created the Non-Scheduled Flying Advisory Committee, charged with investigating all aspects of private aviation and making recommendations for bringing CAA regulations in line with the needs of the industry. By 1947, Wright had helped streamline the licensing of private pilots, but his efforts to get the industry to concentrate on improvements to lightplane design and construction had little effect. Under Wright, the CAA spent $150,000 developing a castered crosswind landing-gear system and initiated plans for a national airport network including large numbers of landing fields with unidirectional runways.[13]

William T. Piper, president of Piper Aircraft, was skeptical about government regulation in general and the policies of the CAA in particular. Knowing enough about the lightplane business to understand its vagaries, and weary of the enticing wartime dreams of an exciting new age of aviation, he thought it was time to "reappraise private flying in the light of cold hard facts." Specifically responding to Geisse's article, he admitted that personal aviation had been "oversold" and dismissed optimistic predictions about the size of the future lightplane market as nothing more than "wild guesses." There was no chance that lightplane production would ever compare with the volume of automobile production. But he took exception to Geisse's criticism that lightplane manufacturers had not done all they could to offer new and better aircraft. The Piper company had 10 percent of its personnel working in research and development and was paying particular attention to the improved safety and efficiency of its products. At the same time, he did not see how his or any other firm could be blamed for "giving the public what we have" after not selling any private aircraft at all during the war.[14]

Piper did not see the CAA playing a constructive role in the postwar lightplane industry. The administration's pursuit of a true low-cost airplane he saw as little more than an ephemeral dead end. The Piper company had designed the single-seat Skycycle, which it hoped to offer at $1,000, only to find that the cost of materials, engine, instrumentation, and dealer fees amounted to $1,000,

7.6. CAA administrator Theodore P. Wright did all he could to encourage the expansion of the lightplane industry in the years immediately following World War II. (Harris and Ewing, courtesy of the National Air and Space Museum)

making the project totally uneconomical. He criticized the CAA's flight instruction program, which did not suit the requirements of the private flier. He did not like the CAA's efforts to develop crosswind landing gear; it was far better, according to Piper, to design and build landing fields with safe, multidirection runways. Piper dismissed the NACA as having done "very little" to assist the industry, although he admitted "prospects of NACA aid" were better now than they had been in the past. On the whole, though, Piper forecast that "the lightplane and private flying will grow and develop," but at a more deliberate pace than they had in the previous few months.[15]

Piper sounded less optimistic later in the year, when he and other lightplane manufacturers gathered at the National Aviation Clinic in Oklahoma City in October 1946. He said that he had seen sales in the early 1930s fall from 6,000 per year to about 500 per year, and he warned that such a contraction "could happen again." He went on to identify government-sponsored flight training through

7.7. Piper Aircraft was one of
the most successful lightplane
manufacturers. Its president,
William T. Piper, warned against
overexpansion of the industry.
(Courtesy of the National Air and
Space Museum; 91-7126)

the G.I. Bill as the principal reason for the boom and pointed out that it was
"problematical" how much longer the expansion would continue. Almost certainly, he predicted, lightplane sales would level off in the near future, with the
result that some of the companies would be forced out of business. Max Karant,
editor of *Flying* magazine, prophesied that the end of the seller's market in the
lightplane business was "not too far off." He said that the manufacturers had to
become more sophisticated in their sales techniques and devise new ways to
make the customer "reach for his check book." But even more important, firms
had to pay more attention to technological developments, safety, and maintenance of their products. [16]

A harbinger of things to come was a slump in lightplane sales in the last two
months of 1946. Statistics from the Aircraft Industries Association showed a
34-percent decline in sales for November, followed by another 31-percent decrease in December. *Aviation News* blamed the fall on the "general economic
scene" and determined that the "market is definitely limited for those who can
afford to pay $2,000 to $3,000 for a personal plane." Hardest hit was Aeronca,

7.8. The Globe Swift assembly line. Despite the appearance of prosperity, Globe
Aircraft was in serious financial trouble by the end of 1946. (*Aero Digest,* courtesy of
the National Air and Space Museum)

which experienced a drop in sales from 717 in November to only 231 in December. Two companies, Globe and ERCO, ceased production altogether.[17]

Nevertheless, there was still room for optimism. Statistics showed that the
backlog of orders, while declining for two-place airplanes, fell off only margin-
ally for three- and four-passenger models. Part of the backlog had been due, as
well, to potential customers who had placed duplicate orders earlier in the year.
When they finally took delivery, they canceled the second order. Journalist Alexander McSurely surveyed the scene in December, finding a "general softening" of the lightplane market, but seeing nothing particularly alarming. Lightplane sales had always been seasonal, generally declining in the winter months.
He surmised that in the "snowbelt" many customers who had placed orders
were waiting for warmer weather before taking delivery.[18]

At the National Aircraft Show in Cleveland at the end of the year, manufacturers put on the best face possible. While acknowledging that the industry was
undergoing a "reorganization," during which "some heads must fall," W. T.
Piper insisted that the market was not saturated, that his company still had a

backlog of 7,000 orders, and that "new models designed for practical transportation will create unprecedented demands upon the aircraft industry." Aeronca reported that sales of its two-place Champion were off, but it was accepting a good number of orders for its larger Chum, due to be certificated early in 1947. Turning out 30 airplanes per day in its Wichita plant, Cessna thought the market was generally healthy.[19]

Whatever residual hope persisted that the market would soon right itself largely evaporated in early 1947. Reporting a $400,000 loss for his company in fiscal year 1946, W. T. Piper told his employees that the losses had been incurred despite the production of record numbers of airplanes. The outlook was bleak for 1947, which promised to be a "struggle" for the company. After a two-month shutdown, ERCO resumed production of the Ercoupe, but in much smaller numbers than previously. The company limped through the first half of 1947 before selling off all its Ercoupe parts, materials, tools, and distribution rights. In early 1948, ERCO abandoned the lightplane business altogether. As for Globe, it fell prey to financial mismanagement, and when the Securities and Exchange Commission began investigating its 1946 stock sales, the company declared bankruptcy. So did Taylorcraft, which succumbed after seeing its output fall from 30 airplanes per day to fewer than 40 per month by February 1947. North American ceased Navion production in May after producing only 1,100 of the airplanes since June 1946. The Ryan company in San Diego bought the rights and tooling to the Navion and reintroduced an improved version of the airplane later in the year.[20]

In the midst of the growing crisis in the industry, W. T. Piper again took stock of the situation. He thought it was important for everyone to understand that "aviation is not a mass-production industry, either from the manufacturing or the customer viewpoint." To realize genuine economies, an aircraft manufacturer had to gear up for the production of at least 50,000 airplanes per year, and "we do not anticipate such a demand for as far into the future as we can see." "Let's face it," Piper wrote, "there isn't a mass market. There can't be now or in the foreseeable future. If the past 20 years have taught us anything, they should have taught us that only a relatively few people can take advantage of the utility or pleasure of the airplane. They add up to a lot of people but not to the millions sometimes envisioned." But Piper could still not shake his belief that there were "excellent prospects" for the industry "now and for at least the next two decades." He expected his company to sell about 4,000 airplanes in 1947.[21]

Total industrywide production in 1947 was about 16,000, far fewer than in 1946, but not too far off some estimates that ran as high as 20,000. Piper led with more than 3,500 airplanes, but the company lost more than a half million

7.9. Ercoupes in production. The bus body under construction on the left suggests that ERCO was seeking diversification in anticipation of a downturn in lightplane sales. (Courtesy of the National Air and Space Museum; 77-14062)

dollars and furloughed two-thirds of its employees. Nearly bankrupt, Piper underwent a traumatic reorganization during which the board of directors muscled aside the company's founder and replaced him with a former Chrysler executive, whose only instructions were to pinch pennies and hold off the firm's creditors. Cessna and Beechcraft fared better. Cessna recorded a nearly 70-percent increase in the dollar volume of sales in 1947 over that of 1946, in addition to a profit in excess of $370,000. But the firm's gains were due in large part to a contract with the army to manufacture furniture and to substantial earnings from large subcontracts with Boeing in Wichita. Beechcraft sold 1,200 Bonanzas worth nearly $8 million in 1947, indicating that there was a clear shift in the market to higher-performance, four-place airplanes.[22]

Things got much worse during the next two years. In 1948 lightplane sales dropped precipitously, falling to less than 7,000, or 45 percent of what they had been in 1947. Cessna took first place in the depressed market with total sales of

1,600 airplanes. Lacking airplanes in the upper range of the four-passenger market, Piper acquired Stinson and its popular Voyager model from Consolidated-Vultee in late 1947. The firm also introduced the four-place Clipper, priced at less than $3,000, hoping to undercut its competitors, whose lowest-priced models cost close to $5,000. But it was to little avail; Piper trailed Cessna with only about 1,400 airplanes delivered in 1948.[23]

If 1947 and 1948 were bad for the lightplane industry, the next few years were disastrous. In 1949, characterized by a recession that saw a fall in the GNP and a sharp increase in unemployment, manufacturers sold fewer than 3,400 lightplanes, less than half the number of the previous year. Sales in 1950 started off slowly but picked up as the year went on, culminating in deliveries of about 100 more airplanes than in 1949. Cessna continued to lead Piper by a slight margin, selling about 20 more airplanes than its competitor. The two combined to take two-thirds of the lightplane market. In 1951, sales bottomed out at 2,300.[24]

What happened? Or perhaps a more appropriate question: What did not happen?

One consideration is that all manufacturers assumed that "pent-up demand" from the war years would spill over into sales of lightplanes. To be sure, there was an increase in per capita income during the war, rising to $1,600 in 1946, and there was a shortage of consumer durables, but that did not translate into immediate demand for personal airplanes, especially when the lowest-priced J-3 Cub sold for $2,195. Sales of durable goods did go up immediately after the war, but those goods were automobiles, refrigerators, and electric appliances, not airplanes.[25] Many consumers decided their first priority after the war was to put their money into a home. Few saw an airplane as the best way to use their disposable income.

Related to this was the limited utility of the lightplane. Uncomfortable, noisy, and not especially fast, the lightplanes of 1946 and 1947 met entry-level expectations at best. Moreover, there was confusion about where lightplanes fit into the overall transportation picture. Were they to be used as a substitute for the automobile on medium-range and long trips, or were they to provide a fast and convenient alternative to the car for shorter commuter journeys? W. T. Piper thought larger, more expensive private aircraft performed best in long-distance travel in fair weather. But more than just basic transportation was involved. Many prospective buyers of lightplanes were initially attracted to them for their recreation potential. Flying was fun, and an affordable airplane seemed to be a perfect alternative to a new set of golf clubs. But when these consumers looked at what $2,500 bought them, they were discouraged. In comparison, a shiny new MG sports car cost $1,800 in 1946—still a lot of money, but a purchase that had far more utility and entertainment value than a J-3 Cub. The lightplane simply could not match the automobile on either a practical or amusement level.[26]

Lightplanes were tied to airports, of which there were never enough despite constant entreaties from the industry and sincere if limited efforts by the CAA to expand the number of landing fields. In late November 1944, the administration had presented an ambitious national airport plan that included 2,900 landing fields to meet the needs of private pilots. The Federal Airport Act of 1946, much more modest in scope than the CAA plan, was aimed at assisting big-city airports served by the major airlines. In any case, restricted congressional appropriations and a small CAA airport planning staff hindered the act's rapid implementation. It is also possible the CAA put the cart before the horse in viewing airport development as a stimulus to lightplane production and sales. Using the automobile as an analog, widespread automobility preceded the construction of highways and related supporting infrastructure.[27]

Market forces worked against the lightplane industry, too. Proponents of low-cost private aircraft often pointed to the automobile industry as a model to be followed; all that had to be done was to manufacture and sell lightplanes in sufficient quantities and at a low enough price to generate hundreds of thousands if not millions of sales. But traditionally, aircraft had been sold in a protected "hot-house" climate, where both the producer and the consumer (normally the military) were experts and worked closely with each other on what would now be called product development. The automobile market, in contrast, was far more open, characterized by producers who often dictated to inexpert customers what products they thought they wanted.[28] It was impossible for the lightplane industry to bridge the gulf between such disparate market environments.

The failure of the lightplane to command a large market in the postwar era was also due in part to the limitations inherent in the technology and structure of the industry. Entry into the market was deceptively easy. All it took to design and produce a lightplane was a fundamental knowledge of aerodynamics and some understanding of welding steel and shaping light alloys. Initial capital costs were low, but as the volume of sales expanded, manufacturers soon faced the need to build and equip larger plants. Having entered the business with marginal capital reserves, many competitors were not in a position to generate and sustain the capital needed for longer-term requirements. In 1946–47, there were 14 major companies in the business, far too many to compete successfully in a limited market. Even the few relatively prosperous firms were slow to grasp the possibilities of new materials and power plants.[29]

Finally, the lightplane industry during this period suffered from noneconomic and nontechnical problems that can best be defined as philosophical and cultural. Many of the leaders of the industry were independent-minded, stubbornly insisting on going it alone, and maintained a steadfast resistance to government involvement or interference. Only grudgingly did lightplane manufacturers go along with the requirements of the military during the war, and as soon as the emergency was over, they hoped and expected to return to their old ways of doing things. The CAA did little to improve the situation, limiting itself during the late 1940s to sponsoring developments in parts and components rather than stimulating manufacturers to come up with more fundamental innovations that might have sufficiently improved the product and broadened its appeal. Nor was the NACA much help. In 1949, Grover Loening, a pioneer aircraft manufacturer and consultant to the NACA, pointed to the success of the XS-1 supersonic airplane as an example of what government-industry cooperation could accomplish. In contrast, he could recall only "two or three instances" in the previous year where the NACA had worked with the lightplane industry to solve technical problems. He went on to defend the NACA, stating that it had concentrated on research beneficial to the industry, only to find that most lightplane manufacturers had dismissed the NACA's contributions as too expensive or too impractical to implement.[30]

Reduced to its fundamentals, the cause of the debacle was the failure of anyone in or out of government in the late 1940s to understand the essential symbiotic relationship between government regulatory and research agencies and the lightplane industry. Lack of vision, the pursuit of narrow bureaucratic or short-term economic objectives, and unwillingness or inability to comprehend how government and industry can and should work together in the quest for advanced technology led to the collapse of the dream of personal aviation in the post–World War II years.

NOTES

1. Roger E. Bilstein, *Flight in America, 1900–1983: From the Wrights to the Astronauts* (Baltimore and London: Johns Hopkins University Press, 1984), 195–96; Carl F. B. Roth, "Lightplanes Seen Vital for Defense," *Aviation Week* 56 (Feb. 25, 1952): 89.

2. Devon Francis, *Mr. Piper and His Cubs* (Ames: Iowa State University Press, 1973), 77; John R. M. Wilson, *Turbulence Aloft: The Civil Aeronautics Administration Amid Wars and Rumors of Wars, 1938–1953* (Washington, D.C.: Department of Transportation, Federal Aviation Administration, 1979), 97–102.

3. *Aviation News* 7 (Apr. 7, 1947): 15; Nick A. Komons, *Bonfires to Beacons: Federal Civil Aviation Policy under the Air Commerce Act, 1926–1938* (Washington, D.C.: U.S. Department of Transportation, Federal Aviation Administration, 1978), 244–48.

4. Fred E. Weick and James R. Hansen, *From the Ground Up: The Autobiography of an Aeronautical Engineer* (Washington, D.C.: Smithsonian Institution Press, 1988), 172–84, 221.

5. Clark G. Reynolds, *Admiral John H. Towers: The Struggle for Air Supremacy* (Annapolis, Md.: Naval Institute Press, 1991), 474; Francis, *Mr. Piper,* 120.

6. John Paul Andrews, *Your Personal Plane* (New York: Eagle Books, 1945), 23–39, 126–40.

7. Bilstein, *Flight in America,* 195; Francis, *Mr. Piper,* 124; *Aviation News* 5 (Mar. 4, 1946): 42.

8. *Aviation News* 7 (Jan. 27, 1947): 12–13; ibid. 6 (Nov. 18, 1946): 20.

9. John C. Swick, *The Luscombe Story* (Terre Haute, Ind.: SunShine House, 1987), 91–92; *Aviation News* 6 (July 8, 1946): 14; Alexander McSurely, "Beech Bonanza Certificated; Fast Deliveries in December," ibid. 6 (Nov. 25, 1946): 13–14. On Bendix, see ibid. 6 (Sept. 30, 1946): 27. For an overview of the lightplane market in late 1946, see Franklin F. Page, "Private Plane Who's Who Compiled," *National Aeronautics* 25 (Nov. 1946): 2–3, 10, 13–14.

10. Alexander McSurely, "Private Aircraft Manufacturers Facing Severe Material Shortages," *Aviation News* 5 (Apr. 22, 1946): 12; ibid. 5 (Feb. 18, 1946): 17; ibid. 6 (July 15, 1946): 24.

11. *Aviation News* 5 (Mar. 25, 1946): 22; ibid. 6 (Aug. 12, 1946): 21; ibid. 7 (Apr. 21, 1947): 20.

12. *Aviation News* 5 (Jan. 21, 1946): 18; ibid. 6 (Nov. 4, 1946): 17–18; John H. Geisse, "Is Private Flying Oversold?" *Flying* 38 (Mar. 1946): 22, 100.

13. Wilson, *Turbulence Aloft,* 145, 147–48, 164–67.

14. William T. Piper, "Let's Be Realistic about Private Flying," *Flying* 38 (May 1946): 21, 119–22.

15. Ibid.

16. Alexander McSurely, "Warnings on Lightplane Future Are Sounded at National Clinic," *Aviation News* 6 (Oct. 21, 1946): 25–26.

17. *Aviation News* 7 (Jan. 27, 1947): 12–13; ibid. 6 (Nov. 18, 1946): 36.

18. *Aviation News* 7 (Jan. 27, 1947): 12–13; Alexander McSurely, "Lightplane Leaders are Optimistic Despite Seasonal Market Slump," ibid. 6 (Dec. 2, 1946): 23–24.

19. McSurely, "Lightplane Leaders," 24–26.

20. Weick and Hansen, *From the Ground Up,* 234, 237–38; *Aviation News* 7 (Jan. 20, 1947): 14; ibid. 7 (Apr. 21, 1947): 11, 20; ibid. 7 (Feb. 17, 1947): 24; ibid. 7 (May 26, 1947): 13.

21. "Mr. Piper Counts the Score," *Flying* 41 (Aug. 1947): 17–18, 75–76.

22. Francis, *Mr. Piper,* 136, 139, 148; *Aviation Week* 48 (Jan. 5, 1948): 26; ibid. 48 (Feb. 2, 1948): 31.

23. Alexander McSurely, "Cessna in Front," *Aviation Week* 50 (Jan. 31, 1949): 30; ibid. 49 (Dec. 6, 1948): 14; ibid. 50 (Feb. 7, 1949): 35.

24. *Aviation Week* 54 (Jan. 15, 1951): 16; ibid. 56 (Feb. 25, 1952): 89.

25. Charles H. Hession and Hyman Sardy, *Ascent to Affluence: A History of American Economic Development* (Boston: Allyn and Bacon, 1969), 782; Alvin H. Hansen, *The Postwar American Economy: Performance and Problems* (New York: W. W. Norton, 1964), 24–25; Francis, *Mr. Piper,* 125–26.

26. "Mr. Piper Counts the Score," 75. Professor Robin Higham brought up the point of the attractiveness of low-priced sports cars in the immediate postwar period.

27. Wilson, *Turbulence Aloft,* 173–86.

28. Ian Lloyd, *Rolls Royce: The Years of Endeavour* (London: Macmillan Press, 1978), 214.

29. *Aviation News* 7 (Jan. 27, 1947): 12.

30. *Aviation News* 7 (Apr. 7, 1947): 15; Grover Loening, "Better Lightplane Design Asked," *Aviation Week* 50 (June 13, 1949): 23–25.

PART THREE

Connections between Military and Commercial Aviation

Richard P. Hallion

Introduction

The history of aviation is replete with examples of the mutually beneficial relationship between military and civilian aviation. Military developments in World War I helped spawn the post–Great War air transport revolution in both Europe and America. Likewise, the push of military technology (particularly in gas turbine and high-speed aerodynamic research) in World War II accelerated the growth of commercial aviation after 1945. Generally speaking, then, there has been a leader-follower relationship between military and civilian technology. For example, the jet engine and the swept wing were initially first applied to technology demonstrators, followed by high-performance fighters, followed by bombers, and then, finally, by commercial aircraft. Today, new-generation jetliners take advantage of materials and electronic flight-control revolutions first pioneered in the 1970s with military systems.

But within this larger framework, the story is far more complex. For example, the development of the pressurized-cabin airplane drew upon nearly simultaneous military and civilian work aimed both at long-range civil transports and long-range bombers. The emergence of blind-flying, advanced navigation techniques, and electronic landing aids received a healthy impetus from the needs of civil aviation. (Indeed, at the time of the airmail fiasco of 1934, American civil air transport crews and airplanes were far better equipped for foul-weather flying than their military counterparts, as resulting accident statistics tragically highlighted). In one notable case, the refinement of design practice in the 1920s and 1930s in the United States resulted in pre–World War II American commercial aviation's actually outstripping American military aviation in terms of the overall performance of in-service aircraft. The design configuration of these new monoplane transports—such craft as the Lockheed Orion, Northrop Alpha, Boeing 200 Monomail and 247, and Douglas DC-2/3—inspired both military and civilian successors worldwide. When the American military built up its airlift capacity for combat support operations in World War II, it drew directly upon the fruits of this civilian work—notably the Douglas DC-3 and DC-4, which served by the thousands in all wartime theaters as the ubiquitous C-47 and C-54—rather than developing specifications for militarily unique designs. This is a classic case of the way in which civilian technology's "push" preceded military requirement's "pull." In similar fashion, the dramatic Swissair Orion service around Europe directly influenced the development of the quasi-military Heinkel He70 Blitz and the overtly military He111.

In America, the civil monoplane revolution typified by the work of Northrop, Lockheed, and Boeing in the "Golden Age" of aviation inspired the trend-setting Martin B-10 bomber and, eventually, the four-engine B-17. In the case of the former Soviet Union, the outright copying of Boeing B-29 bombers that force-landed in the U.S.S.R. during American raids against Japan led to the emergence of the postwar Soviet long-range bomber force, beginning with the Tupolev Tu-4. The refinement of this technology base, and the addition to it of the jet engine and the swept wing, spawned the first long-range Soviet jet bomber, the Tupolev Tu-16. In turn, this airplane led to a civil transport derivation, the Tu-104, and from that point, the interplay between military and civilian technology generated more capable and sophisticated civil transports, notably the Tu-134 and Tu-154 family.

The four papers in Part Three, first presented at the International Conference on the History of Civil and Commercial Aviation, offer detailed perspectives on four little-known cases where military and civilian aviation interests have come together: Nazi Germany, wartime Japan, Sweden, and the former Soviet Union. The distinguished scholars who have undertaken these studies are as interesting and diverse as the subjects they treat. John H. Morrow, Jr., a noted historian of early German aviation, examines the often tortuous and intricate relationships among the Junkers, Heinkel, and Dornier design concerns and the German government and military.[1] Eiichiro Sekigawa, a prolific and world-renowned journalist and historian of Asian aviation, examines the virtually unknown story of Japanese commercial aviation and its operations in support of the far-flung Japanese empire in the tumultuous years of World War II. Genrikh Novozhilov, a gifted aircraft designer and student of aviation history, in a trailblazing and most welcome post–cold-war presentation, gives an incisive look into the workings of one of the former U.S.S.R.'s most notable civil and military aircraft manufacturers. And, finally, Klaus-Richard Böhme, a professional military officer and historian, traces the intriguing story of how one technologically adept neutralist nation pursued joint civil and military aims. These four illuminating studies do much to dissipate the murky fog of civil-military aviation relations.

NOTE

1. Dr. Morrow was unable to attend the conference in Lucerne; his paper was delivered in absentia.

John H. Morrow, Jr.

Connections between Military and Commercial Aviation in Germany

Junkers, Heinkel, and Dornier through the 1930s

In the era from the dawn of powered heavier-than-air flight in 1903 to the out-break of World War II in 1939, the airplane became a potent military weapon and a viable commercial vehicle. The careers of Hugo Junkers, Ernst Heinkel, and Claudius Dornier, three of the world's most famous pioneers in aircraft design and manufacture, span the first half of the twentieth century. Because their factories produced aircraft for civilian and military aviation in Germany and abroad, these three entrepreneurs personify the intertwined development of military and civilian aviation in Germany through the beginning of the Second World War.

Before World War I the airplane was too embryonic for commercial use. It was the vehicle of the few sportsmen who could afford it, and aviation sport competitions were the preserve of the tiny industry and a handful of pilots. Between 1912 and 1914, as war loomed on the horizon, the German army used its influence on aviation sport organizations to transform the contests into overland reconnaissance trials for military aircraft types fielded by aircraft companies.

World War I brought a concentration on military aviation and the airplane's emergence as a reliable and important weapon of war. The war led to improvements in the speed, load-carrying ability, range, and reliability of standard airplane types. In the fall of 1917, after three years of war, serious discussion of air transport began within the German military establishment, when Chief Q.M. Gen. Erich Ludendorff agreed that the commanding general of the Air Forces (Kogenluft) would represent the German High Command in official discussions of air transport. Ever the ardent militarist, Ludendorff advocated military control of civil aviation, to the extent of using military subsidies to preserve competition within the aircraft industry. He proposed a central agency, evolved from Kogenluft and subordinate to the chief of the General Staff, which would administer and coordinate all aspects of aviation, military and civil.[1]

Substantial financial interests in Germany also expressed interest in commercial aviation. Through the Imperial Postal Ministry, the Deutsche Bank sponsored preparations for commercial aviation. In 1917 AEG (Allgemeine Elektrizitäts Gesellschaft) founded an air transport company, Deutsche Luftreederei, because the firm's directors believed that air links using multiengined craft would be particularly useful over long stretches of water and in areas where other modes of transportation were not feasible.[2]

Kogenluft, determined to assure Germany a leading position in postwar commercial aviation, began experimental airmail flights in February 1918. By October 1918 the Imperial Naval Office envisaged routes not only to Scandinavia but also Asia Minor and Persia, although it was not certain whether national interests would be sufficiently involved to warrant state-run enterprises.[3] The highest agencies of the German government, both civilian and military, thus favored promoting commercial aviation. Their plans, however, were of a general nature, the one firm point being the high command's insistence on military control over civil aviation.

The interest in commercial aviation stemmed from the necessity of creating a civilian aircraft market to compensate for the anticipated drastic reduction of military contracts in peacetime. With the end of the war rapidly approaching, and Germany's loss of the conflict imminent, it was obvious that military contracts would support only a handful of small firms. Before the war the army had crushed any diversion of resources to civil aviation in its drive to develop an air force and an aircraft industry. Now a postwar civilian market was indispensable to sustain an industry bloated on wartime contracts. Yet these plans for the postwar era would be upset by the cataclysmic end of hostilities and the severity of the ensuing peace, which would nearly wipe out German aviation.

Junkers, Heinkel, and Dornier, names that aviation historian William Green considered "virtually synonymous with the resurgence of German aircraft design between the world wars,"[4] were already at work during the war of 1914–18. Junkers, the oldest of the three, was born the son of the owner of a weaving mill in 1859 in the Rhenish industrial city of Rheydt. An educated engineer, he was already a noted inventor with interests ranging from engines to boilers when he turned to aviation in the years before the war. During the war he invented and built all-metal aircraft with cantilever wings that served successfully with the German air force and established his reputation as the pioneer and dean of all-metal aircraft construction by the war's end in 1918. In 1917 the army arranged the formation of the Junkers-Fokker Works for the serial production of all-metal airplanes.

Claudius Dornier, born the son of a businessman in 1884 in Kempten, like Junkers was a product of Germany's superb system of technical schools. The young engineer joined the test institute of the Zeppelin firm in 1910 and went on in World War I to design giant floatplane and flying boat prototypes and an all-metal fighter plane prototype.

Ernst Heinkel, the youngest of the three, was born in 1887, the son of a master craftsman from Grunbach in Württemberg. He finished four semesters at a technical high school in Stuttgart and then left to build airplanes. After prewar stints with major German aircraft manufacturers Luftverkehrsgesellschaft and Albatros, Heinkel became the chief designer for the Hansa-Brandenburg works during the war. He was particularly noted for his exceptional biplane and monoplane floatplane fighter designs, which served with the German navy in 1917 and 1918, although he also built landplane fighters and observation aircraft for the Austro-Hungarian air service.

How had the war affected German aviation science, technology and production in general, and the work of these three designers in particular? East German aviation historian Gerhard Wissmann contended unreservedly that the war hindered the progress of aviation science and technology because capitalist systems and imperialistic wars, of necessity, hinder scientific progress. The war forced aviation to live from "hand to mouth," resulting in piecemeal improvements that left the "aerodynamically unfavorable conception of the externally braced wooden biplane" basically intact. Progressive concepts that would take years to mature did not interest the manufacturers or the military, and by 1918 material and labor shortages ensured the rejection of such advanced concepts as the all-metal airplane. If the war prompted increased funds for aviation, scientific agencies like the German Research Institute for Aviation received precious little of them, because the emphasis on large-scale serial production limited the possibilities of further progress.[5]

Manufacturers Heinkel and Junkers held more positive opinions. Heinkel suggested that four and a half years of war equaled six years of peacetime evolution, while Junkers, perhaps the most accomplished scientist among the Ger-

man manufacturers, was convinced that the war would greatly hasten technological and industrial development.[6]

In fact, the war both hindered and promoted the evolution of aviation science
and technology. It exerted more pressure for speedy technological progress, but
the necessity for haste often did not allow sufficient time to verify developments, ponder facts, and draw logical conclusions from them. Wartime shortages did place a premium on ease of construction, not incorporation of the most
advanced aviation knowledge, and hindered pursuit of such concepts as all-
metal aircraft.

Despite wartime constraints, the German manufacturers pursued their own
methods of construction quite successfully. They generally resisted wartime
pressures more than did their French and British counterparts, who compro-
mised greatly with wartime necessity by keeping their airframe structures
simple, persisting in wooden construction and relying primarily upon increased
engine power for improved performance. German aircraft manufacturers like
Junkers and Dornier did not relinquish their pursuit of advanced aviation
knowledge. Anthony Fokker's reproach to Junkers—that the older man refused
to compromise his all-metal construction with the wartime necessity for simplicity and mass production—is the best proof of the engineer's perseverance
under adverse conditions. Consequently, German airframe technology at the
end of the war was clearly superior to that of the Entente, a superiority that
would benefit German civil aviation in the interwar years. The all-metal construction and cantilever wings of Dornier and Junkers craft were major examples of German pioneering efforts. Wartime haste and pressures may have favored trial-and-error designers like Fokker and Heinkel, but they did not halt
the efforts of their more scientific colleagues.

Certain wartime developments promoted aviation progress. The German Research Institute for Aviation accumulated and disseminated knowledge to the
manufacturers. The army and navy encouraged and promoted the development
of large airplanes, thereby enabling Dornier's early development of his giant
flying boats. The war thus enabled manufacturers to test their ideas at the public
expense. The relative lack of powerful engines in Germany forced the aircraft
manufacturers there to rely more on advanced airframes than did the Allies in
the quest for air superiority. Furthermore, the wartime emphasis on mass serial
production fueled the industry's tremendous expansion and necessitated its rationalization of production.

As the wartime plans for postwar commercial aviation indicated, the government expected a severe contraction. What it did not anticipate was the drastic
effect of international political circumstances upon the contraction of military

aviation and the transition to civil flight. The disclosure of the terms of the Versailles Treaty on May 8, 1919, was devastating, as the Allies sought to crush German military aviation permanently and aircraft production temporarily. German military aviation was dismantled under the direction of the Inter-Allied Aviation Control Commission, which began its duties on February 22, 1920. Though the Germans ultimately surrendered some 15,000 aircraft and 27,000 engines, the commission deemed the pace of disarmament too slow and had evidence of continued aircraft manufacture in Germany. The six-month prohibition on construction stipulated at Versailles, which was due to end on July 10, 1920, was consequently extended until a future date when the commission would judge that Germany had fulfilled the disarmament provisions and destroyed or yielded all matériel. The signing of the Versailles Treaty on June 23, 1919, consequently signaled the death knell of the German air force and wartime aircraft industry.[7]

Various prohibitions continued to confound German aircraft manufacture in general until the mid-1920s, and military aircraft manufacture in particular until the end of the Weimar Republic. Although these prohibitions exacerbated the contraction to the extent that most of the German aircraft firms collapsed, a few of the best designers survived, and German aircraft manufacture never ceased. German constructors established small branches abroad—Junkers and Heinkel in Sweden, Dornier in Holland and Italy—while they maintained their design offices in Germany. Claudius Dornier, who was designing small seaplanes with some 50 men at Seemoos, began work on a large flying boat, the famous Dornier Wal (Whale), at an Italian subsidiary after the Allied Control Commission's protests had forced him to scuttle a new six-passenger flying boat off Kiel in April 1920. At the Karl Caspar firm in Travemünde, Ernst Heinkel designed seaplanes for foreign powers and had the parts assembled in Sweden, where the navy had been buying his floatplanes since the end of 1918.[8]

Hugo Junkers in particular wasted no time undertaking the transition to commercial aviation. When the Junkers-Fokker Works dissolved in December 1918, Junkers assumed all the shares and in April 1919 actually increased the capital of the joint-stock company from 900,000 marks to 3.5 million marks. During the intervening period, the firm's production of its all-metal warplanes peaked as it turned out 12 of 47 monoplane D1 fighters in February, and 11 of 44 C11 attack fighters in March 1919. More important for the near future, the prototype Junkers F13, an all-metal six-seater cabin monoplane that was destined to become the most widely used transport airplane in the world in the 1920s, flew on June 25, 1919, two days after the signing of the Versailles Treaty. The

8.1. The all-metal Junkers F13 monoplane first flew in 1919 and became the world's most widely used transport in the 1920s. (Courtesy of the National Air and Space Museum, 90-13116)

airplane's fine performance enabled the Russians and Japanese to use it for military operations.

The Junkers F13 is often termed the first pure transport airplane, as opposed to other aircraft, which were converted warplanes. Junkers biographer Richard Blunck made the distinction between warplanes, which were designed primarily for the highest performance, with cost and safety considerations secondary, and transport craft, which required speed, safety, load-carrying ability, range, and economy for success. In Blunck's opinion, the achievement of a truly economical transport for people and freight meant freeing design completely from wartime construction.[9] Two design principles that Junkers had pioneered during the war, all-metal construction and the low-wing monoplane, were the essential foundations of the design of the record-setting F13 and of future aircraft design in general.

Author Fischer von Poturzyn likened the comparison between the pure transport and the modified warplane to that between a personal automobile and a tank. Poturzyn emphasized the differences between military and commercial aviation, their different tasks requiring different aircraft. He referred to British aviation authority C. G. Grey, who observed that while transport airplanes would have use in war, the more progress that was made in civil aviation, the greater the divergence would be between transports and warplanes, just as between the warship and the passenger liner. Others pointed out that it took more than putting guns and bombs on a civil aircraft to make it a warplane.[10] In fact, the state of large-aircraft design in the 1920s and early 1930s was sufficiently embryonic that the divergence between transport and military aircraft was often small.

The French undersecretary of state for aviation issued a comprehensive report on German aviation on January 18, 1921, indicating how sorely disturbing he found the continued progress of German aviation technology. The French were particularly concerned about Zeppelin's (Dornier's) continued development of giant airplanes and Junkers's five-seat "advanced experimental all-metal limousine" (the F13), the "craft of the future." The report cautioned that larger factories like Junkers and Zeppelin had retained most of their original personnel, and consequently:

> From the time the Junkers and Zeppelin corporations can put their aircraft on the market, commercial aviation will progress with an incredible swiftness. . . .
> To place the enormous number of factories capable of producing aviation equipment on a footing to produce new material will require no more than three months; to enable them to produce again at full capacity, no more than nine months to a year. Consequently, the terms of the Treaty of Versailles which forbid all aeronautical construction in Germany for six months will have no appreciable effect on the subsequent volume of Germany's aeronautical production. The only present restriction to Germany's assuming aviation supremacy is her financial and economic situation.[11]

French fears were exaggerated, because the large majority of German aircraft firms collapsed, but the French attempted to postpone the inevitable resurgence of German aviation for as long as possible. Ironically, the continued aviation restrictions ultimately redounded to the benefit of German military aviation. German government officials committed to a civil aviation distinct from military aviation fell victim to public dissatisfaction with the Versailles Treaty, because the German aviation manufacturers blamed these officials for the continued ban on aircraft production. As of early 1921 the man in charge of the Transport Ministry's aviation department was Capt. (ret.) Ernst Brandenburg, who had won the Pour le Mérite as a bomber commander during the war and was prepared to use German civil aviation as a vehicle for the reconstruction of the German air force.[12]

The Allies' attempt to destroy German military aviation aided its survival at the expense of German civil aeronautics. The German Defense Ministry's secret rearmament project in Russia enabled it to evade the total ban on military

8.2. This view of the Junkers F13 on skis epitomizes the versatility of the plane. (Courtesy of the National Air and Space Museum; A 42718)

aviation, while the restrictions on commercial aviation forced the few remaining German aircraft firms back into the clutches of the army if they desired contracts. After constant French harassment forced Junkers to suspend the operations of his airmail line late in October 1921, he agreed to construct an aircraft and aero engine plant in Russia for the army. In 1922–23, the army approached Heinkel for the Russian venture. The Allied bans restored the symbiotic relationship between the military and the aircraft industry, which had disintegrated in the crisis of early 1919, at a much more rapid rate than might have occurred had they left German civil aeronautics alone to prosper in peace. The restrictions had severely crippled the German aircraft industry and the air arm, but the few firms that survived and the new ones that arose in the 1920s were invariably and indissolubly linked to the German army in the clandestine rearmament of the Reich.

Allied shackles on German aviation endured in the civilian realm until 1926 and in military affairs until their repudiation by the Nazi regime, but they did not prevent the rebirth of the German aircraft industry and the air force. The new industry's guiding designers included Junkers, Dornier, and Heinkel, who had survived by concentrating on scientific and technological advances and civil aircraft, while not relinquishing the development of military airplanes.

After the F13, Junkers was forced to stop work on an advanced cantilever-wing monoplane transport because of the restrictions on the performance of German airplanes. Junkers's participation in the Defense Ministry's Russian venture at Fili yielded experience in air transport because the firm was preparing aviation links to Asia. Junkers's staff at his research institute at Dessau included a military expert to watch the development of the Luftwaffe so that his airplanes could keep abreast of changes in military technology.[13]

According to historian William Green, Junkers appreciated that the military market was as lucrative as the commercial and thus designed all future aircraft to be "dimorphic"—each commercial model would have a military counterpart, and vice versa. The factory's aircraft designs of the 1920s exemplified this principle: The light transport airplane A20 of 1923 was also a tactical reconnaissance craft for the Soviet, Iranian, and Turkish governments; the G24 transport had a bomber version built in Sweden; the A32 and A35 two-seat postal and photography aircraft of 1926 had light-bomber and reconnaissance-fighter counterparts, while the W34 light transport had a light-bomber counterpart; the S36 twin-engine transport of 1927 was built as a warplane in Japan; and the Junkers four-engine G38 transport of 1929 was built in limited numbers as a heavy bomber in Japan. The two-seat K47 fighter of 1928, which was the progenitor of the dive bomber, was also built in civilian guise.[14]

Ultimately, the Fili agreement collapsed because the German army did not supply sufficient funds, and the Russian government did not place sufficient orders. Junkers was using the military subsidies to pay wages at Dessau, so the Fili plant lost money and was forced to close in 1927. But Junkers had commercial ventures to sustain him because the company had founded its own airline, which was one of two merged by order of the Air Office in 1925 to create Deutsche Lufthansa.[15]

After the armistice, while Zeppelin-Lindau built observation planes for the Swiss air arm, Dornier built a six-passenger flying boat, the GsI, with the inherently stable broad-beam hull and sponsons that characterized his later boats. The craft was a success, but after a demonstration in the Netherlands, the Allies demanded its destruction because the Control Commission had forbidden that category of aircraft. The GsI was sunk off Kiel in 1920. Consequently, for the next few years Dornier built in Germany only small commercial planes, the Komet and the Merkur, the latter for two pilots and six to eight passengers, which conformed to the commission's stipulations. Meanwhile, Dornier commissioned the firm's Italian subsidiary to continue development and construction of the forbidden type. The GsII, the famous Wal, which flew in 1922, was built under license in Japan, Netherlands, and Spain and would evolve through the 1920s and into the 1930s. Between the first production Wal of 1923 and the military type of 1932, the airplane's wingspan increased greatly, its engine power more than doubled, and its loaded weight rose from 8,820 to 22,000 pounds. It was used for civilian mail service and long-range reconnaissance, and the commercial and military models differed little. In 1926, Dornier located his main center of activities across Lake Constance at Altenrhein, Switzerland, and began the development of the Superwal, the four-engine DoR with two passenger cabins for 20 passengers, and then the gigantic 12-engine DoX, intended for transatlantic travel. Dornier also pursued the clandestine development of military aircraft, including the DoH Falke and Seefalke all-metal cantilever high-wing fighter monoplanes in 1922 and the DoD twin-float torpedo bomber monoplane in 1926.[16]

For the aviation industry in general and Ernst Heinkel in particular, the cooperation between the ministries of defense and transport (Reichswehrministerium and Reichsverkehrsministerium) was important. Not only did the transport ministry allot funds for civil aviation, it also gave the army financial support for aviation. The ministry ordered airplanes that were in fact built for the army and navy. Many of its contracts for Heinkel aircraft were for naval reconnaissance, torpedo, and fighter planes. Furthermore, the difference between civil and military versions was not always evident, and several airplanes were used for civil and military tasks without any modifications. The HD30 was listed variously as a sea rescue airplane for high seas fisheries, a mail plane, and a naval reconnaissance aircraft. Heinkel developed the mail seaplane HE12 for launching by shipboard catapult to deliver the mail in late 1920s, and Heinkel built catapults and catapult planes for commercial purposes. Yet this equipment could be, and later was, used by the naval air arm. Heinkel developed his fast airplanes in close cooperation with civilian and military aviation agencies, while his numerous foreign contracts from Japan, Sweden, Denmark, and the U.S.S.R. were of an overwhelmingly military nature.[17]

By the late 1920s, Junkers, Heinkel, and Dornier were the leaders in German aircraft production, although in the absence of any demand for large numbers of airplanes, no firm was prepared for large-scale serial production. Junkers's general director, Gotthard Sachsenberg, argued in 1928 and 1929 that because the Allies knew that Germany was evading the military restrictions by building civil aircraft, the military should openly establish the basis for large-scale serial production by building a large fleet of fast transport-bombers along the lines of Junkers all-metal transports. Sachsenberg's ideas anticipated the Nazi government's first large building program, but they were too radical for the officers of the Weimar government's Ordnance Office, who were divided over the use of commercial aircraft as bombers and unconvinced of the wisdom of having a bomber force.[18]

With Hitler's coming to power in 1933, German rearmament ceased to be a clandestine undertaking, although the increased emphasis on military airplanes did not mean the total eclipse of transport airplanes, especially in the early 1930s. The year 1931 witnessed the appearance of the Junkers Ju52 all-metal trimotor, the most widely used multiengined transport airplane of the time. Thirty airlines in 25 countries made it their standard medium-range airliner, and it equipped the new Luftwaffe's transport squadrons. Yet the Luftwaffe also adopted the "Tante Ju" as an auxiliary bomber (*Behelfskampfflugzeug*) in October 1933, and because of problems in the development of the Do11 bomber, the Ju52 equipped many of the Luftwaffe's bombing units as well as its transport squadrons in the mid-1930s, serving in both roles during the Spanish Civil War.[19]

The Heinkel factory brought out the Heinkel He70 Blitz transport in 1932. When the Blitz was officially presented at Tempelhof field, its speed of 362 kilometers per hour made it not only the fastest commercial airplane of the time, but also faster than contemporary foreign fighters. The four-passenger airplane,

8.3. Introduced in 1931, the sturdy all-metal Junkers Ju52 trimotor was one of the most widely used transports of the 1930s. (Courtesy of the National Air and Space Museum; 87-15114)

8.4. The Heinkel He70 Blitz was a high-performance four-passenger transport used on European express routes. (Courtesy of the National Air and Space Museum; 75-12129)

with its elliptical wings positioned low on its duralumin monocoque fuselage, was the premier high-speed transport of its day on European express routes, but it served also in Germany and abroad as a high-speed communications and liaison airplane and reconnaissance bomber.[20]

Meanwhile, Dornier was building multiengined bomber prototypes, demonstrated as commercial transports but in fact steps in the development of a heavy-bomber prototype, which emerged as the Do19. In 1932, the firm began to build large aircraft on the German side of Lake Constance with the Militär-Wal 33 and in late 1933 the first Do11 bomber. Perhaps Dornier's best-known airplane of the 1930s was the Do17, which served as a Luftwaffe bomber in World War II. Yet the Do17 was designed solely as a commercial transport, developed in response to a Lufthansa requirement for a high-speed mailplane carrying six passengers for express services. After Do17 prototypes flew in 1934, Lufthansa decided in 1935 that the airplane's passenger accommodation was too small. An Air Ministry liaison officer who was also a Lufthansa pilot suggested that the addition of more keel area would make the plane a stable bombing platform, so the Air Ministry's Technical Office tested the Do17 and ordered a bomber prototype.

8.5. The He70, shown here in high-speed, low-level flight, served in transport, communications and liaison, and as a reconnaissance bomber. (Courtesy of the National Air and Space Museum; 72-5805)

There is some disagreement about the origins of the Do17's contemporary, the Heinkel He111. Some authors suggest that the He111 was designed as a bomber and unveiled as a commercial transport. Yet historians William Green and Edward Homze argue persuasively that the Heinkel, like another Luftwaffe bomber, the Junkers Ju86, was that rare bird, an aircraft designed from the outset to fulfill the roles of both bomber and commercial transport without any fundamental structural changes. Green dismisses accusations of German subterfuge, saying that the transport was merely a bomber in disguise. He points out that the design was conceived to fulfill both civilian and military tasks and that the commercial transport and bomber versions evolved in parallel. The Air Ministry and Lufthansa had collaborated in framing the specifications for a modern twin-engine high-speed medium bomber and a 10-passenger airliner, although the design emphasis was on military potential rather than economy.[21]

In any case, with the Nazis in power, the focus of German aircraft design turned unabashedly to military aviation. The responses of the three designer-manufacturers to the Nazis differed. The Nazis drove Junkers from his factory because he had become an ardent democrat and pacifist, and they wanted the firm for rearmament. The Junkers firm was nationalized, and Junkers died in 1935. Dornier, though he had excellent connections with the German military and navy, was circumspect toward the Nazi regime until it was entrenched in power. Heinkel, the most closely linked of all three to the secret rearmament of the 1920s and early 1930s, was among the first and most enthusiastic supporters of the Nazis' aerial rearmament.[22]

The Nazis financed the expansion and encouraged the rationalization of the aircraft industry. Junkers, Heinkel, and Dornier, which had been the largest German aircraft manufacturers at the end of the 1920s, grew even larger under the tutelage of the Nazis. Furthermore, the Junkers firm, based on its development of the diesel engine for aviation in the 1920s, was also one of three dominating aircraft engine firms. Heinkel, with his experience designing a diversity of types for the air force and navy in the 1920s, was best equipped to profit from the turn to military aviation. Of 14 aircraft types in the Third Reich's first aircraft production program of 1934–35, 12 were built by these three firms, 8 by Heinkel alone. The 25 types in the production plan of 1935 included 12 from Heinkel, 5 from Dornier, and 4 from Junkers. Heinkel also backed the development of the first rocket and jet airplanes, the He176 and He178, although Ernst Udet of the Air Ministry blocked their development because he was convinced that they were unnecessary and would divert Heinkel from bomber production. In October 1938, as Germany prepared for another war, Dornier employed more than 15,000 workers, Heinkel more than 18,000, and Junkers nearly 26,000.[23]

The experience of the firms of Hugo Junkers, Ernst Heinkel, and Claudius Dornier, three of the greatest aviation designers, clearly shows the intertwined links between commercial and military aviation in Germany in the 1920s and 1930s and demonstrates that any attempt to distinguish between civil and military aircraft development in the interwar years is probably an exercise in futility. Before World War I the power of the military in German society had led to its control of sport aviation, a situation that continued in the interwar era in the use of glider associations to indoctrinate youth in military air-mindedness. It was clear in 1918 that the German military intended to play a controlling role in the development of commercial aviation in the postwar era. Even with the overt demise of German military aviation after Versailles, during the Weimar years German commercial and military aviation were linked financially, technologically, and politically, as the covert rearmament, like a parasite, fed from its civilian host. In those years civil and military aeronautics were essentially inseparable, especially in the important realm of transport and bomber aviation, because the bomber, not the fighter, enjoyed the priority of military development until the mid-1930s.

German success in civilian air technology in the interwar era fed the same notions of cultural superiority that success in aviation sport nurtured in the prewar era and military air technology aroused during the war. Consequently, when the Nazis came to power, the industry and the German people had little or no difficulty transferring their concentration from civilian to military aviation. A manufacturer with reservations about the resurgence of military aviation under the Nazis, such as Junkers apparently had, could be removed. Ernst Heinkel and Claudius Dornier continued to manufacture aircraft for the Nazi regime throughout the Second World War. Heinkel died in 1958, and Dornier, after passing his company on to his son, died in 1969. He was the last of the great pioneer designers whose work had set the standard for the interwar design of German commercial and military aircraft.

NOTES

1. Hans Radandt, "Hugo Junkers—Ein Monopolkapitalist und Korrespondierendes Mitglied der preussischen Akademie der Wissenschaften," *Jahrbuch für Wirtschaftsgeschichte* (hereafter *JfW*), pt. 1 (1960): 94–95.

2. Ibid.

3. Correspondence between the Imperial Office of the Interior, Imperial Naval Office, and AEG, in volume stock no. 5714, set III.5.1, Naval Archive, German Federal Archive.

4. William Green, *Warplanes of the Third Reich* (Garden City, N.Y.: Doubleday, 1970), 258.

5. Gerhard Wissmann, "Imperialistische Krieg und technischwissenschaftlicher Fortschritt," *JfW*, pt. 2 (1962): 145–58.

6. Ernst Heinkel, *Stürmisches Leben,* ed. Jürgen Thorwald (Stuttgart: Mundus-Verlag, 1953), 69. Richard Blunck, *Hugo Junkers: Ein Leben für Technik und Luftfahrt* (Düsseldorf: Econ-Verlag, 1951), 89.

7. Karl-Heinz Völker, *Die Entwicklung der Militärischen Luftfahrt in Deutschland, 1920–1933* (Stuttgart: Deutsche Verlags-Anstalt, 1962), 120–30. Edward Homze, *Arming the Luftwaffe: The Reich Air Ministry and the German Aircraft Industry, 1919–1939* (Lincoln: University of Nebraska Press, 1976), 2.

8. Völker, *Die Entwicklung,* 130; Homze, *Arming the Luftwaffe,* 11; Walter Zürl, *Deutsche Flugzeugkonstrukteure: Werdegang und Erfolge unserer Flugzeug- und Flugmotorenbauer* (Munich: Pechstein, 1942), 94; David Irving, *The Rise and Fall of the Luftwaffe: The Life of Field Marshal Erhard Milch* (Boston: Little, Brown, 1973), 130.

9. Blunck, *Hugo Junkers*, 113–14.

10. Fischer von Poturzyn, ed., *Junkers und die Weltluftfahrt: Ein Beitrag zur Entstehungsgeschichte deutscher Luftgeltung, 1909–1934* (Munich: Pflaum Verlag, 1935), 40–41, 53.

11. French Sub-Secretary of State for Aeronautics, *Germany: A Compilation*, Bulletin no. 19 (1921): 11–28.

12. Homze, *Arming the Luftwaffe*, 12.

13. Blunck, *Junkers*, 167, 171, 188.

14. Green, *Warplanes*, 404.

15. Homze, *Arming the Luftwaffe*, 10; Irving, *Rise and Fall*, 14–17.

16. Green, *Warplanes*, 109; Zürl, *Deutsche Flugzeugkonstrukteure*, 95, 101.

17. H. Dieter Köhler, *Ernst Heinkel: Pionier der Schnellflugzeuge* (Koblenz: Bernard & Graefe, 1983), 58–59, 70, 75, 77, 82–85, 97.

18. Homze, *Arming the Luftwaffe*, 26, 32.

19. Blunck, *Junkers*, 212, 226; Irving, *Rise and Fall*, 27; Green, *Warplanes*, 405.

20. Köhler, *Ernst Heinkel*, 104, 111; Homze, *Arming the Luftwaffe*, 65; Green, *Warplanes*, 280.

21. Green, *Warplanes*, 287, 414; Homze, *Arming the Luftwaffe*, 120.

22. Homze, *Arming the Luftwaffe*, 63–64.

23. Köhler, *Ernst Heinkel*, 150; Irving, *Rise and Fall*, 76; Homze, *Arming the Luftwaffe*, 73, 77, 79, 81, 105, 107, 128, 183, 185.

 Eiichiro Sekigawa

Japan's Commercial Air Transportation and Military Missions in World War II

An established theory among Japanese historians is that poor logistics caused by insufficient transport capability, particularly air transport, accelerated Japan's defeat in the Pacific War. Since the introduction of their first aircraft in 1910 and 1912, respectively, both the Imperial Army and the navy had not been interested in applications of transport aircraft. A further example of this shortcoming was that when the army decided on an ambitious air power expansion program in August 1939 to increase the number of air squadrons to 162 before 1942, no air transport unit was included in the plan—although the plan was amended later to provide for such elements.

Traditionally, the army expected future battles to occur only in China and Siberia, and consequently had planned to use railways for logistical support. The navy had usually depended upon civilian vessels for its supply train. The army, however, was interested in a possible aerial link between Japan's home islands and Dalian (Dairen), a city in the southernmost part of Manchuria, which was then a leased territory of Japan.

The first commercial air transport service in Japan began in 1922, and three minor carriers maintained limited operations between several domestic cities. Then, following the example of major European countries, the government decided on the need for a national flag carrier. It formed Japan Air Transport Corporation (JAT) in 1928, and this company absorbed the existing three carriers.

In creating JAT, the government decided to commit a subsidy of 19.97 million yen to the new carrier during the first 11 years—the equivalent of more than $1 billion at today's prices. In exchange, a contract between the government and JAT included an article permitting the government free use of the aircraft, personnel, and facilities of the carrier in the event of a national emergency. Wanting to use JAT for transportation between the Japanese homeland and Dalian, the army proposed the requisition article as a means of becoming the airline's shadow administrator in case of war. Thus, from the time of its founding, JAT was destined to be the army's tool.

The army implemented a requisition of JAT equipment and staff for the first time in September 1931, when it invaded Manchuria. Before the operation, the army expected to use railways for logistics as planned, but Chinese forces destroyed the railroads in several key places. Subsequently, the army ordered JAT to allocate several Fokker Super Universals with pilots and mechanics to help in the operation. In the beginning, the JAT fleet was operated mainly for the evacuation of wounded soldiers and food supply. As a result of the success of these operations, the army expanded the missions of the JAT fleet to include transport of ammunition and other equipment and, later on, even reconnaissance and bombing. The army then ordered JAT to start provisional scheduled service for the forces in Manchuria in December 1931, establishing a basis for the creation of Manchurian Airways the following year.

After the first requisition, the army cast about for another air carrier that it could control more effectively than JAT. The army made considerable use of the JAT fleet under the requisition but was sometimes reluctant to do so because JAT was under the administration of another government agency, the Ministry of Communications. As a result, following the formation of the Manchurian Empire in March 1932, the army formed Manchurian Airways in September of that year with a joint investment by the Manchurian government and two Japanese business firms.

Although Manchurian Airways was a commercial carrier, it was virtually controlled by the army. The new carrier, much closer to the army than JAT had been, was effectively an air transport division of the army in Manchuria. After the foundation of Manchurian Airways, the army mobilized the airline for military roles more than 10 times before 1938, usually in response to local outbreaks such as the Namonhan conflict.

Following the establishment of Manchurian Airways, the army formed another carrier, Huitong Airways, in Tianjin, China, in November 1936. A joint

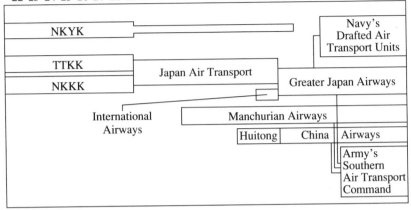

'22 23 24 25 26 27 28 29 30 31 32 33 34 35 36 37 38 39 40 41 42 43 44 45

NKYK

Navy's Drafted Air Transport Units

TTKK

Japan Air Transport

NKKK

Greater Japan Airways

International Airways

Manchurian Airways

Huitong | China | Airways

Army's Southern Air Transport Command

9.1. Japan's air carriers.

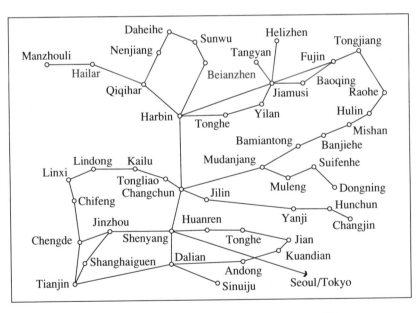

9.2. Manchurian Airways' commercial service network (October 1939).

investment by Manchurian Airways and the local Chinese government, Huitong was operated on a comparatively small scale, its primary purpose being to
pave the way for the army's invasion of north China. Subsequent events showed
that after the invasion, the airline's capability was inadequate to fulfill the
army's ever-increasing military transport demands. Consequently, the army
formed a larger carrier, China Airways, in December 1938, with a joint investment by JAT and three Chinese puppet local governments created by the army.
The new airline absorbed Huitong. With China Airways and Manchurian Airways, the army's intention to build up its own air transport network in China
had been accomplished.

Leaving military missions in Manchuria to Manchurian Airways, JAT concentrated on commercial business from 1933 onwards; but the carrier had suffered from heavy losses caused by low traffic until 1935 and barely maintained
operations even with the government subsidy. The situation began to change,
however, and JAT's revenues improved after 1936 with the addition of new
routes; the introduction of the 14-passenger Douglas DC-2, the first modern
airliner in Japan; and the inauguration of an express service between Japan and
Manchuria. The outbreak of the Japan-China War, or Sino-Japanese conflict, in
July 1937 accelerated the trend. As a result of the war, military passenger traffic

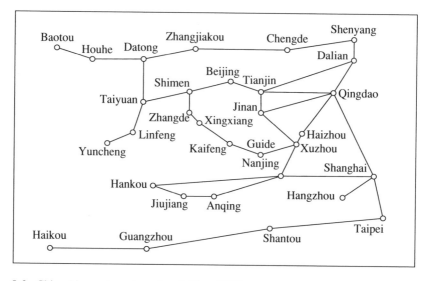

9.3. China Airways' service network (June 1941).

between Japan and China increased quickly. Higher demand brought substantial profits to JAT, illustrating what became a close relationship between expansion of the air transport business and war in Asia and the western Pacific
(Table 1).

A new reservations system introduced by the army and the navy contributed
to the upturn in JAT's business. In the new system, the military services reserved a certain number of seats on every JAT flight between Japan and China
and between Japan and Manchuria and paid full fares for all the reserved seats
whether the seats were filled or not. Due to the expanding military utilization of
the airline, the passenger-load factor of most JAT flights soared to 100 percent,
and military payments reached 38.9 percent of the company's total income in
November 1938. This appropriation inevitably limited civilian patronage because ticket procurement became difficult for other than military passengers.
JAT carried 69,268 passengers in 1938, representing 2.6 percent of the world's
air passenger traffic that year (Table 2).

The huge military payment stabilized JAT's business and opened the door to
the possibility of financial independence without government subsidy. Nevertheless, the government continued its support even after 1939 because of a
silent struggle among the Ministry of Communication, the army, and the navy,
all of which intended to maintain their influence in the carrier and supported
continuation of the subsidy. Through the Manchurian conflict and the Sino-

TABLE 1
JAT Financial Results and Subsidy

Year	Total Income	Government Subsidy	Share	Operating Income	Share
1929	Yen 3,642,464	Yen 3,317,679	91.1%	Yen 324,784	8.9%
1930	3,447,661	3,120,504	90.5	327,157	9.5
1931	3,316,081	2,777,067	83.7	539,013	16.3
1932	3,274,311	2,374,949	72.5	899,361	27.5
1933	2,029,446	1,368,886	67.5	660,559	32.5
1934	1,838,680	954,041	51.9	884,638	48.1
1935	1,949,202	1,020,282	52.3	928,919	47.7
1936	3,348,583	1,508,959	45.1	1,839,624	54.9
1937	7,853,174	3,984,709	50.7	3,868,464	49.3
1938	9,623,218	3,744,546	38.9	5,878,672	61.1

Yen (million)

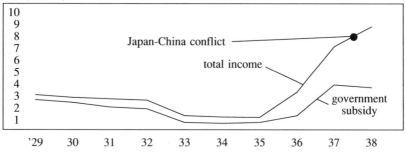

9.4. JAT financial results.

TABLE 2
JAT/GJA Operation Results

	Year	Flight Cycle	Operation Rate	Passengers Carried	Kilometers Flown		
					Scheduled Service	Others	Total
J	1929	2,574	77.93%	2,755	1,033,582	331,422	1,365,004
	1930	4,548	89.09	7,642	1,683,285	209,352	1,892,637
	1931	4,868	93.72	6,766	1,767,108	433,746	2,200,854
	1932	5,298	94.04	10,716	1,767,558	507,082	2,274,640
A	1933	5,497	92.60	10,992	1,734,238	217,302	1,951,540
	1934	5,586	89.81	12,187	1,679,038	237,476	1,916,514
T	1935	5,873	90.60	10,822	1,863,177	311,669	2,174,846
	1936	9,425	82.81	18,955	2,871,626	728,033	3,599,659
	1937	16,195	84.37	47,342	5,087,265	1,460,669	6,547,934
	1938	17,328	76.03	69,268	6,243,505	2,602,189	8,845,694
	1939	20,202	76.31	—	7,335,579	2,588,373	9,923,952
G	1940	19,487	73.77	—	7,227,179	2,306,113	9,533,292
	1941	—	—	—	—	—	10,198,376
J	1942	—	—	—	—	—	13,181,067
	1943	—	—	—	—	—	17,741,974
A	1944	—	—	—	—	—	10,452,139
	1945	—	—	—	—	—	—

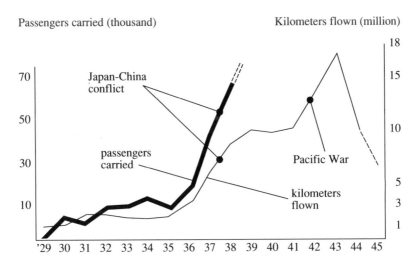

9.5. JAT/GJA operation results.

Japanese War, JAT played a major role in military missions and virtually became the transport arm of the army and the navy. The armed services then began to compete for a dominating influence in the company.

In the meantime, the army negotiated with the German government, through Manchurian Airways, for the possible inauguration of scheduled service between Tokyo and Berlin via China and Manchuria. On the face of it, the negotiation called for a commercial service, but the real intention was for mutual military collaboration in the case of emergency. The two countries signed an agreement to this effect in November 1936. To initiate the proposed service, the army formed a new carrier, International Airways, in August 1937 as a subsidiary of Manchurian Airways, although International ended up being only a "paper" company.

In the interservice power struggle for control over JAT, the navy had fewer advantages than the army. To strengthen its position, the navy planned to form another nominally civilian carrier, tentatively named Oceanic Airways. It was to function as an auxiliary force within the navy, but it never materialized. As the army and navy jockeyed for position, the Ministry of Communication began to fear that its administrative role in the air transport industry might become meaningless. A government regulation gave JAT monopolistic rights in the na-

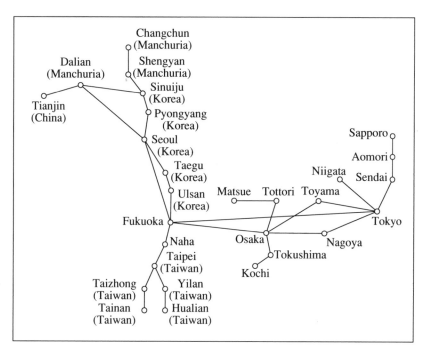

9.6. JAT's commercial service network (April 1937).

tion's air transport industry. The attempts to form International Airways and Oceanic Airways violated this monopoly, at least according to the ministry.

As a compromise, the ministry proposed the creation of an entirely new carrier by a merger of JAT, International, and Oceanic. The army and the navy decided to go along with the proposal, and as a result, Greater Japan Airways (GJA) was formed in December 1938 as a new flag carrier to replace JAT. In a concession to the navy, the Ministry of Communication created the Oceanic Division within GJA, specifically to work for the navy in fulfilling its transport requirements. Outwardly, with the creation of GJA, the power struggle seemed to have come to an end, but in fact, rivalry between the two military services intensified, and the ministry's influence in the company gradually declined.

The new flag carrier continued commercial services and services for the army and the navy between 1939 and 1941. During this period, GJA made efforts to expand its long-range overseas operations and its China routes. To begin, the carrier tried to inaugurate a flying boat service to the Micronesian is-

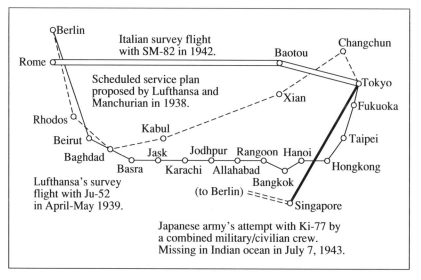

9.8. GJA's commercial service network (April 1941).

lands administered by Japan under a League of Nations mandate. A scheduled service between Yokohama and Saipan and Palau was also successfully inaugurated in April 1939. This two-year period was the most brilliant episode in GJA's years as a commercial operator. Behind the scenes, however, in August 1939, the government changed GJA from an independent company to a half state-owned corporation to facilitate more direct control over the airline and its operations.

Continued military expansion into French Indochina and Thailand led to pressure on the governments of those countries to sign air agreements with Japan, under which GJA inaugurated scheduled services to Bangkok in June 1940 and to Hanoi and Saigon in April 1941. These services expanded the carrier's operating role and sphere of influence, although the agreements were signed by the French and Thai governments under the army's threat. On the other hand, because of ever-increasing requisition of aircraft and crews by the military services, GJA found it nearly impossible to maintain the previous level of commercial operations, and the airline had to terminate all local domestic services by September 1941.

The military services, though still heavily dependent on GJA, China Airways, and Manchurian Airways for transport aircraft, began building up their

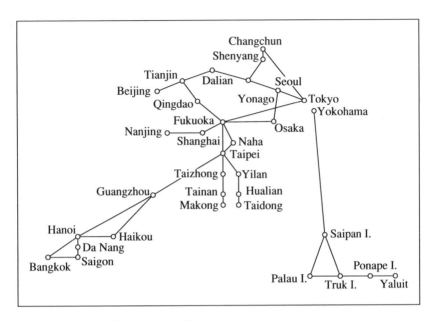

9.7. Planned Japan-Europe liaison flights.

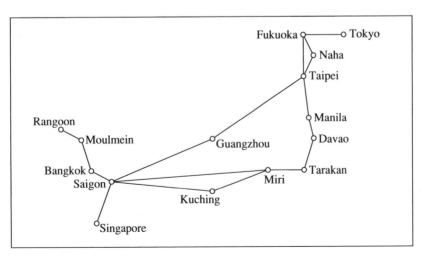

9.9. An example of GJA's provisional scheduled service network for the army (February 1942).

own transport fleets by 1940. Following the 1937 Type 97 transport, a military version of the eight-passenger Nakajima AT-2 airliner, in 1940 the army introduced a second transport model, the Type 100, a military version of the Mitsubishi MC-20 11-passenger airliner. At the same time, the navy introduced the Type 0 transport, a Showa-built version of the 21-passenger DC-3. Both the Type 100 and the Type 0 were passenger airliners, and the services did not yet consider the feasibility of adapting them for carrying heavy cargo. Although the army introduced the first cargo transport, the Kawasaki Type 1, in 1941, the aircraft was again a military version of the 13-passenger Lockheed 14 airliner, and it had a maximum payload of only 3 metric tons. With the new aircraft, the services achieved a measure of independence in air transport for the first time, but in quantity and quality the Japanese transport fleets were much inferior to those of the Allied forces. One reason was that the armed services were still not too concerned about providing airlift capability by themselves and continued to leave most of the transport missions to the civilian airlines, intending to reserve as many flight crews as possible for combat roles (Tables 3 and 4).

Early in 1941, the army and the navy began to think that a war with the United States and Great Britain was unavoidable and started to plan accordingly. In July 1941, the two services scrutinized GJA's capability and decided on a plan to utilize the carrier in the coming conflict. As originally drawn up, the plan stipulated that a part of GJA's fleet and crews would be reserved for commercial operations, but after the outbreak of the war, the services found that was impossible, and all aircraft and crews were mobilized for the war effort. Consequently, GJA had to terminate all its commercial services by January 1942.

Under the mobilization plan, the navy drafted some of GJA's aircraft and crews in August 1941, forming the 1st Drafted Air Transport Unit, which went to Hainan Island, China, for local transport missions. Based on the success of the first unit, the navy formed five more drafted units, numbered from the 2nd to the 6th, by February 1942. The six units were equipped with about 75 aircraft and had about 1,200 personnel at their peak. They put in excellent service and satisfied the navy far beyond its original expectations.

The army also drafted aircraft and crews from GJA, Manchurian Airways, and China Airways, and formed the Southern Air Transport Command in July 1942 as an element in the army's Southern Command. Although 95 percent of the Air Transport Command's personnel were civilians, the army treated them as military personnel. The Air Transport Command was a larger organization than the navy's Drafted Air Transport units. In the beginning, the army planned to equip the command with 450 aircraft and assign 4,000 personnel to it, but in fact, the command at its peak had only about 120 aircraft and 2,000 personnel. The command operated its own maintenance center and a flight school.

TABLE 3

Aircraft Operated by JAT and GJA

Aircraft Type	Number Bought	JAT										GJA						
		29	30	31	32	33	34	35	36	37	38	39	40	41	42	43	44	45
Super Universal	50+	▪	▪	▪	▪	▪	▪	▪	▪	▪	▪	▪	▪	▪	▪			
Fokker F7b3m	10	▪	▪	▪	▪	▪	▪	▪	▪	▪	▪							
Nakajima P-1	8				▪	▪	▪	▪	▪	▪	▪	▪	▪	▪				
Airspeed Envoy	15					▪	▪	▪	▪	▪	▪	▪	▪	▪				
Douglas DC-2	4							▪	▪	▪	▪	▪						
Beech CI7E	14						▪	▪										
Nakajima AT-2	33								▪	▪	▪	▪	▪	▪	▪	▪	▪	▪
Douglas DC-3	70+										▪	▪	▪	▪	▪	▪	▪	▪
Lockheed 14WG	10+										▪	▪	▪	▪	▪	▪	▪	▪
Heinkel He-116	2											▪	▪					
Mitsubishi Type 96 modified	?											▪	▪	▪	▪	▪	▪	▪
Kawanishi Type 97 modified	18										▪	▪	▪	▪	▪	▪	▪	▪
Mitsubishi 21	?												▪	▪	▪	▪		
Mitsubishi MC-20	60+													▪	▪	▪	▪	▪
Kawanishi Type 2 modified	4																▪	▪

Note: Of the GJA fleet, 38 DC-3s, 16 Type 97s, 33 MC-20s, and 2 Type 2s remained in Japan when the war ended. Numbers outside Japan are not known.

TABLE 4
Types and Numbers of Transport Aircraft Operated in Japan

Aircraft Type	Crew/ Passengers	Operator				
		Army	Navy	JAT/GJA	Manchurian Airways	China Airways
Dornier Wal	4/10	—	—	3	—	—
Super Universal	2/ 6	5	—	50+	35+	some
Fokker F7b3m	2/ 8	—	—	10	—	—
D.H. Pussmoth	1/ 2	5	—	—	25	—
BFW Typhoon	1/ 3	—	—	—	some	—
Beech C17E	1/ 4	—	—	20	—	—
Junkers Ju-160	2/ 6	2	1	—	3	—
Manshu Hayabusa	1/ 5	—	1	—	35	20
Airspeed Envoy	2/ 6	—	some	15	—	—
Nakajima AT-2	3/ 8	318	2	33	some	some
Junkers Ju-86	3/10	—	—	—	10+	—
Douglas DC-2	4/14	1	—	4	—	—
Douglas DC-3	4/21	—	400+	70+	some	some
Lockheed 14WG	4/13	65	—	10+	—	some
Heinkel He-116	4/ 2	—	—	—	2	—
Douglas DF	4/32	—	1	—	—	—
Mitsubishi Type 96 modified	4/ 8	—	13	some	—	—
Kawanishi Type 97 modified	8/18	—	20	18	—	—
Mitsubishi 21	4/ 8	some	—	some	some	some
Mitsubishi MC-20	4/11	400+	—	60+	20+	20+
Kawasaki Type 1	3/—	121	—	—	—	—
Nihon Kokukogyo Type 1	3/ 8	50+	—	—	—	—
Kawanishi Type 2 modified	9/64	—	32	4	—	—

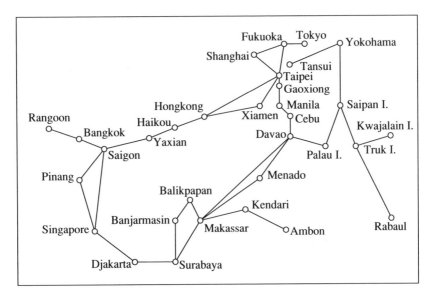

9.10. The Navy Drafted Air Transport units' service network (March 1942).

The army treated the Air Transport Command no differently from other units. The command itself consisted of a mixed force of personnel from the three airlines. Because they had worked under three different flight and maintenance procedures before the war, there was not always complete cooperation. Furthermore, the Air Transport Command operated more than eight different types of aircraft, causing maintenance and repair problems, dropping the rate of aircraft utilization, and leading to frequent accidents.

In contrast to the army, the navy left responsibility for all the aircraft and crews of the Drafted Air Transport units to the operating company, GJA, and provided only minimal oversight. All operational procedures, for example, were the exclusive responsibility of GJA. Under the circumstances, the personnel in the navy drafted units benefited from freer working conditions, enjoyed better operational efficiency, and had fewer accidents than the army command.

Both the army's Southern Air Transport Command and the navy's Drafted Air Transport units were fully committed to the war effort, flying within all the occupied areas in Southeast Asia and the western Pacific. The total distance of the army command's scheduled service reached 25,000 kilometers early in 1943, and the monthly flight time of the crews frequently exceeded 130 hours.

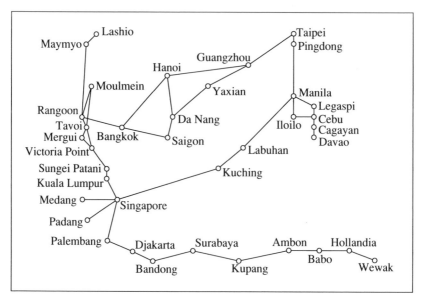

9.11. The Army Southern Air Transport Command's service network (December 1942).

As a matter of course, the civilian flight crews mostly flew transport missions, but most of army's career officers discriminated against the civilian crews, and sometimes they were forced to participate in more dangerous assignments. A typical example of this discrimination occurred when the army's staff officers planned to sweep out Allied interceptors that still remained around Rangoon, Burma, in January 1942, to pave the way for the bomber force. The staff officers tried to utilize some of the civilian crews and unarmed transports of the Southern Air Transport Command as decoys to entice the Allied fighters. The idea was to fly the transports in first, with the fighter force following close behind. The staff officers thought that when the transport force approached Rangoon without fighter escort, Allied fighters would take off to intercept them, and the Japanese fighters could ambush them and easily shoot them down. The staff officers deceived the civilian crews by ordering them to drop supply goods to friendly forces near Rangoon. As planned, the fighter force took off not far behind the transport force. During the flight to Rangoon, however, a leader of the transport force became aware of the trick and told his compatriots to return. The transports returned and landed without damage, and the lead pilot reported to the staff officers that the transport force had been unable to reach Rangoon because of bad weather. The navy was much better than the army in not practicing such misuse, but a part of the Drafted Air Transport units was mobilized for antisubmarine patrol missions sometime during the later stages of the war.

Full-scale operations of the civilian air fleets in the army and the navy continued, but from mid-1943, air superiority in the war theaters gradually shifted to the Allies, and attacks by Allied fighters against Japanese transport aircraft increased. Japan's fighter forces were busy in frontline battles, and the transports always had to fly without escort. Subsequently, from early 1944, the loss of aircraft in the Southern Air Transport Command and the Drafted Air Transport units began to increase significantly, with many civilian crew casualties. Also, it became difficult to maintain scheduled operations because of the constant attacks.

In addition, both the army command and the navy units suffered from the low quality of newly delivered aircraft and the low skill level of young pilots fresh out of training. Late in 1942, the government mobilized most students into various production plants, including aircraft manufacturing, to offset serious shortages in the labor force. Frequent problems arose in aircraft assembled by nonskilled students. Also, many inexperienced young pilots, hurriedly trained after the outbreak of the war, were assigned to frontline duty in the army command and the navy units, and they were frequently involved in accidents.

By the end of 1944, Japan's air power was seriously diminished. Allied attacks intensified, and effective operations by both the army command and the navy units became almost impossible, particularly between Japan's home islands and the occupied areas in the south. The operations were virtually terminated by the early months of 1945, and in August, Japan was defeated.

The mobilization of civil air carriers for wartime use occurred in many countries. The role of the airlines as a reserve air fleet in times of war can be accepted as an inevitable obligation and their destiny, given the unique capabilities that air carriers can bring to bear in wartime. The responsibilities forced upon the Japanese airlines and the risks and hardships they suffered before and during World War II were the most tragic and excessive examples of what happens when airlines, whose missions should be for peaceful purposes, are misdirected for purely political and military purposes.

AIR TRANSPORT CHRONOLOGY OF JAPAN

1922

November 3. Nihon Koku Yuso Kenkyujo (NKYK, Japan Air Transport Institute, formed privately by Choichi Inoue) inaugurated Japan's first commercial air service between Sakai and Tokushima.

1923

January 11. Tozai Teiki Koku Kai (TTKK, East-West Scheduled Air Service Association) inaugurated service.
July 1. Nihon Koku Kabushiki Kaisha (NKKK, Japan Airways Corporation) inaugurated service.

1927

January 1. Japan's first civil aviation law became effective.

1928

October 30. Nihon Koku Yuso Kabushiki Kaisha (JAT, Japan Air Transport Corporation) was formed by the government as a national flag carrier and an independent company. Under a government policy, TTKK and NKKK terminated operations while NKYK was allowed to continue, but only in short-haul services.

1929

April 1. JAT inaugurated cargo and mail service.
July 15. JAT inaugurated daily passenger service.

1931

August 25. Haneda Airport, Tokyo, was completed and opened.
September 18. Manchurian conflict broke out.
September 20. Under army direction, JAT sent Super Universals and crews to Shenyang to help the army operations. The dispatch was the first mobilization of civil aircraft crew by the military in Japan.
December. Under army direction, JAT inaugurated provisional scheduled service for the army.

1932

March 1. Manchurian Empire was created.

September 26. Manchurian Airways (MA) was formed as a joint investment of the Manchurian government and Japanese business firms.

September 27. A JAT Super Universal force landed during a liaison flight for the army in Manchuria, and all eight persons on board were killed by a local Chinese force. The incident was the first time civilian crew members lost their lives in a military mission.

November 3. MA began operations.

1933

February 22. The army began a new operation in Rehe, west Manchuria, then invaded north China. Aircraft and crews of MA were mobilized to help the operation.

1934

March. The army forced MA's flight crews to participate in combat training, including bombing, reconnaissance, and gunnery.

1936

April 1. JAT introduced the DC-2 (14 passengers).

October 1. JAT inaugurated four domestic local services.

November 7. Under army policy, Huitong Hangkong Gongsi (Huitong Airways) was formed in north China with a joint investment by MA and a Chinese local government as an army tool. The new carrier inaugurated services on November 17.

November 25. Japan and Germany signed an aviation agreement.

1937

June 1. JAT introduced the eight-passenger Nakajima AT-2.

July 7. The Sino-Japanese conflict broke out.

July 12. Under army direction, JAT and MA sent aircraft and crews to the Chinese theater.

July 29. The mobilized MA aircraft were forced again to participate in bombing operations against a Chinese force in Taiyuan.

August. Under army policy, MA formed Kokusai Koku (International Airways) as a wholly owned subsidiary in preparation for the proposed inauguration of mutual service between Tokyo and Berlin with Lufthansa, but the program never materialized. At almost the same time, the navy planned to form another civilian carrier as its tool for long-range oceanic operations.

November 13. The army captured Nanjing.

1938

April. Japan's Ministry of Communications began large-scale training of civilian pilots.
August 1. JAT introduced the Lockheed L-14WG (13 passengers).
October. Japan's government decided to form a new national flag carrier with a merger of JAT and Kokusai Koku.
October 5. JAT introduced the DC-3 for the first time in commercial operation.
October 21. The army captured Guangzhou.
November 30. JAT was closed.
December 1. Dai Nippon Koku (Greater Japan Airways, GJA) was formed as a new national flag carrier from a merger of JAT and Kokusai Koku. The carrier was an independent company at its founding.
December 16. Under army policy, Zhonghua Hangkong Gongsi (China Airways) was formed as a joint investment by GJA and three Chinese local governments as a more effective army tool in China, replacing Huitong Airways.

1939

January 25–February 5. GJA provided a goodwill flight to Bangkok with a Heinkel He116 for long-range flight training.
February 10. The navy captured Hainan Island.
April 1. GJA inaugurated cargo and mail service.
April 9-May 28. GJA sent a Mitsubishi Type 96 modified transport (eight passengers) to Tehran, Iran, to celebrate the wedding of the Iranian crown prince and for long-range flight training.
May 11. The Namonhan conflict broke out in Manchuria. The conflict continued until September 5, and many MA aircraft and crews were mobilized for logistic and evacuation missions.
August 31. The government changed GJA to a half state-owned company.
September 1. World War II broke out.
September 22. The army sent forces to French Indochina (Vietnam).
October 1. MA inaugurated Changchun-Tokyo service via Seoul, the only foreign air service based in Japan before the Pacific War.
November 30. Japan and Thailand signed an aviation agreement.
December 23–January 23, 1940. CJA provided a goodwill flight to Rome with a Mitsubishi Type 96 modified transport for long-range flight training.

1940

March 6. GJA inaugurated passenger service.
June 10. Under the agreement with Thailand, GJA inaugurated Tokyo-Bangkok service.
October. Along with the commercial service, GJA inaugurated provisional scheduled service for the army.

1941

June. China Airways inaugurated passenger service.

August. Under navy direction, for the first time GJA sent its aircraft and crews to Haikou to help a navy operation.

September. GJA suspended all domestic local services due to shortages of crew and equipment.

October. Under army direction, GJA formed an extra transport group and sent it to French Indochina in preparation for war. MA and China Airways also formed similar groups for the army.

December 8. The Pacific War broke out. The navy informed GJA that all of its DC-3s, Type 96 modified transports, and Type 97 modified flying boats were to be administered by the navy.

December 25. The army captured Hong Kong.

1942

January 2. The army captured Manila.

January. GJA suspended all its commercial services.

January 10. The army landed in Indonesia.

February 15. The army captured Singapore.

February. GJA inaugurated several provisional scheduled services for the army between Japan and captured southeast Asian cities.

February. Under navy direction, GJA formed six groups and sent them to captured areas in Southeast Asia to set up a provisional scheduled service network for the navy.

April. GJA reformed its company structure and created two new divisions: one for the army, and one for the navy.

June 5. The navy sustained a heavy defeat in the Battle of Midway.

July 10. The army formed the Southern Air Transport Command in Singapore with aircraft and crews of GJA, MA, and China Airways.

August 7. U.S. forces landed at Guadalcanal Island.

1943

February 7. The army retreated from Guadalcanal.

March 8. Activities of the army's Southern Air Transport Command and the navy's Drafted Air Transport units reached a peak.

At least 15 civilian flight crew members were killed when shot down or bombed by Allied aircraft during 1943.

1944

June 15. U.S. forces landed at Saipan Island.

July 4. All GJA crew members left on Saipan Island were killed.

October. Services of the drafted transport units in both the army and the navy began to be curtailed gradually by losses of aircraft and crews in operations.

October 20. U.S. forces landed at Leyte in the Philippines.

November 24. The first B-29 bombing raid against Tokyo.

Late 1944. Activities of the army and the navy drafted transport units decreased to a minimum level because of the threat of Allied interception. At least 73 civilian flight crew members were killed when shot down or bombed by Allied aircraft during 1944.

1945

January. The Southern Air Transport Command lost 41 transports on the ground at Clark Field, Manila, in a U.S. bombing raid.

June 26. U.S. forces captured Okinawa.

August 15. Japan surrendered.

October 31. GJA was disbanded. At least 94 civilian flight crew members were killed when shot down or bombed by Allied aircraft during 1945.

JAPAN'S AIR TRANSPORT COMPANIES AND MILITARY ELEMENTS

Japan Air Transport Corporation

Formed: October 30, 1928; closed November 30, 1938
Employees at peak period: 1,500
Aircraft at peak period: 80
Total distance of service network: 12,800 km
Service area: Japan, Korea, Taiwan, Manchuria, and China

Greater Japan Airways Corporation

Formed: December 1, 1938; closed October 31, 1945
Employees at peak period: 5,000
Aircraft at peak period: more than 120
Total distance of service network: 31,000 km
Service area: Japan, Korea, Taiwan, Manchuria, China, French Indochina, Thailand, and Marshall/Caroline islands.

Manchurian Airways Corporation

Formed: September 26, 1932; ceased operation August 15, 1945
Employees at peak period: 3,000
Aircraft at peak period: 140

Total distance of service network: 13,000 km
Service area: Manchuria, Japan, China, and Korea

China Airways Corporation

Formed: December 16, 1938; ceased operation August 15, 1945
Employees at peak period: 4,000
Aircraft at peak period: 100
Total distance of service network: 12,000 km
Service area: China and Manchuria

The Army Southern Air Transport Command

Formed: July 10, 1942, with aircraft and personnel of Greater Japan Airways, Manchurian Airways, and China Airways
Employees at peak period: 2,000
Aircraft at peak period: 120
Total distance of service network: 28,000 km
Service area: Taiwan, China, the Philippines, French Indochina, Thailand, Malaya, Singapore, Indonesia, Burma, and New Guinea

The Navy Drafted Air Transport Units

Formed: August 1941, with aircraft and personnel of Greater Japan Airways
Employees at peak period: 1,200
Aircraft at peak period: 75
Total distance of service network: 35,000 km
Service area: Japan, Taiwan, China, the Philippines, French Indochina, Malaya, Singapore, Indonesia, Burma, and Marshall/Caroline islands

■■■
■■
■■■ Genrikh V. Novozhilov

The Design of Military and Passenger Aircraft in Russia

Most historians will agree today that the key figure in the early development of civil aviation in Russia was Igor Sikorsky. Under his direct leadership, the famous Russian Knight airplane was designed and built in early 1913. Better known in the West as the Sikorsky Le Grand, the airplane had impressive load-carrying capability and featured enclosed crew and passenger compartments to protect the occupants from airflow. In this respect, the airplane was quite different from and considerably more advanced than all its contemporaries. The Russian Knight, which featured four 100-horsepower, wing-mounted engines, can be considered the first aircraft capable, due to its design, of carrying seven to ten passengers over a distance of 150 kilometers while providing a high level of safety and comfort, at least by the standards of the day.

In late 1913, Sikorsky designed and manufactured the four-engine Ilya Muromets to take the place of the Russian Knight. First flown in late 1913, the aircraft had more advanced aerodynamics and a fuselage structure with sufficient room for the cockpit, cabin, and sleeping compartment. Its layout was a major improvement in passenger comfort; all the airplane compartments were lighted by electricity and heated by engine exhaust gas. In addition, at the rear of the cabin there was a separate room for the toilet and washstand.

190

The performance of the Ilya Muromets improved significantly over that of the Russian Knight. The airplane set a number of world records, including some remarkable long-distance flights. Sikorsky was the first to create aircraft capable of carrying significant numbers of passengers over long distances while maintaining unparalleled levels of safety and comfort.

On account of World War I, which broke out in August 1914, the Ilya Muromets did not get a chance to demonstrate its superior capabilities as a passenger aircraft. Shortly after the beginning of the war, the Russian army adapted it for use as a long-range reconnaissance and bombing aircraft. In December 1914, the first air force formation of heavy bombers—the so-called Airship Squadron—was built up with Ilya Murometses, and the unit took an active part in military operations. Having a bomb capacity of 410–500 kilograms (heavy for those days) and a defensive armament consisting of three and later eight machine guns capable of 360-degree fire, the airplanes were effective on offensive missions deep behind the enemy's front lines.

In the early 1920s, the reequipped Ilya Murometses—by then largely obsolete and at the end of their service lives—were used once again to carry passengers, but soon their flights were prohibited because the aircraft wore out and were deemed unsafe.

After October 1917, the Soviet Union made great efforts to create a powerful aviation industry. As a result, a number of design bureaus and research centers specializing in aerodynamics, hydrodynamics, aircraft engines, and materials were set up. Also, various aircraft and engine manufacturing facilities were built, as well as many factories producing aircraft components and flight instruments. As a whole, these efforts resulted in an infrastructure that before World War II supported research and development and the production of aircraft for the air force and civil air fleet that were comparable in performance to those found elsewhere in the world. Nevertheless, the structure of the industry was such that it could not support separate military and civil aircraft design and production. Soviet civil aircraft, therefore, strongly resembled military designs, especially the larger passenger airliners, which were basically modifications of existing bombers.

Such an approach to creating civil aircraft allowed a reduction in the development time, production schedule, and expenses associated with aircraft manufacture. The philosophy also brought some reduced operating costs. As a rule, the aircraft designed on the basis of bombers had the same wings, power plants, empennages, and landing gear used in the military aircraft, but new fuselages allowed for passenger seating.

For a long time, Andrei Tupolev led this trend in the design of Soviet pas-

Sikorsky heavy aircraft

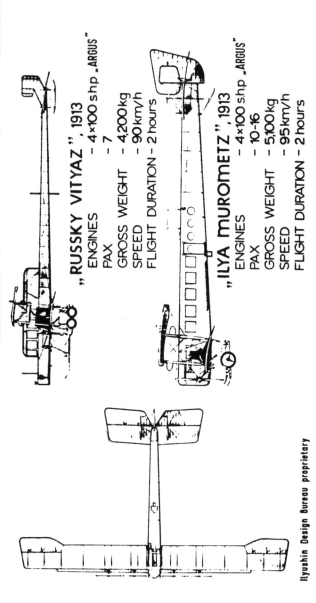

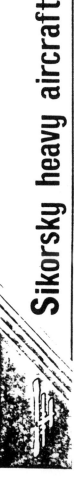

„RUSSKY VITYAZ", 1913

ENGINES — 4×100 s.h.p. „ARGUS"
PAX — 7
GROSS WEIGHT — 4,200kg
SPEED — 90km/h
FLIGHT DURATION — 2 hours

„ILYA MUROMETZ", 1913

ENGINES — 4×100 s.h.p. „ARGUS"
PAX — 10-16
GROSS WEIGHT — 5,100kg
SPEED — 95km/h
FLIGHT DURATION — 2 hours

Ilyushin Design Bureau proprietary

10.1. Igor Sikorsky designed and manufactured the Ilya Muromets, superior in aerodynamics and passenger comfort to the Russky Vityaz (Russian Knight), his previous creation. (Courtesy of Ilyushin Design Bureau)

senger aircraft. Under his direct leadership the TB-1, the first all-metal two-engine heavy bomber, was built as early as 1925. In 1929, S. A. Shestakov and his crew flew a TB-1, named *Land of the Soviets,* from Moscow to the Far East, then across the Pacific to the United States. The Red Army adopted the airplane and put it into service, along with a transport version designated the G-1. The G-1 transport was also used by Dobrolet, the state airline, both as a cargo and passenger aircraft. It is interesting to note that the design accommodated 10 passengers in special cabins suspended under the fuselage and secured by shackles.

The TB-1 airframe and some components of the twin-engine multipurpose military aircraft known as the R-6, which was designed on the basis of the TB-1, were used in the nine-passenger, three-engine ANT-9, developed in 1929. The outer wings, empennage, and power plant of the R-6 were transferred into the production version of the ANT-9, which was designated PS-9. A total of 75 PS-9s were built, and they successfully operated on short-haul routes by Dobrolet and its successor after 1932, Aeroflot. Due to their powerful engines, they were particularly effective in high-altitude conditions and hot climates.

The basic design of the TB-1 received a further development in the construction of the four-engine TB-3 (ANT-6), Tupolev's famous heavy bomber, which began flight tests in December 1930. The TB-3 won a reputation for simplicity and reliability, so in 1931, its basic design was carried forth with the five-engine, 36-seat ANT-14. The ANT-14 was meant to complement the successful PS-9. The ANT-14's high seating capacity and impressive size made it one of the largest passenger aircraft of the time, with performance roughly the same as that of the Junkers G-38, designed in Germany a year before. Pilots greatly appreciated the ANT-14 for its stability and ease of handling. Unfortunately, the aircraft was not put into production because of the lack of production capacity of the fledgling Soviet aviation industry, the depressed state of the Soviet economy in the early 1930s, and the relatively small volume of passengers due to the high cost of air travel. But right up to World War II, the ANT-14 prototype was intensively used as a propaganda aircraft and flew sightseeing passengers over Moscow.

Aeroflot made the most use of the G-2, another version of the TB-3. The fuselage and wing torsion box of this airplane allowed for fitting cargo tie-down equipment or passenger seats. A large airplane, the G-2 was capable of carrying up to 50 passengers or 4,000 kilograms of cargo. Several such airplanes were modified for operation in the arctic latitudes. In May 1937, these airplanes made the first landing on the ice in the vicinity of the North Pole, delivering

TB-1 heavy bomber

TB-1 (ANT-4), 1925

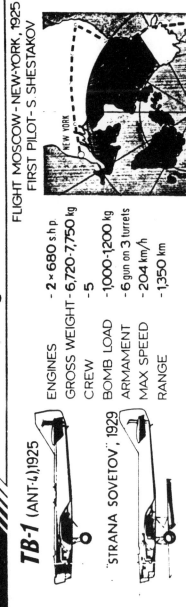

FLIGHT MOSCOW - NEW-YORK, 1925
FIRST PILOT- S.SHESTAKOV

"STRANA SOVETOV", 1929

G-1, 1932

Ilyushin Design Bureau proprietary

ENGINES	- 2 × 680 s.h.p.	
GROSS WEIGHT	- 6,720-7,750 kg	
CREW	- 5	
BOMB LOAD	- 1,000-1,200 kg	
ARMAMENT	- 6 gun on 3 turrets	
MAX SPEED	- 204 km/h	
RANGE	- 1,350 km	

PAX	- 10-12	
TROOPERS	- 12-16	
WOUNDED ON STRETCHES - 8		

TOTAL PRODUCTION AIRCRAFT – 216

FLIGHT DISTANCE 21,242 km

10.2. Andrei Tupolev developed the TB-1, the first all-metal two-engine heavy bomber. One of these aircraft, *Strana Sovetov* (*Land of the Soviets*), flew from Moscow to New York in 1929. The G-1 was a transport version of the TB-1. (Courtesy of Ilyushin Design Bureau)

equipment to a scientific expedition that was setting up the drifting station called North Pole One. It was a significant achievement for those days. Continuing to develop the concept of the heavy bomber from the TB-3, the Tupolev Design Bureau in July 1933 began flight tests of the six-engine heavy bomber TB-4 (ANT-16), which was capable of carrying up to 10 tons of bombs and had a formidable defensive armament. The distinctive feature of this aircraft was the location of its engines above the fuselage in three nacelles, each having two engines arranged in tandem with tractor and pusher propellers.

Subsequently, the design of this heavy bomber was used as the basis for the eight-engine ANT-20 Maxim Gorky, the prototype of which was built as a propaganda airplane, but which could also be used for carrying passengers. It was determined that the military version of the aircraft was to be used as a bomber and command post for the army's general headquarters.

In its passenger configuration, the ANT-20 could carry up to 80 people— 8 crew members and 72 passengers. It is noteworthy that passengers could enter the cabin by using the airstairs built into the rear fuselage, similar to the arrangement used years later on the Boeing 727, Sud Aviation Caravelle, and other jet passenger aircraft.

The ANT-20 made its first flight in June 1934. The flight tests were successful on the whole, but in its final flight—just before being approved for service—the airplane had an accident caused by a collision with an escorting aircraft that had violated flight procedures. Despite the mishap, the decision was made to produce a passenger version of the airplane. The production model improved on the prototype. For instance, due to the employment of higher-rated engines, the concept of the above-fuselage tandem power plant was abandoned. Production ANT-20s used six engines mounted separately in the wings.

Serial production of the ANT-20 took place at the Kazan aircraft production plant number 124, which was built especially for this purpose. For some reason, however, the first production aircraft, ANT-20 *bis,* designated PS-124 (the number of the production plant), was not rolled out until May 1939. Later, this aircraft, in the 64-seat layout, operated for a long time on the route from Moscow to Mineralny Vody.

The distinctive feature of all the airplanes (PS-9, ANT-14, and ANT-20) designed in the first half of the 1930s was their substantial growth in size and seating capacity and their almost unchanged cruising speed of 200–235 kilometers per hour. Such a low cruising speed was the result of relatively low wing loading (73–95 kilograms per square meter) and the use of corrugated metal skin and fixed landing gear.

While engineers were working on the development of fairly low-speed pas-

Giant aircraft of the thirties

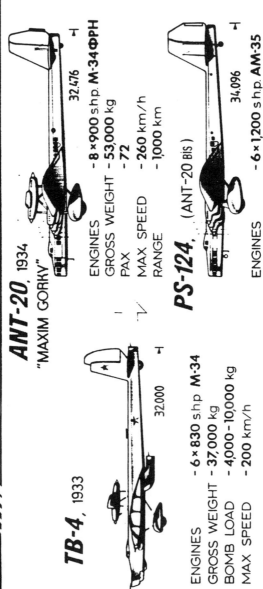

TB-4, 1933

32,000

ENGINES – 6 × 830 s.h.p M-34
GROSS WEIGHT – 37,000 kg
BOMB LOAD – 4,000–10,000 kg
MAX SPEED – 200 km/h

ANT-20, 1934
"MAXIM GORKY"

32,476

ENGINES – 8 × 900 s.h.p. M-34ФРН
GROSS WEIGHT – 53,000 kg
PAX – 72
MAX SPEED – 260 km/h
RANGE – 1,000 km

PS-124, (ANT-20 Bis)

34,096

ENGINES – 6 × 1,200 s.h.p. AM-35
GROSS WEIGHT – 45,600 kg
PAX – 64
MAX SPEED – 296 km/h

Ilyushin Design Bureau proprietary

10.3. The design of the six-engine heavy bomber TB-4 was the basis for the eight-engine ANT-20 (Maxim Gorky), also intended as an army command post in its military configuration. The production aircraft, PS-124, did not appear until 1939. (Courtesy of Ilyushin Design Bureau)

senger aircraft, they were also designing high-speed examples. In October 1932, the first Soviet high-speed passenger aircraft, designated the KhAI-1 and featuring retractable landing gear, made its first flight. This six-seat aircraft, designed by the Kharkov Aviation Institute, featured a smooth airframe skin and a cowled air-cooled engine. The aircraft could reach a maximum speed of 324 kilometers per hour. It had been put into production and later successfully operated on Aeroflot routes. During flight tests, the KhAI-1 showed a maximum speed exceeding that of fighters then in service. It speaks highly of the original design that the high-speed reconnaissance KhAI-4, and later the more advanced reconnaissance R-10, which was manufactured in significant numbers until 1939, were based on the KhAI-1 passenger aircraft.

In 1934, the Tupolev Design Bureau developed the all-metal two-engine high-speed SB-1 bomber, whose design realized all the scientific and technological advances in the fields of aerodynamics, materials, and mechanics. The major features of the aircraft were the smooth airframe skin, retractable landing gear, and efficiently cowled air-cooled engines. The aircraft could develop a speed up to 418 kilometers per hour. Serial production of this aircraft continued up to the beginning of World War II.

In 1935, the 10-passenger ANT-35 was designed on the basis of the SB-1 bomber. Primary attention was paid to the fact that the flight speed of the aircraft had to be similar to or even higher than that of the best American aircraft designs. The urge to obtain high flight speeds dictated a fuselage cross section that was as narrow as possible. This decreased airframe drag to a minimum but created other problems. During its flight tests the ANT-35 achieved a maximum speed of 390 kilometers per hour; unfortunately, due to its narrow fuselage, the cabin height was too small—less than an average man's height. Taking this into account, the fuselage of the production aircraft, designated PS-35, was somewhat heightened. Doing so, however, cut the PS-35's payload to no more than 1,050 kilograms, and the limitations of the landing gear brought over from the SB-1 precluded any further increases in the capacity of the aircraft. This was the main reason production was limited to only nine aircraft. The PS-35 nevertheless operated on some of Aeroflot's transcontinental routes.

Another high-speed two-engine passenger aircraft, known as Steel 7, was developed under Roberto Bartini in 1936. This airplane also featured a small cabin capable of accommodating up to 12 passengers. It could attain a maximum speed of 450 kilometers per hour, and its range was more than 5,000 kilometers. This performance was such that the airplane was considered as a prototype of a long-range bomber. The bomber, designated Er-2, was actually built and used by the Soviet air force in World War II. During the war, on Stalin's

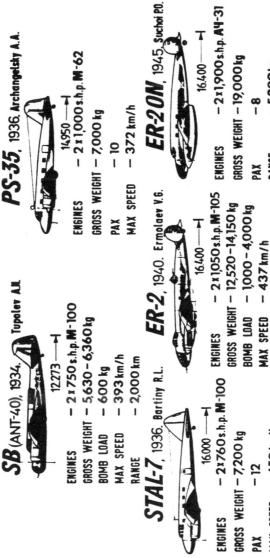

High-speed aircraft

SB (ANT-40), 1934. Tupolev A.I.

ENGINES — 2 x 750 s.h.p. M-100
GROSS WEIGHT — 5,630 – 6,360 kg
BOMB LOAD — 600 kg
MAX SPEED — 393 km/h
RANGE — 2,000 km

STAL-7, 1936. Bartiny R.L.

ENGINES — 2 x 760 s.h.p. M-100
GROSS WEIGHT — 7,200 kg
PAX — 12
MAX SPEED — 450 km/h
Ilyushin Design Bureau proprietary

PS-35, 1936. Archangelsky A.A.

ENGINES — 2 x 1,000 s.h.p. M-62
GROSS WEIGHT — 7,000 kg
PAX — 10
MAX SPEED — 372 km/h

ER-2, 1940. Ermolaev V.G.

ENGINES — 2 x 1,050 s.h.p. M-105
GROSS WEIGHT — 12,520 – 14,150 kg
BOMB LOAD — 1,000 – 4,000 kg
MAX SPEED — 437 km/h
RANGE — 4,000 km

ER-2ON, 1945. Suchoi P.O.

ENGINES — 2 x 1,900 s.h.p. AV-31
GROSS WEIGHT — 19,000 kg
PAX — 8
RANGE — 5,200 km

10.4. The fast, technologically advanced SB-1 bomber evolved into the PS-35, which flew some of Aeroflot's passenger routes. Inversely, the Stal-7 (Steel-7) was designed as a passenger aircraft and became the prototype of a long-range bomber, the Er-2. During World War II, on Stalin's orders, the Er-2 was reconverted into a passenger aircraft, the Er-2ON. (Courtesy of Ilyushin Design Bureau)

orders, this bomber was modified once again into a passenger aircraft and used for special missions. Although a promising design, the Er-2 was not developed further.

In the Soviet Union before the war there was also a trend toward smaller and slower passenger aircraft designed specifically for civilian use. In the 1930s, the most successful of these designs was the eight-seat single-engine K-5, developed under Konstantin Kalinin in 1930. A total of 260 aircraft were built, and the K-5 became the main passenger aircraft in Aeroflot's inventory up to 1939. The cruising speed of this aircraft was 170 kilometers per hour.

In the prewar years, research and development in the field of efficient high-speed passenger aircraft was not successful. The Soviet bureaucracy in charge of aviation, taking into account that the design bureaus could not entirely devote themselves to the development of the new passenger aircraft, made the decision to buy the license to produce the American Douglas DC-3, which had been designed in 1935. This aircraft, powered by engines rated the same as those used on the PS-35, could carry twice the payload of the PS-35, although at a lower speed. In an effort to improve the strength of the aircraft and use as much domestic materials and equipment as possible, the Myasishchev Design Bureau in 1939 changed the structure of the DC-3. Soon, the modified aircraft, designated PS-84, became Aeroflot's main airliner. The military transport version of this aircraft, known as the Lisunov Li-2, saw considerable use in World War II.

In the postwar years, the two main trends in the development of passenger aircraft were revived, and designers created both specialized passenger models and ones derived from military aircraft. The Ilyushin Design Bureau, for instance, developed passenger aircraft optimized to carry out specific transport missions. From the very beginning of his activity in the field of civil aircraft design and manufacture, Sergei Ilyushin adhered to the dual approach in building up a passenger aircraft fleet. The 27-seat, twin-engine Il-12, for medium-haul air routes; and the pressurized 66-seat, four-engine Il-18, for longer hauls, reflected Ilyushin's approach to specially designed airliners. The Il-12 made its first flight on August 15, 1945; a year later, on August 17, 1946, the Il-18, powered by four ASh-73 radial engines, flew for the first time.

In the postwar years, the second trend was the design and development of passenger aircraft based on bombers, notably the Pe-8, Er-2, and Tu-4. The most successful was the Tupolev Tu-70, the development of which coincided with the building of the first Tu-4 bomber, a derivative of the Boeing B-29. The Tu-70 was designed to carry 72 passengers and their baggage and had six crew members. This aircraft adhered to the aerodynamic design of the Tu-4 as a whole but differed in having a low-wing configuration instead of the bomber's mid-wing layout. In addition, the greater diameter of fuselage caused a change in the distance between the inboard engines and, accordingly, an increase in the wing span and area. The aircraft featured a pressurized cabin.

The Tu-70 made its first flight on November 27, 1946, half a year before the Tu-4. This discrepancy is explained by the Tu-70's use of the wings of one of three Boeing B-29s in the Soviet Union at that time. Up to 75 percent of the structural components of the Tu-70 and Tu-4 were common to both aircraft.

Compared to the Tu-70, the Il-18 was characterized by rather less load ratio, because its structure was optimized for the operating conditions of the aircraft (Table 1). There was no serial production of either the Il-18 or the Tu-70. In 1957, Nikita Khrushchev determined that the advanced turboprop-powered Il-18 should take priority over its piston-engine predecessor. Test pilot Vladimir Kokkinaki told Khrushchev about Stalin's great interest in the first Il-18. One day Stalin had summoned Sergei Ilyushin to ask him about the new aircraft in detail and said, in conclusion: "Comrade Ilyushin, can you assure me that your aircraft will not crash? Now, when an aircraft crashes and only 25 persons are lost it is a great sorrow. But if 70 persons were lost it would be a tragedy for the whole country, you know." Ilyushin, of course, could not guarantee that the Il-18 would not have an accident, and all work on the Il-18 with reciprocating engines was stopped.

Table 1
Comparison of the Il-18 and the Tu-70

	Il-18	Tu-70
First flight	Aug. 17, 1946	Nov. 27, 1946
Engine type	ASh-73	ASh-73
Takeoff power (hp)	2,400	2,400
Wing area (sq m)	140	166.1
Number of passengers	66	72
Takeoff weight (kg)	47,500	60,000
Empty weight (kg)	28,490	38,290
Empty weight per passenger (kg/passenger)	432	532
Range (km)	4,000	4,900
Speed (km/hr)	565	568
Takeoff run (m)	746	670

Many thought aircraft in the Soviet Union were created in accordance with specific tasks assigned to the individual design bureaus. This was not so. The development of aircraft of the same type used to be given to several design bureaus at a time, with the idea of subjecting prototypes to intense competition. Moreover, it was Sergei Ilyushin's style to begin working on aircraft on his own initiative. This was the case with the twin-engine Il-4 (DB-3) long-range bomber, the famous armored close-air-support aircraft Il-2 Sturmovik, and the Il-12 passenger aircraft. Also on his own initiative, Ilyushin created the frontline jet bomber Il-28, although the official task had been given to the Tupolev Design Bureau.

The Tu-73, later designated Tu-14, emerged from the Tu-2 bomber, which was powered by reciprocating engines, and it inherited the Tu-2's defensive armament layout of two separate rearward-firing guns protecting the upper and lower portions of the aircraft. This armament layout, in addition to the four-man crew, dictated an increase in the dimensions and weight of the aircraft, which in turn resulted in adding a third engine in the rear fuselage with the air intake at the fin root. Thus, the Tu-14 was the first airplane to use the layout that many years later was applied to the Boeing 727, DeHavilland DH-121 Trident, and other passenger aircraft.

The major feature of the Il-28 was the single defensive gun installation at the rear fuselage. Developed by Sergei Ilyushin, the installation was thought to be excellent in repulsing hostile fighter attacks from the rear of the aircraft. Smaller and lighter than the Tu-14, the Il-28 demonstrated better all-around performance and was placed in mass production.

In the early 1950s, however, the Ilyushin Design Bureau lost out to the Tupolev bureau in creating a medium jet bomber. Primary conceptual decisions based on the use of a straight wing, which had proved its value in the Il-28 light-bomber program, were not relevant to a medium bomber intended for longer-range operations and higher speeds. In this respect, the twin-engine Tu-16 bomber, with a swept wing and formidable defensive armament, was more successful. Due to its large dimensions, the Tu-16 was capable of carrying a heavier weapons load over a longer range than the Il-46, which Ilyushin had submitted as the bureau's entry in the design competition.

By the mid-1950s, the Soviet Union needed to develop and put into service new, more advanced and efficient aircraft whose performance would completely satisfy the requirements of Aeroflot's domestic and transcontinental air routes. Taking into account the possibilities of gas-turbine engines, the decision was made to design and put into service a new class of turbojet and turboprop aircraft. Accordingly, the Tupolev and Antonov design bureaus took on the high-priority tasks of developing the Tu-104 and An-10 passenger aircraft. Sergei Ilyushin, for his part, had concentrated on the design and development of the turboprop variant of the Il-18. Each of the proposed aircraft was meant to satisfy the specific operating requirements of different Aeroflot domestic and transcontinental air routes.

On June 17, 1955, the twin-turbojet Tu-104 airliner made its first flight. In March 1957, the four-turboprop An-10 took off for the first time. And three months later, on July 4, 1957, the Il-18 with four turboprops made its maiden flight. In October of that year, the Tu-114, at the time the world's largest passenger aircraft, was turned over for flight tests.

The Tu-16 medium bomber was the basis for the Tu-104, which was capable of carrying 70 to 100 passengers on medium-haul routes. In its design and manufacture, the Tu-104 borrowed the wings, landing gear, engines, and a great portion of the systems and equipment from the Tu-16 bomber. Only the fuselage and some of the systems and other equipment necessary for passengers were designed from scratch.

Such an approach allowed Aeroflot to have a high-speed multiseat jet airliner much earlier than if an entirely new aircraft had been designed and built. But due to its high empty weight and powerful turbojet engines, characterized by high specific fuel consumption at cruising speeds and altitudes, the Tu-104 was not as efficient as some of its Western contemporaries. The DeHavilland Comet and Sud Aviation Caravelle were better suited to passenger operations, although the Caravelle appeared somewhat later than the Russian and British aircraft (Table 2). The economic effectiveness of the Tu-104 was considerably improved in later years, first by creating the Tu-104B version, with a stretched fuselage for seating capacity up to 100 passengers, and then with the Tu-110 modification, which featured four D-20 engines and had a specific fuel consumption at cruise of 0.684 kilograms per kilogram/hour.

The same principles were adhered to in creating the long-haul Tu-114 passenger aircraft, designed on the basis of the Tu-95 strategic bomber, with the wings, landing gear, power plants, and other systems and equipment transferred directly from the military airplane. Largely due to powerful and economical Kuznetsov NK-12 engines, considered the best turboprops of the era, the cruising speed of the Tu-114 was high (on the order of 780–800 kilometers per hour at an altitude of 7,000 meters), and its commercial range was up to 8,000 kilometers with a payload of 14.4 tons. At the time, knowledgeable observers considered the Tu-114 an important engineering achievement because of its flight performance and good fuel economy, despite its somewhat excessive weight.

A comparison of the Tu-114 and the four-jet Ilyushin Il-62, which was de-

Table 2

Comparison of Aircraft by Fuel-Efficiency Factors

	Tupolev Tu-104/Tu-104A	DeHavilland Comet Mk IV	Sud Aviation Caravelle Mk IV
First flight	1955/1958	1958	1958
Engines	2	4	2
	AM-3M-500	RR Avon Mk 525	RR Avon Mk 531
Takeoff thrust (kg)	2 × 9,700	4 × 4,767	2 × 5,670
Cruise-specific fuel consumption (kg/kg hr)	1.05/1.05	0.775	0.762
Number of passengers	70/100	81	70
Takeoff weight (tons)	76/76	71.7	47
Equipped empty weight (tons)	42.3/43.3	33.9	26.8
Equipped weight per passenger (kg/passenger)	604/433	419	383
Commercial range (km with payload, tons)	3,000/2,500 7.0/10.0	4,500 8.0	3,000 7.0
Fuel consumption (g/seat-km)	97.8/67.0	66.6	62.8

Note: These fuel-efficiency factors were not being used in those days.

signed by the Ilyushin company, is given in Table 3. Throughout its service operation until it was retired in 1976, the Tu-114 maintained a good reputation as a highly reliable aircraft, providing the greatest level of flight safety while carrying out regular passenger transportation.

The aim of designing the An-10 was to obtain an aircraft capable of operating on short-haul routes of 500 to 2,500 kilometers. Such a relatively short flight range was a result of the derivation of the An-10 from the An-12 military transport. The fore- and mid-fuselage sections, wings, landing gear, and engines of the An-10 were the same as those of the An-12, the only difference being a new rear fuselage and a pressurized cabin with an ordinary unstrengthened floor.

Table 3
Comparison of the Tu-114 and the Il-62

	Tu-114	Il-62
First flight	1957	1963
Engines	4	4
	NK-12MB	NK-8-4
Takeoff thrust	4 × 15,000 shp	4 × 10,500 kg
Cruise-specific fuel consumption (kg/kg hr)	0.166	0.78
Number of passengers	170	186
Takeoff weight (tons)	173.5	160
Equipped empty weight (tons)	94.5	67.9
Equipped weight per passenger (kg/passenger)	556	365
Maximum payload (tons)	22.5	23
Commercial range with maximum payload (km)	5,000	5,800
Cruising speed (km/hr)	780	820
Fuel consumption (g/seat-km)	57.8	56.2

The comparatively large proportions of the An-10, with a fuselage diameter of 4.1 meters, resulted in low lift-drag and high load ratios. Its indisputable advantage, however, which largely compensated for the above-mentioned short-coming, was the takeoff and landing performance inherited from the An-12. This was important, considering the standards of Soviet civil aviation at the time, because the An-10 could be used from unprepared airfields, thus allowing regular air services to be established between a great number of populous districts and industrial centers that did not have well-developed airports. For example, at the time even Borispol Airport in Kiev had no concrete runway.

Compared to the An-10, the Il-18 had to meet somewhat different requirements. The Il-18 should have become the main medium-haul airliner, competing with any aircraft in the world market in economy, comfort, and flight performance. It was much better than the An-10 both in fuel efficiency and flight performance, and though slightly deficient in distance required for takeoff, it was superior in rate of climb (Table 4).

Looking back, it should be recognized that the development program of Soviet passenger aircraft from 1955 to 1957 took a qualitative leap from relatively

10.5. First flown in 1963, the four-engine Il-62 was Aeroflot's main long-haul airliner, capable of carrying 186 passengers. A total of 250 were produced. (Courtesy of Ilyushin Design Bureau)

low-speed, low-capacity airplanes powered by reciprocating engines (for example, the Li-2, Il-12, and Il-14) to high-speed, gas-turbine-powered aircraft with high seating capacity. The widespread early adoption of turboprop and turbojet aircraft ensured the rapid modernization of the Soviet civil air fleet.

Table 4
Comparison of the An-10A and the Il-18B

	An-10	Il-18B
First flight	1957	1957
Engines	AI-20K	AI-20K
Takeoff thrust (shp)	4 × 4,000	4 × 4,000
Number of passengers	112	110
Takeoff weight (tons)	56	61.2
Equipped weight (tons)	31	33.54
Maximum payload (tons)	14	14
Commercial range (km)	2,260	4,460
Cruising speed (km/hr)	650	650
Takeoff run (m)	900	1,300
Fuel consumption (g/seat-km)	46.8	34.5

The sharp rise in seating capacity, performance, and operational efficiency that characterized the first wave of Soviet gas-turbine passenger aircraft occurred at the cost of such parameters as weight, fuel consumption, noise level, and so forth. These changes came about as a result of the decision to enter jet aircraft based on military designs into the Soviet passenger fleet.

This explanation did not apply to the Il-18, however, because from the beginning its requirements and design features had been determined by the assumption that it would be used as a passenger aircraft only. This approach, as well as the experience of the Il-12, Il-14, and Il-18 with ASh-73 engines, led to the decision to equip the new aircraft with turboprops. The result was that the Il-18 was one of the most successful passenger aircraft of its time. Its most distinctive features were its high levels of safety and reliability, passenger comfort, maintainability, and cost effectiveness. It was the only Soviet commercial aircraft of the time capable of competing in the world market of gas-turbine aircraft.

No doubt the program of creating Soviet passenger aircraft on the basis of military designs in 1955–57 played a positive role in the history of Soviet civil aviation. The program allowed the Soviet Union, which had lagged behind the West in civil aircraft development, to catch up, and it provided Aeroflot with more up-to-date equipment than it would have had otherwise. In addition, as a

10.6. The Ilyushin Il-86 was the first Soviet wide-body airliner, making its first flight in 1976. More than 100 of the 350-passenger aircraft have been manufactured. One of its unusual features is the availability of integral stairs, allowing passengers to board at airports lacking jetways or other boarding facilities. (Courtesy of Ilyushin Design Bureau)

result of the adoption of these aircraft, air transport became a means of mass conveyance, generally available to broad sections of the public at reasonable cost. The creation and adoption of these aircraft also promoted improvements in the infrastructure of air transport. New airports and runways were built, and air traffic control systems and economic and other organizations of the Soviet civil air fleet were established.

Altogether, these new aircraft formed the basis for further advances by Aeroflot as a whole and of its aircraft and accompanying equipment in particular. Airframes came to be designed only on the basis of technical specifications. Such specifications began to reflect the peculiarities of passenger aircraft operation, although at times they meant the aircraft had to carry extra equipment, which was necessary because of deficiencies in the ground infrastructure (navigation and other facilities) needed for air transport in the Soviet Union.

SOURCES

"Aviation Industry in the USSR from 1917 to 1945." Moscow: TSAGI, 1992.

Davies, R. E. G. *Aeroflot: An Illustrated History of the World's Largest Airline*. Rockville, Md.: Paladwr Press, 1992.

Gunston, Bill. *Aircraft of the Soviet Union*. London: Osprey, 1983.

Novozhilov, G. V., ed. *Ilyushin Aircraft*. Moscow: Mashinostroeniye Publishers, 1990.

Stoud, John. *Soviet Transport Aircraft since 1945*. London: Putnam, 1965.

Klaus-Richard Böhme

Connections between Commercial and Military Aviation in a Neutralist Country

The Case of Sweden

Swedish military authorities became interested in aviation some years before the outbreak of World War I. About 1910 the army and the navy organized flying corps, both of which expanded during the war, especially that of the army. During the war, there were also plans to start civil airlines, using airships for the most part, but according to some ideas employing airplanes. Nothing came of these plans, largely because no airships were manufactured in Sweden, and during the war hardly any could be purchased abroad. Neither could military aircraft, but military aircraft and, under license, aircraft engines were produced in Sweden. Aircraft were manufactured both by private companies and in army and navy factories. Engines, however, were produced only by one private company.

After the war all private production of aircraft matériel ceased because the companies involved took the view that they would be quite incapable of coping with foreign competition. The military factories, on the other hand, continued to manufacture aircraft, mainly because the military wanted to keep a body of trained workers and engineers. Both private industry and the state, however, retained an interest in encouraging domestic aircraft production.

The question was discussed by four public bodies in the immediate postwar years: the War Materials Commission, which was appointed in 1915, and three organizations set up in 1919—the Air Commission, the Air Traffic Commission, and the Defense Review Commission. The members of all these commissions agreed in principle that domestic aircraft production ought to occur for strategic reasons. Major Karl Amundson, the commander of the army flying corps, who was also chairman of the Air Commission and a member of the Air Traffic Commission, placed particular emphasis on the need to manufacture engines in Sweden. He also thought aircraft equipment should be produced by private companies, while the military workshops, in principle, should be restricted to maintenance and repair work. These opinions were shared by all four commissions. Their general outlook was that domestic aircraft production ought to be sustained, that it ought to be primarily in the hands of private firms, and that priority should be given to the manufacture of engines.

It was also clear that the private aircraft industry would be entirely dependent for its survival on orders placed by the armed forces. The Air Traffic Commission took the view that civil aviation, even if heavily subsidized by the state, would be unable to provide the necessary level of support for the military. Political authorities—that is, all governments regardless of political orientation—and the Riksdag (Swedish parliament) on several occasions accepted the principles concerning domestic aircraft production put forward by the various commissions.

As a prerequisite for domestic air equipment production, the military had to present proper procurement planning. By the defense resolutions of the Riksdag in 1924 and 1925, the army and naval flying corps were united into an independent armed service. In 1922, Capt. Carl Florman, one of the country's leading experts on aviation, had been appointed as an assistant to the Swedish military attaché in London with special responsibility for aviation. British arguments in favor of an independent air force made a strong impression on him. He was summoned to appear before the Riksdag when the organization of the air units was discussed. Influenced by Florman's arguments, the politicians decided that an independent air force should be established on July 1, 1926.

The politicians, however, agreed on an independent air force mainly for economic, not military reasons. Their primary interest was to keep defense costs low, and they considered the new organization a means of rationalizing the armed forces. But, as it resulted, the funds to maintain the matériel and replace obsolete and destroyed aircraft were insufficient and based on inaccurate calculations. Military experts went along with the unification plan, despite its defects. By accepting an independent air force, the military avoided making a commitment on air doctrine, because the army and navy held widely divergent views on this matter. The army advocated defensive fighter protection, and the navy was in favor of offensive bombing raids against enemy bases.

In 1925, after the Riksdag had definitely decided to establish the air force as an independent service, some large Swedish companies were interested in starting aircraft production, provided the commander-in-chief of the air force, Amundson, by now a major general, could present a procurement plan. Amundson could not. He was an enthusiastic and highly respected expert on air power, but he was not staff trained, nor did he have the personality and will to exercise real leadership. But most seriously, he and his subordinates failed to realize the initial necessity of developing a doctrine and plan for the use of air power.

The formation of a doctrine was necessary for proper matériel procurement planning. Such planning was vital not only to the buildup of the air force, but also to start private domestic aircraft production. The large companies wanted to know exactly what they could sell, and, more important, they wanted to be sure of continuous production. When the air force, due to the lack of a doctrine, failed to be precise on these points, the companies gave up the idea of aircraft production. Incidentally, not before 1934, when a new commander-in-chief, Maj. Gen. Torsten Friis, was appointed, did the air force finally formulate a doctrine and present proper procurement planning.

In 1925, only two small private factories were producing aircraft in Sweden, both of them opened illegally by the Germans. The Versailles Treaty forbade Germany to manufacture any air force matériel whatsoever, and a number of German manufacturers established themselves abroad to evade these restrictions. Sweden, neutral during the war, was attractive to German producers, especially because Sweden was also interested in German military aircraft and aviation know-how. In 1921, the naval Flying Corps approached Ernst Heinkel and helped him to form Svenska Aero AB, which produced military aircraft for the Swedish navy, the German armed forces, and export, although on a very small scale.

Three years later, Hugo Junkers gained a foothold in Sweden by starting a commercial airline. He, like many other American and European manufacturers, tried to create a guaranteed market for his airplanes by setting up private commercial air companies. One stage in Junkers's empire building was the creation of the Finnish aviation company Aero OY in November 1923. At the same time, Junkers made contact with Capt. Carl Florman and his brother, 1st Lt. Adrian Florman. By this time, the Florman brothers had resigned from the military to start a commercial airline.

Since 1917, six commercial airlines had been started in Sweden. Mainly due to financial weakness, none of them survived for very long. On March 27,

1924, the Florman brothers founded the seventh, Aerotransport Company (Ak-tiebolaget Aerotransport, or ABA). This company is still in existence as the Swedish part of the Scandinavian Airline Systems (SAS). It is not possible to say with certainty when the first contacts were made between Junkers and the Florman brothers, or who took the initiative, but it is clear that by May 1924 agreement had been reached jointly to set up a commercial airline company and an aircraft factory in Sweden. Junkers put up 56 percent of the share capital of 356,000 crowns in ABA. By March 1925, the share capital had been increased twice and stood at 996,500 crowns, of which 82 percent belonged to Junkers.

Under the terms of a 1916 law, foreigners could not own more than just under one-fifth of the shares in a Swedish firm. From the outset a part, and from January 1925 all of the shares in ABA were therefore put in the names of Swedish citizens. Foremost among these were the Florman brothers and Friedrich Treitschke, a German by birth who had been given Swedish citizenship in 1920. The law did not forbid using such legal and financial fictions. As a result, ABA was now officially a purely Swedish firm, and the Florman brothers did all they could to present it as such.

It was necessary to use this approach if the subsidies and interest-free loan to purchase aircraft for which ABA had applied to the government in October 1924 were to be secured. The aircraft in question were to be bought from the factory that Junkers founded in Sweden. Carl Florman was particularly assiduous in putting forward this arrangement. The experts appointed to report on the application, the military authorities, and the minister of communications all accepted this point. When the Riksdag approved state support of ABA, it added the condition that the company should use Swedish aircraft material as far as possible. Florman had succeeded in securing a change in the generally held earlier belief that Sweden's need for civil aircraft was too limited to sustain a domestic aircraft industry. Florman and Junkers were naturally both aware that this belief was correct. They realized perfectly well that the existence of an aircraft industry depended almost entirely on military orders, but all orders were welcome, especially during the initial phase.

Junkers seems to have had in mind that his Swedish factory would establish itself more easily if it began as a repair workshop. But he had big plans for the future of the factory, as is clear from a letter that one of his directors, Eberhard Milch, wrote to Carl Florman on December 22, 1924. According to Milch, the factory would produce aircraft mainly for export, and they would be equipped with engines manufactured by the British firm Blackburn. The factory was to be located in a free-port area of a coastal town to make it easier and cheaper to import Blackburn engines, raw materials, components, and miscellaneous equipment, as well as completed aircraft. Milch was clearly thinking of Malmö. The choice of a coastal city was also a precondition for cooperation with Blackburn, which insisted that the factory had to be within the range of British naval artillery in the event of war. Blackburn imposed this condition because the company knew it would be helping Junkers to evade the Versailles Treaty.

On the other hand, Milch realized that locating the factory in a coastal town might deter the Swedish armed forces from relying on it as a supplier. He was also aware that the Swedes might be reluctant to commit themselves to Junkers aircraft because they were built from duralumin, an alloy that was not manufactured in Sweden. But Milch thought this objection could be met if enough aluminum could be stockpiled in Sweden to assure the production of 1,000 aircraft and the factory could be evacuated inland within one to two weeks in the event of war. Despite all these efforts, nothing came of the idea of cooperating with Blackburn. Nor did Junkers accept a contract drawn up by the Malmö municipal council agreeing to the use of certain land for the construction of a factory employing at least 2,000 people. It remained clear that the existence of the Swedish factory had to be assured through ABA's subsidized purchase of the aircraft it produced and through orders placed by the Swedish air force.

Flygindustri Company Ltd. (Aktiebolaget Flygindustri, or AFI) was formed on January 15, 1925, by six Swedish citizens, headed by Treitschke. The share capital was set at a minimum of 150,000 crowns and a maximum of 450,000 crowns. The shares were in the names of the founders, but all belonged to Junkers. AFI began by assembling Junkers aircraft but soon switched to manufacturing under license. It used a factory in the Limhamn shipyards outside Malmö. The company's development was initially rapid. It had a staff of about 20 at the outset, but the figure rose by late 1925 to about 450 workers and salaried employees. The number fell, however, to about 200 in 1926 and sometimes declined even more during the following years, reaching far less than 100 on certain occasions.

The reason for this state of affairs was that the large orders the company hoped to receive never materialized. The company's records seem to have been destroyed, and it is therefore impossible to say how many aircraft left the factory during its 10-year life. There is some evidence that the total was just over 100. Ten civil airliners were supplied to ABA, and one ambulance plane to the Swedish Red Cross. The remainder were exported.

AFI was on the verge of bankruptcy by about 1927 or 1928 at the latest, but it was kept alive by switching to other forms of production in the hope that better times would come. In these circumstances the company placed its hopes even more than it had earlier on orders from ABA, that is, on state assistance to civil aviation, and from the air force. But, despite persistent efforts, AFI had still not succeeded in selling any aircraft to the Swedish armed forces. In the years before 1932, the air force was primarily interested in obtaining fighters, and Junkers never succeeded in designing a fighter. The main reason, however, why the Swedish air force avoided buying Junkers aircraft was that they were primarily made of duralumin. The air force avoided acquiring aircraft made from this alloy for strategic reasons, preferring airplanes made of wood, steel, and fabric. An additional consideration was that Junkers aircraft were between 30 percent and 50 percent more expensive than other airplanes.

An unsatisfactory financial position, hastened by certain political measures in Sweden, forced closure of the company. On behalf of Junkers the Florman brothers had tried to secure orders by persuading the politicians to buy civil aircraft instead of bombers, particularly because the Junkers airplane could easily be used as such. This attempt to gain a backdoor entrance to the Swedish military market had definitively failed by 1930. That same year, Junkers lost its monopoly on orders from ABA, and the company could now freely choose what aircraft equipment to buy in the future. In 1934, the War Materials Committee, appointed in 1932, presented its findings and recommendations. The government now introduced stronger legislation against the use of fictitious stock ownership in the armaments industry. The new law, which came into force on July 1, 1935, was explicitly directed against AFI. Neither the state nor private Swedish interests were prepared to buy out Junkers, and AFI went into liquidation on May 17, 1935.

The government took an opposite view of ABA from the one taken of AFI. Although from the outset, ABA had been on the verge of bankruptcy, the company soon earned a good professional reputation. In 1928, the government appointed a new air traffic committee, which presented its findings in 1930. Junkers was now forced to withdraw from the company. But the government not only wanted ABA to survive, it even wanted the company to open new flight routes. The state promised to increase its subsidies, provided the company was restructured financially with an infusion of 500,000 crowns of private Swedish money and the government was allowed to name the chairman of the board. Carl Florman stayed on as managing director, while his brother had to leave. Carl found the money, and ABA stayed in business. Now financially solvent, ABA continued to operate Junkers airplanes, as well as aircraft manufactured by Fokker.

What then was the effect of ABA on Swedish military aviation? First, in case of war, the company's airplanes could be used as military transports. During World War II, ABA airplanes, mainly of Junkers design, made up the bulk of the air force's transport fleet. Second, at the outbreak of the war in 1939, ABA pilots were far better trained and much more experienced in instrument and night flying than the pilots of the Swedish air force. During the war they were called up by the air force and became highly appreciated and essential instructors.

An indirect effect of ABA, however, might have been of greatest importance to Swedish aviation. Since 1919, several committees had stressed the importance of domestic production of aircraft and, especially, of aircraft engines. The Academy of Engineering Sciences, set up in 1919, supported this view. Its by-laws declared that its purpose was to encourage technological research and, by so doing, to promote the interests of Swedish industry and the utilization of Sweden's natural resources. When ABA applied for state support in the autumn of 1924, the academy set up an aeronautical committee. Its members were renowned professors, civil engineers, and industrialists, among them the famous inventor Gustaf Dalén. The committee elected the governor of Gävleborg County, Carl Lübeck, as chairman. Lübeck had graduated from the Stockholm Institute of Technology as a civil engineer but became a politician. He was one of the Conservative party's experts on communications, serving as minister of communications from 1923 to 1924. Lübeck had been approached by Florman previously in 1923 to secure state support for the commercial airline he intended to start.

Lübeck and Dalén were particularly emphatic that no subsidy could be allowed to lead to a situation in which Swedish civil aviation became linked to a single factory. Dalén openly stated that it was important to ensure that Junkers did not gain a foothold in Sweden because that would be damaging to the development of a national aeronautic industry. In its statement on the issue, the committee emphasized that if there were to be any state subsidies, they must contribute to the emergence of a domestic aircraft industry. It was clearly dissatisfied when the government resolved in favor of ABA's application for state support. The debate on how public funds could be used most effectively to develop aviation did lead, however, to the aeronautical committee's adoption of a more concrete research program. Until 1932, research on aero engines and other kinds of aircraft equipment was carried out by two subcommittees.

During the same period, the aeronautical committee persuaded the political authorities that a chair in aeronautics and an aerodynamics laboratory should be established at the Stockholm Institute of Technology. In 1928, the Riksdag accepted the creation of a chair in aeronautics but rejected an aerodynamics laboratory. The first holder of the new chair was Ivar Malmer, a member of the aeronautical committee. In 1930, a small aerodynamics laboratory was linked to his chair. The aeronautical committee's efforts then turned mainly to establishing an aeronautical test center, which it regarded as essential if Swedish industry were to move from manufacture under license to the production of aircraft designed in Sweden. The committee in this context stressed the point that Sweden had to develop both commercial and military aircraft. In 1938, the Riksdag voted for the creation of the Aeronautical Research Institute, which started its work in 1940. Malmer became its first director.

There can be no doubt that through its aeronautical committee the Academy of Engineering Sciences made a large contribution to advancing aeronautical research in Sweden. It is fair to suggest that not the least of the academy's contributions was its decisive role in ensuring that an aeronautical test center be set up before the outbreak of World War II. Without such a center, it would have been difficult, if not impossible, to design and develop Swedish military airplanes during the war. In due time the academy certainly would have taken such steps anyhow. But there can be no doubt that thanks to ABA's application for state support, the academy acted earlier and more resolutely than would have been the case otherwise. In this way, Junkers's Swedish commercial airline, without its even being realized at the time, made its most important contribution to Swedish military aviation.

SOURCES

This paper is based on my article "AB Aerotransport, Junkers och flygvapnet," *Militärhistorisk Tidskrift* (1980): 63–95; and my book, *Svenska vingar växar: Flygvapnet och flygindustrin, 1918–1945* (Stockholm: Militärhistoriska Förlaget, 1982). The English version appeared as *The Growth of the Swedish Aircraft Industry, 1918–1945* (Stockholm and Manhattan, Kans.: Sunflower University Press, 1988). The other principal source is Klaus-Richard Böhme, "Swedish Air Defense Doctrine, 1918 to 1936," *Aerospace Historian* 24 (June 1977): 94–99.

PART FOUR

Great Pioneers in the Development of Commercial Aviation

 Nick A. Komons

Introduction

The three articles presented here deal with events that took place on three continents—Europe, North America, and Australia—during commercial aviation's infancy. One might expect that events so widely scattered by distance, if not time, and taking place independently of each other, would lack a strong common thread. That, it turns out, is not the case.

Of course, the details do differ. Commercial aviation did not develop around the world as if it had sprung from a single source. The precise approaches taken in the Netherlands differed from those taken in Australia or the United States. But what I find striking is what commercial aviation in these three countries had in common, not the differences. In each case the development of commercial aviation was invariably linked to government policy. Indeed, it was hopelessly dependent on it. All three studies may not emphasize this point with equal force, but government's presence is clearly in evidence, both in the shadows and in the spotlight. And in all cases, government is lending a fostering hand— granting direct or indirect subsidies, regulating safety, or developing airways.

We learn from Marc Dierikx that Albert Plesman managed to persuade a laissez-faire-oriented Dutch government to violate its economic tenets and pass out subsidies to the Netherlands' chosen instrument, KLM. F. Robert van der Linden gives us a glimpse of Herbert Hoover's aviation policy in the United States. There we find Hoover's postmaster general, Walter Folger Brown, trying to bring stability to the airline industry through the judicious use of airmail contracts—contracts heavily laden with generous subsidies—during a period in American history when sermons on self-help were delivered from the rooftops. And, in the final article, Leigh Edmonds leads us through Edgar Johnston's struggles in Australia to bring the regulatory arm of government to bear on civil aviation activity.

What do these similarities tell us? At the risk of belaboring the obvious, they tell us that commercial aviation is a dependent industry.

Look up at an airliner climbing overhead. It appears to be as free as a bird in flight. In reality it is as dependent on terrestrial devices as any earthbound creature. Air traffic controllers, electronic technicians, and weathermen are engaged in making its passage aloft possible by manning an intricate air navigation and air traffic control system.

The dependence of that airliner serves as a metaphor for the dependent nature of the airline industry itself. And, as we shall see in the following articles, that dependence on governmental benefaction was first recognized by those who pioneered commercial aviation's development.

Marc Dierikx

"Hard Work, Living off the Air"

Albert Plesman's KLM in International Aviation, 1919–1953

It is doubtful that Albert Plesman would have liked historians to dig into his life and airline achievements, for this entrepreneur of Dutch air transport was a man who single-mindedly looked toward the future. In 1948, when questioned by the Dutch official Parliamentary Commission on Wartime Conduct about KLM's record in 1940–45, Plesman commented with bitterness that he found the whole investigation into past events "so utterly unpractical and of such unbelievably little value" that the whole effort seemed profoundly useless to him. To Plesman, it was "looking into a past that no longer exists."[1] Nonetheless, it is fitting to pay tribute he. ⁀ to this aviation entrepreneur, who managed, in the scope of his working career, tʋ build up his airline, KLM, not only once, but twice.

As a person to lead one of the world's first (and soon to be foremost) airlines, Albert Plesman was an unlikely candidate by any standard. So how did the conglomerate of large banks, financial institutions, and shipping lines that founded the Koninklijke Luchtvaart Maatschappij voor Nederland en Koloniën, better known by its English name, KLM Royal Dutch Airlines, choose this 30-year-old air corps lieutenant, who had no formal training in commerce, to lead their costly, high-risk venture into air transport in the autumn of 1919? To answer this question, one must go further back in time to find out how Plesman came to the fore of the aeronautical scene in the Netherlands.

Albert Plesman was born on September 7, 1889, the seventh child of shop-keepers in The Hague. He later described his father, Jan, as an authoritarian brute,[2] which may go some way to explain how the stammering young Albert grew into such a muscular rogue. Yet apart from that, his childhood years were as average as those of the boy next door. At school he excelled in arithmetic and sports. And even though he was born a city kid, Albert was very much an out-door boy, haunting the nearby dunes. The surroundings of his early youth would shape his later years. For most of his life, Plesman, director of an inter-national airline that, in his own words, came to "unite the peoples of the world," lived and worked within the same square mile that had formed his childhood environment.

Like many teenagers, Plesman was fascinated by the army and joined as a junior cadet. The officer's career he yearned for was not normally open to some-one from his social background, and, boarding away from home, he took the first step out of the ordinary world he had lived in. In 1909, he enlisted at the Military Academy at Breda, and it was during his academy years that he had his first encounter with aeronautics. In June 1911, the French paper *Le Journal* or-ganized a European tour for airplanes, for which one of the staging points was the tiny airstrip of Gilze Rijen, some six miles east of Breda. Plesman went to look and, according his biographer, Anthony van Kampen, was absolutely fas-cinated by what he saw.[3] His admiration for the daring heroes who piloted air-planes would never disappear.

Four years later, in 1915, the army offered him his first opportunity to fly. At that time Plesman was posted to a novel (and also very Dutch) army unit—the bicyclists. In October, Plesman's bicyclists made a trip to Holland's only mili-tary airfield at that time: Soesterberg. Here, Plesman was among the lucky ones who were taken for a short ride in one of the air corps' Farman F.20s. His pilot that day, Willem Versteegh, who later became his friend, distinctly remem-bered the difficulty the ramshackle air corps had in providing someone of Ples-man's stature with a large enough flying kit.[4]

Shortly afterwards, Plesman was posted to the air corps as an observer. By that time he had already built up a reputation within his army unit as a relentless organizer of sporting events. By those who knew him in this capacity, he was also considered stubborn. This willfulness, which was to characterize him in later life, was especially apparent in his marriage to Suze van Eijk on Decem-ber 27, 1916, before a district court judge. Her parents, well-to-do cheese mer-chants, had refused to give their daughter permission to marry the young "fly-boy" without any prospects of future wealth. Some months later, he managed to get commissioned for pilot training. Although he earned his pilot's license, flying did not come naturally to Plesman. During his many years as director of KLM, he appeared to have no inclination to pilot any of his airplanes. His real strength lay in his capacities as an organizer, and he proved these before a nationwide audience in 1919.

Although Holland largely missed out on the aeronautical developments of World War I, these had nonetheless given rise to an inner circle of visionary aviation enthusiasts who were trying to focus public attention on the enormous potential for civil use of airplanes. These protagonists of Dutch aviation were united in the Koninklijke Nederlandse Vereeninging voor Luchtvaart (Royal Netherlands Aeronautical Society), presided over by the former minister of war, then director-general of the Anglo-Dutch Shell oil company, Hendrik Colijn. The society published a journal, *Het Vliegveld (The Airfield),* which found wide readership among the decision-making elite in The Hague, the seat of government.

Among its less prominent subscribers, Lt. Albert Plesman was caught by the bright future for air transport foretold in the journal's columns and in various brochures on the subject published in 1918. Before long, Plesman and a fellow officer, Marius Hofstee, embarked upon an ambitious plan to stage a major international aeronautical exhibition in the Netherlands. The idea soon caught on and received high-ranking support, notably from the former supreme commander of the Dutch Land and Naval Forces, retired Gen. Cornelis Snijders, himself one of those belonging to the inner circle of believers in the future of aviation. In one of the brochures advertising the forthcoming event, an exceptionally eloquent Plesman stated his typical belief that "civil aviation is only a matter of organization."[5] Mainly as a result of Plesman's single-minded persistence as a fund-raiser and canvasser for political support, and the daunting number of hours he put into the scheme, the ELTA exhibition (Eerste Luchtverkeer Tentoonstelling Amsterdam, or First Air Transport Exhibition Amsterdam), indeed materialized. Among its subsidizers were the Ministry of Waterworks (75,000 guilders) and the city of Amsterdam (130,000 guilders). Queen Wilhelmina officially opened its gates on August 1, 1919. More than a half million paying visitors followed in her footsteps before the exhibition closed six weeks later.

The enormous success of the ELTA enshrined Plesman's name once and for all in the annals of Dutch aeronautical history. At the age of 30, he had made his name nationwide. And what was more, organizing the ELTA had brought his skills to the attention of the financiers who were at that time hammering out plans for the founding of a Dutch air transport company. Even though these people from the world of high finance were far removed from the social circle of an air corps lieutenant of common descent, they decided that Plesman was just the kind of person they needed for the everyday running of their envisaged air transport company. When asked on September 17, three days after the close of the ELTA, Plesman immediately said yes. An honorable discharge from the air corps was arranged to allow him to become the administrator of the airline.

The management of the company, it was thought, would be entrusted to a small body of delegates from the Board of Executives (Raad van Bestuur) made up of the directors of Royal Dutch Shell and the banks, investment companies, and shipping lines that were the founders of the airline. So, when on October 7, 1919, the official memorandum of incorporation of KLM was signed in The Hague, Plesman was not even present. But if the executives around him had thought they could keep him in check, they were quickly proved wrong. Plesman put in more hours and more work than anyone. Within months, this omnipresent, relentless, authoritarian bully became the virtual embodiment of KLM. Despite constant clashes with the financiers around him on the board, henceforth Plesman, and not they, set the course for KLM's development.

Although the initiators of KLM had entertained high hopes of future profitability, the airline held out for no more than five months before having to turn to the Ministry of Waterworks, responsible also for civil aviation in Holland, with a request for subsidy in early April 1920. That was before a single KLM flight had left the ground. Moreover, KLM did not even possess any aircraft of its own and had only with great difficulty been able to reach a charter and pool agreement with British Air Transport and Travel (AT&T) for starting a joint air service between Amsterdam and London on May 17.[6] Nonetheless, Plesman stimulated the request for subsidy by referring to a government-sponsored study that recommended active state involvement in an airline that would maintain a service between Amsterdam and Batavia, the capital of the Netherlands East Indies, as a means of tightening the bond between the colony and the mother country.[7]

Contrary to what might be expected from a conservative government, whose economic policies were (and remained) characterized by a predominantly laissez-faire attitude, the question of whether or not to subsidize the national aviation effort was quickly resolved. The minister of waterworks, Adriaan König, himself enthusiastic about the future of civil aviation, strongly supported the request. With Plesman, König heartily agreed that Holland would immediately have to seize its place in international civil aviation if it did not want to be left out completely.[8] In June 1920, it was acknowledged that, as a temporary

12.1. This early photo of Plesman was taken after he became the "administrator" of KLM, about 1923. (Courtesy of KLM)

provision, Waterworks would cover two-thirds of the company's losses to a maximum of 200,000 guilders over 1920 and 1921.[9]

This measure marked the start of KLM's financial dependence on the government, which would only increase as the years went by. Less than six months later, even the concept of maximizing the subsidy had to be abolished because KLM's actual losses turned out to be much higher than expected. At the end of the two-year period, the government had already paid KLM 406,313 guilders, more than double the amount agreed upon initially.[10] The government agreed to provide these sums because of the importance it attached to a future Dutch air service to the East Indies.

Another dependency of KLM also began in 1920. The new airline needed aircraft of its own, and so came about its famous relationship with Fokker. Dutch-born aircraft constructor Anthony Fokker had spent the four wartime years building observation and fighter planes for the German military in his factory in Schwerin, Mecklenburg, north of Berlin. Learning of the backhanded praise his products had received by being singled out as military equipment to be handed over to the Allied powers forthwith in the armistice agreement of

November 1918, Fokker lost little time making preparations to transfer most of his aircraft construction activities to his native Holland in the first months of 1919—an enormous gamble, which, however, paid off.

Having lost his German customer, Fokker was in desperate need of aircraft orders. The founding of KLM appeared to be a godsend for his efforts to resettle his commercial base in Holland. Civil aviation, it was widely recognized at that time, held enormous prospects as a market for airplanes, and Fokker just happened to have the right concept under development in his Schwerin works at that time: the V.44/V.45, later redesignated F.II. For this single-engine, four-passenger, high-wing monoplane, he used the construction methods he had developed during the war: wooden wings with a fuselage consisting of welded steel tubes covered by fabric. The cramped cabin barely seated four passengers on lightweight cane chairs with, as one early passenger put it, "four times two knees pressed hard against each other."[11]

Nevertheless, the F.II was a novel and generally efficient concept for those days. Fokker had the airplane on offer to KLM at a price some 60 percent below what the comparable DeHavilland DH-18, for example, would have cost.[12] Not surprisingly, KLM accepted this tempting offer. Yet, as Plesman was to learn the hard way in his subsequent dealings with this other self-styled Dutch aviation entrepreneur, Fokker had not told him all. The two airplanes KLM had ordered were to be built in Fokker's German works, thereby violating the re-

12.2. The Fokker F.II was KLM's first airliner and the model for all subsequent Fokker passenger aircraft (1920). (Courtesy of KLM)

12.3. KLM's first scheduled flight arrived in Amsterdam from London on May 17, 1920. The aircraft is a DeHavilland DH-18 chartered from the British company Air Transport and Travel. Plesman is on the left wearing the bowler hat. (Courtesy of KLM)

strictions imposed on German aircraft construction under the Versailles Treaty. With the legally binding contract signed, Plesman had several uneasy months awaiting the reaction of the ex-Allies towards this sale. The British let him fry, and it was only by a risky flight to London with one of the new Fokkers that Plesman found out they would not impose any sanctions on KLM because of the make of its aircraft.

Even after that, all was not well between KLM and Fokker. Although KLM recognized the technical attractiveness of the Fokker concept, there were constant troubles over the quality of the aircraft Fokker delivered. An angry Plesman remarked before delegates of his board on June 7, 1921: "The Administrator has to remark that the Netherlands Aircraft Factory [as Fokker had wisely called his Dutch subsidiary] tries to deliver bad materials, such as old tyres, bad airscrews, bad glazing, etc. The Administrator has repeatedly complained about this to the factory and has informed the Board of the contents of his most recent letter in this respect."[13]

12.4. Albert Plesman and Anthony Fokker appeared to be in a friendly mood at
Schiphol Airport in early 1932. (Courtesy of KLM)

Problems between KLM and Fokker slowly spiraled upwards. Bad aircraft
and bad finances were sources of continuous turmoil during most of the 1920s.
Still, Plesman and KLM battled on from their small office above the Odeon
Cinema in The Hague. Even though profitability would remain an ever-distant
goal, the possibility of establishing an aerial connection with the East Indies
materialized in the next few years. In 1924, a private committee managed to
interest both Plesman and Fokker in having an airplane attempt to fly to Batavia.
It took the crew more than a month, and two engines, to complete their mission.
The aircraft, an F.VII, was shipped back to Holland to continue its career, flying passengers for KLM in Europe.

It was another three years before there were further developments in the air
route to the East Indies. In February 1927, Plesman agreed to charter an airplane to the American newspaper millionaire Van Lear Black, owner of the *Baltimore Sun,* who hoped to become the first airline passenger to fly across the
Atlantic. Instead, Plesman offered to fly him to Batavia, an offer the American
gladly accepted. Using a reengined Fokker F.VIIa, the crew took two weeks to
complete the trip. Later that same year, the earliest of the three-engine Fokkers

made the first airmail return flight to Batavia as the result of another private venture.

In retrospect, it is ironic that these promising developments should coincide with KLM's virtual bankruptcy. In 1923, Plesman had managed to convince the government to sign a three-year subsidy contract upon his solemn promise of achieving profitability at its expiry, December 31, 1926. It had been agreed that the subsidy would enable the airline to survive until it could sustain itself. As was the case with all airlines in Europe at that time, however, KLM's losses had continued to mount at roughly the same pace as the expansion of its services. When the contract expired, KLM was at least as far away from profitability as it had been in 1923. The Ministry of Finance was less than pleased and refused further payments to KLM.

In early February 1927, an acute shortage of money arose, and Plesman came within days of having to apply for bankruptcy protection. Even though the company was thereafter saved from going out of business by the government, the price demanded for its continued financial support fell heavily on Plesman. In

12.5. Plesman (with hat) boarding one of KLM's Fokker F.III airliners in 1922. (Courtesy of KLM)

exchange for a new long-term subsidy contract, and as a sign of the private sector's confidence in aviation as a serious business proposition, the government demanded a substantial increase of private investment in the airline.[14] This proved nearly impossible to come by. It took Plesman six months to find enough money to satisfy the Ministry of Finance, which had demanded the increased private stake in KLM. Under the new subsidy agreement, with growing governmental influence in KLM, the airline now took on the status of a semistate enterprise. Representatives of the Ministry of Waterworks were given a decisive vote on the board, and the government became a major shareholder.[15]

These continuing financial difficulties gave rise to a growing dissent in Dutch financial circles, where not everyone was convinced that Plesman's guidance of the airline was sound. Indeed, critical financiers nearly split the board when they joined forces with a group of colonial investors to establish a separate airline in the Netherlands East Indies in the spring of 1927. Communist-inspired uprisings in Java and Sumatra in 1926 had caused considerable concern in Dutch businesses with interests overseas. It was hoped that by providing rapid means of transportation to far-off corners of the Indonesian archipelago, an air transport company could be instrumental in maintaining colonial order.[16]

Given the poor state of KLM's finances, there was little Plesman could do to stop these developments, since KLM lacked the financial means to offer an alternative. Before long he was forced to accept the inevitable: KLM had to give up its aspirations for a subsidiary in Batavia. The right to carry out commercial air transport in the colony went to the Koninklijke Nederlandsch-Indische Luchtvaart Maatschappij (KNILM), formally incorporated in Amsterdam on July 16, 1928. The founding of KNILM involved Cornelis van Aalst, one of KLM's most influential board members and president of Holland's largest financial institution, the Nederlandsche Handel Maatschappij. Plesman saw the founding of KNILM as a betrayal of KLM. Still, he managed to get something out of it in the end: the investors who established KNILM agreed to buy 200,000 guilders of KLM shares, which was very important for Plesman in his efforts to keep KLM afloat. The deal was confirmed in a "gentlemen's agreement" between the two airlines that also recognized Plesman's unique position in Dutch aviation by making him a statutory director of KNILM. Nevertheless, KLM and KNILM would remain independent businesses, with KNILM's network virtually confined to the Dutch East Indies.[17] It was not surprising that Plesman remarked in KLM's Annual Report of 1927 that the first six months of that year had been "the most critical phase in KLM's existence."[18]

The expansion of the international reach of Dutch civil aviation from 1927 onwards forced the government to develop an international aviation policy. The

Hague had been slow in realizing the importance of international political and legal issues in air transport. In a mistaken gesture of isolationist neutrality, the Netherlands had not adhered to the Paris Convention relating to International Civil Aviation, of October 13, 1919, which was drawn up by the victorious Allies.[19] The Paris Convention established two essential principles in international air transport. First, it recognized absolute national sovereignty in the airspace above the territory of any signatory state (Article 1). Second, it required prior permission by the state overflown before a scheduled air service could be operated (Article 15). Much to the disgust of Plesman, who early on acknowledged that aviation diplomacy might become an obstacle to KLM's development, Holland had remained largely passive in bilateral contacts with Britain, France, Germany, Belgium, and the Scandinavian countries about the introduction of scheduled air services.

With plans now under way to establish a KLM service between Amsterdam and Batavia, two things became obvious. First, Holland could no longer postpone recognizing the Paris Convention as the legal basis of international aviation. Second, foreign rights of passage and commercial rights would have to be secured for KLM along the route. The latter were crucial if the service was to be economically viable for a small country like Holland. Partly because of Plesman's growing concern about these issues, a liberal position regarding international civil aviation was taken up in 1929.

The need for a clear-cut policy quickly became evident when KLM's plans for the establishment of its Amsterdam-Batavia service met with British opposition. Both the British Air Ministry and the British government in India, over-conscious of imperial prestige, regarded it as unthinkable that a Dutch airline should precede a British service to India.[20] Given the lack of suitable British aircraft to enable Imperial Airways to start such a service, Britain embarked upon a policy of obstructing the Dutch plans.[21]

Suitably enough, the trouble started on Friday, September 13, 1928. On this day the first of four Fokker F.VIIb aircraft of the now officially established KNILM took off from Schiphol Airport near Amsterdam to be flown out to Batavia as a relatively inexpensive way for KLM to gather more practical experience on the air route to Java. Permission to pass through British airspace over India and the use of RAF ground facilities had been accorded by the British Foreign Office without too many questions. But the British did not know that the aircraft carried 276 kilos of mail, destined for delivery both in the East Indies and at various stops along the route. The news took London by surprise. Although it had been understood beforehand that the KNILM aircraft would be carrying mail, no specific mention had been made regarding the places of delivery, and the British had assumed that all mail was destined for the Dutch East Indies. Now, questions were raised regarding the nature of the flights. The Air Ministry concluded that the flights damaged British imperial prestige because the Dutch had beaten Imperial Airways in delivering airmail to India. Anxiety grew when it became clear that Plesman was already planning for 12 further trial flights, to be conducted at regular intervals in 1929. The director of civil aviation, Sir William Sefton Brancker, himself not ill-disposed towards the Dutch plans, warned Plesman urgently to desist if he wanted to avoid KLM's being proscribed from flying over India.[22]

Plesman urged the government to take a strong position on the issue. If KLM were to be banned from the skies over British territories, he believed the Netherlands should do the same regarding the passage of British airplanes across the Netherlands East Indies to Australia. Plesman was convinced that any show of weakness now would create bigger problems later concerning the operation of the Amsterdam-Batavia route.[23] Valuing its good relations with Britain, however, the Dutch government declined to take action in the matter.

Despite growing concern on both sides of the North Sea, the flights continued. Not all went well. Only two of the four KNILM planes reached Batavia by air. The other two ran into trouble along the route and had to complete their voyage by ship. Towards the end of December 1928, matters came to a head. Plesman and the Dutch postmaster general, Marinus Damme, decided to reschedule one of the twelve flights planned for 1929 to carry Christmas mail to Batavia. Considering the irritation the airmail delivery in India had caused, the prospect for British approval of the flight was bleak. But in London Brancker seemed to be offering a helping hand by advising the Dutch to take up the matter directly with the British air secretary, Sir Samuel Hoare, who offered a deal through the Dutch envoy in London, Reneke de Marees van Swinderen: Hoare would allow the Christmas flight to take place, but after that KLM would have to stay away until "improvements" could be effected at several airfields along the route, notably the one in Baghdad. These improvements were scheduled to be completed by the end of April 1929. The envoy, speaking on behalf of the Dutch government, readily agreed to these terms.[24]

In The Hague, Plesman was furious. It was no coincidence that the date KLM would be allowed to continue its operations coincided with the start of a competing Imperial Airways service to Karachi, in British India. Hoare was not going to allow KLM to take too much of a lead. Yet KLM had spent a considerable amount of money on ordering new airplanes for further flights to Batavia. Plesman made no secret of his opinion that the envoy had not acted in the best interests of KLM.[25] But with things settled between the two governments, there seemed to be little he could do but wait his turn.

An impatient Plesman, backed by his board, reckoned things might be speeded up if KLM applied for a permit to operate a biweekly scheduled service right away. Permission was applied for in London on June 4, 1929. The British government, already anxious about the pace at which KLM wanted to conduct its trial flights across India, bluntly refused, whereupon Plesman tried to take the matter into his own hands. He flew to London to confer with the new British secretary of state for air, Christopher Thomson, convinced he would be able to hammer out a solution. The trip ended in a row between the two men, sending Plesman back to the Dutch envoy steaming with rage.[26] In The Hague, the various government officials involved in civil aviation policy were not amused. The head of Waterworks' Civil Aviation Branch, Emile de Veer, went out of his way to get Plesman fired by his minister for interfering with the government's conduct of policy, and Plesman barely managed to continue as KLM's chief executive.[27]

Only when Imperial Airways initiated its service between London and Karachi in May 1930 did KLM receive a belated green light for its proposed scheduled service to Batavia. Permission came so late, however, that it was impossible to start flying before October of that year. In return for their permission, the British asked for reciprocal rights in advance for a future British service between Singapore and Australia. Without further ado, the Netherlands government accorded these rights in a diplomatic exchange of notes on April 7 and June 3, 1930, which was subsequently interpreted to constitute a bilateral air transport agreement.

The Dutch lived to regret this arrangement, for from that moment on Britain and Australia would successfully use the conditions laid down in the exchange of notes to block attempts by the Netherlands to gain landing rights in Australia, the logical extension of KLM's East Indies service. Instead, the Australian airline QANTAS and Imperial Airways established an air service between Singapore and Brisbane in 1934 through a clever joint venture: Qantas Empire Airways (QEA), which was 51 percent British and 49 percent Australian. QEA was administered and operated by QANTAS using Australian-registered aircraft and Australian crews, but it posed as legally British because of Imperial Airways' majority shareholding and thus could operate under the terms of the British-Dutch bilateral agreement. In this way, Britain and Australia were able to block all attempts to extend KLM's operations beyond Batavia to Sydney, taking the position that any such accord must be conditional on a revised British-Dutch bilateral agreement concerning KLM's commercial rights in India. Because about 40 percent of KLM's passengers on its service to Batavia were British citizens flying to India, KLM stood to lose more than it could gain by offering a through service to Sydney. The Dutch learned aviation diplomacy

the hard way, and Plesman lost no opportunity to put pressure on the government to further the interests of KLM, regardless of the effects it might have on
bilateral relations with Britain and Australia.

So when Britain and Australia decided to reorganize imperial air communications by equipping Imperial Airways and QEA with luxury flying boats, the
Dutch took their turn being obstructive. The idea was that both Imperial Airways and QEA would now operate between Singapore and Brisbane. Provoked
by this intended duplication of services, the Dutch threatened not to build the
required flying boat refueling stations in the Netherlands East Indies. Besides,
they indicated that such a duplication of services would push QEA from under
the umbrella of the 1930 British-Dutch bilateral agreement. In this way the
Dutch were able to secure rights for a service between Batavia and Sydney from
the Australian government in February 1938, nine years after the matter had
first been raised. Yet the Australians had been careful to name KNILM, not
KLM, in the permit.

After so many years of negotiations, everyone in the Dutch camp was convinced KNILM should, for reasons of prestige, start operating as soon as possible. A batch of four Lockheed L-14 Super Electras was acquired for the
service, which was initiated July 3, 1938. The commercial results were disastrous. Competing with the slower, but luxurious, Imperial Airways/QEA flying boats, KNILM's fast but extremely uncomfortable Lockheeds attracted no
more than 104 passengers in 1938. The return flights showed especially disap-
pointing load factors, and many a KNILM airplane left Australia empty.

In an effort to combat KNILM's heavy operational losses, Plesman put pressure on the company to charter DC-3s from KLM's East Indies service to operate between Batavia and Sydney. The scheme, which would have given KLM
access to Australia through the back door, never materialized due to internal
difficulties within the KNILM management and a split between Amsterdam and
Batavia, where Plesman's efforts to run two airlines from one chair were deliberately sabotaged.[28] Although Plesman persisted in his attempts to secure a role
for KLM in the Batavia-Sydney service and mustered considerable political
support in The Hague, the Australians would have none of it. In July 1939, the
Australian minister for external affairs, Sir Henry Gullett, went so far as to
threaten seizure of the first KLM plane to land in Australia.[29] Indeed, not before
December 1951 did a KLM flight touch down on Australian soil.

Plesman's frustration over the denial of Australian landing rights was all the
deeper because the issue also touched upon one of his proudest achievements
with KLM: the policy of aircraft procurement, in which KLM outclassed all its
rivals. Early on, Plesman had convinced his board that it would be vital for

KLM to operate the most modern and economical airplanes available. This meant that the airline expected its material policy to weigh heavily on its annual results. Aircraft were written off in three to five years, allowing for early replacements and balance-sheet profits on the sale of secondhand airplanes, which could still be considered modern. It also meant that Plesman was always in a hurry to get the latest equipment. He personally pressed an unwilling Anthony Fokker to experiment with new aircraft-construction techniques. Fokker was loath to invest substantial amounts of money in aircraft development and had, to give an extreme example, spent no more than 794 guilders on research and development for his F.XVIII airliner.[30] In September 1932, it was Plesman who had to stimulate the Fokker factory to update design experience with an order to modify one of KLM's twin-engine F.VIIIs, incorporating such innovative features as engines built into the wing leading edge.[31]

Dissatisfied with what he saw as a general lack of initiative on the part of the Fokker company, Plesman sent one of his senior pilots, Koene Parmentier (who was to become famous for piloting KLM's DC-2 *Uiver* in the 1934 Melbourne Race), on a fact-finding mission to the United States in October 1933 to study the possibility of speeding up KLM's long-distance routes with night flying. Parmentier also sent Plesman a favorable report on one of the latest American airliners: TWA's novel Douglas DC-2. Plesman, planning expansion of KLM's capacity on the Amsterdam-Batavia service, was then contemplating the purchase of six very large four-engine Fokker 16-to-32-seat F.XXXVIs for this showpiece of KLM's services. The development of the F.XXXVI, however, had fallen seriously behind schedule and was hampered by all kinds of unforeseen technical problems having to do with the sheer size of the aircraft—a wingspan of 108 feet, 2 inches, and a length of 77 feet, 4 inches—reasons for Plesman to regard the F.XXXVI with growing suspicion. Within weeks after receiving Parmentier's report, Plesman suggested to the board that KLM buy at least one DC-2 to see if such an aircraft might offer an alternative solution to the need to expand capacity on the Indies route.[32] When his board agreed, Plesman lost no time getting the consent of the minister of waterworks and placed his order with Douglas. Developing an airplane with similar capabilities in Holland would, according to Plesman, take at least two years and hold no guarantee of a satisfactory product.[33]

There was, however, one crucial problem: KLM had no contacts in the United States with whom to place such an order except Anthony Fokker. Although no longer one of the main players on the American stage in aircraft construction, Fokker was still well placed to act as a middleman between KLM and Douglas. The matter was settled on the evening of the November 28, 1933, board meeting, in which Plesman received the official go-ahead. Plesman had invited Fokker to a private meal at his home, a rare occasion of informality between the two big men of Dutch aviation. Inevitably, the subject got around to the Douglas order again. According to Plesman's youngest son, Plesman indicated he saw a role for Fokker as a go-between for KLM and Douglas. At that moment, the eccentric Anthony Fokker jumped up from the table, enthusiastically grabbing what loose change he could find in his pockets and scattering it on the dining room floor for Plesman's bewildered children.[34] An important deal was in the making. That same evening Fokker set sail for New York to complete the transaction. Satisfied, Plesman wrote to the minister of waterworks the next day that it pleased him to see Fokker so cooperative in acquiring the most modern and economical equipment for KLM.[35]

Yet the cooperative spirit did not last long. Fokker was not only an eccentric; he was also a shrewd businessman. Before long, he reached an understanding with Donald Douglas in which Douglas more or less appointed Fokker as his sales agent in Europe. It appears that Douglas had, at this stage, no knowledge of Fokker's link with KLM in this respect. The months that followed showed just how wise Fokker's instant decision to cooperate with Plesman and acquire the European license and sales rights for the DC-2 had been. Even before KLM's first DC-2 was delivered to be reassembled at Rotterdam's Waalhaven Airport, Plesman and his technical staff made the far-reaching decision to go for a radical change in its fleet by ordering no less than 14 DC-2s—an order of unprecedented magnitude for KLM. The reasons for such a decision were simple enough. For a twice-weekly service operating DC-2s, KLM calculated it would need 1,350,000 guilders—significantly cheaper than the 1,500,000 guilders it would have to pay if it changed its option on six F.XXXVIs into a final order. But there were additional advantages. With a cruising speed of 300 kilometers per hour, the DC-2 was 40 kilometers per hour faster than the big Fokker, and it would be 15 percent more economical on fuel, thus substantially lowering KLM's operating costs (of which fuel was the number one item). Plesman summed it all up before his board, concluding that placing a large order for the DC-2 and making it the mainstay of a modernized KLM fleet both for the Far Eastern service and in Europe offered a shortcut to future profitability.[36]

In early August 1934, KLM's board gave Plesman the official go-ahead to order 14 DC-2s. An enormous row with Fokker followed, for only now did Fokker acquire all sales and license rights for (this and future) Douglas aircraft, and it was not in the interest of Fokker as an aircraft manufacturer to be lenient on the price of his newborn competitor in Europe. Whereas KLM had calculated that Fokker would have to pay about 114,000 guilders for each DC-2 and had made allowances in its financial plans for a 10-percent margin for Fokker on the planes, Fokker demanded at least 160,000 guilders for each aircraft—a margin of no less than 40 percent. The discrepancy meant an abrupt end to the spirit of cooperation in which the DC-2 adventure had started. No matter how angry Plesman got and how heated the negotiations with representatives of the Fokker works became, it was apparent that Fokker had the better of him. Moreover, time was not on Plesman's side. He had already sold off eight of his Fokker planes to other European airlines, with rigid delivery dates written into the contracts. As a result, Plesman found himself forced to sign the contract for his 14 DC-2s at an average price of 166,000 guilders.[37]

Things became even more openly hostile when Donald Douglas himself entered the scene. In May 1935, he visited his European launching customer and instantly became good personal friends with Plesman. At Plesman's request, Douglas went so far as to declare in a formal statement before a notary that he had no recollection of any sales and license agreement with Fokker and maintained that Fokker only acted as an "independent merchant."[38]

It was the last straw. That same afternoon, Plesman had a meeting with his Board of Controllers (Raad van Commissarissen) at which he told those present that KLM would henceforth become strictly a Douglas operator.[39] Fokker, however, remained in the picture. He successfully challenged Douglas's interpretation of their verbal agreement in the United States courts. Without quite knowing it, Douglas had appointed Fokker as his exclusive European agent, responsible for all of Douglas's European sales. At the same time, it was established that Fokker held the sole right (which he never intended to use) for production under license of the DC-2 and future derivative aircraft. Commissions on the sale of Douglas airliners and the maintenance work the Fokker company carried out under the Douglas agreement kept the Fokker factory in business. Nevertheless, as a manufacturer of its own civil aircraft designs, Fokker was finished; another 20 years would pass before the next Fokker airliner, the F-27, left the ground.

With these important issues behind him, Plesman was more or less free to concentrate his efforts upon achieving profitability. Although he managed to make some headway here, things were, again, far from easy. Most of KLM's flights were within Europe, and Europe was in turmoil during the late 1930s. With Plesman's mind on aviation and the role he felt it could play in improving relations between countries and peoples, he seemed to have a curious lack of real understanding of the political and military machinations that were going on around him. Nevertheless, what he did notice must have been extremely worrying. In 1937, the hard-headed Plesman went to Rome in an effort, grotesque as it may seem in retrospect, to promote peace and understanding and talk some sense into Benito Mussolini's head. The interview, arranged by KLM's representative in Rome, was brief and unencouraging. The Anglophile Plesman spoke of peace; Mussolini of his hatred towards the British. A disillusioned Plesman might have known better than to try to crack an even harder nut in early 1940, on the eve, so to speak, of Germany's invasion of the Netherlands, when he attempted to convince Hermann Göring that it was really unwise to wage war.[40] Needless to say, his visit to Berlin was as useless as his journey to Rome.

While KLM's passenger and cargo traffic expanded by 40 percent and 28 percent, respectively, in 1935, the German occupation of the Rhineland in March 1936 and the ensuing heightened political and military tension in Western Europe had a stagnating effect on traffic in the following year: Although air cargo rose by 5 percent in 1937, European passenger transport shrank by 2 percent, to 91,702.[41] If air traffic were on the rise again in 1938, the causes for KLM's increasing numbers of passengers and the volume of goods carried were extremely unsettling. In the weeks after the Munich Crisis of September 1938, KLM was hardly able to cope with the numbers of Czech passengers seeking refuge in Holland. Numerous extra flights had to be laid on. Indeed, right up to the outbreak of the war in September 1939, KLM recorded increasingly high load factors on all its flights from middle and eastern Europe.[42] Although these developments brought KLM close to profitability, they were also the preamble to KLM's downfall in the spring of 1940.

From September 1939 onwards, the operation of KLM's European network became ever more problematical. Because most countries closed their airspace to all foreign aircraft, only rudimentary services remained: to Shoreham by Sea on the English south coast (instead of London), to Brussels, to Copenhagen and Malmö, to Christiansand and Oslo, to Lisbon. In view of the unstable international situation, demand was very high: load factors averaged about 91 percent, and ticket prices went up by more than 100 percent.[43] But operating conditions were difficult. All civil flights were required to meet strict security regulations. Aircraft cabin windows had to be painted with aluminum dope to prevent prying eyes from looking at military secrets. The airplanes themselves were sprayed with orange paint to make it easier to recognize them as civil airliners and prevent them from being fired upon by patrolling fighter aircraft.

For Plesman, the situation was difficult to accept. All he had worked for over the last 20 years was now collapsing. Still, he did not easily admit to being beaten by military realities. In October 1939, he managed to convince an extremely skeptical board of the possibility of establishing a daughter company in Lisbon to operate a service to Angola for the Portuguese, and possibly also to

Paramaribo in the Dutch colony of Surinam, flying DC-3s equipped with extra fuel tanks.[44] During preparations, one of KLM's DC-2s arrived in Lisbon in late December 1939. As it turned out, it would be the only DC-2 in KLM's inventory that survived the war.

The curtain fell on May 10, 1940, when the Luftwaffe bombed most of KLM's fleet in the early hours of the German invasion of the Netherlands. The handful of KLM aircraft that managed to escape destruction converged on Bristol to operate a chartered service to Lisbon for BOAC. Plesman himself remained in Holland, overseeing the dismantling of his airline from his home in The Hague. In May 1941, according to van Kampen, he was imprisoned by the Germans because of his alleged involvement in the escape to Britain of a Fokker G-1 fighter-bomber from Schiphol. They interned him in the nearby prison of Scheveningen, jocularly known as Oranje Hotel (Orange Hotel, after the name of the Dutch royal family, because the prison held many persons involved in resistance activities).[45] After eleven lonely months of deprivation, he was released in April 1942, only to be sent into internal exile to the tiny village of Driene, in the eastern part of the Netherlands. From there, he tried his best to keep in touch with what remained of his former company, always working on plans for a possible resurrection of KLM after the war.

When the village of Driene was finally liberated on April 2, 1945, Plesman was ready. He requisitioned a jeep, drove south to Brussels through the front lines, and boarded the next available plane to London. There he conferred with the Dutch government in exile, and with the tiny group that had kept the Bristol-to-Lisbon operations going. Then he flew to the United States, where, in the next three months, he got the Americans to agree to make 14 C-54 Skymasters available for a Netherlands Government Air Transport organization—the initial form under which Plesman set out to rebuild KLM. The first of these airplanes was delivered in October 1945, a month after KLM had reopened some of its European services. On November 10, 1945, KLM's first postwar flight to Batavia took off; on May 21, 1946, KLM became the first European carrier to operate scheduled transatlantic services to New York. This was Plesman at his best, full of vitality, organizing, rebuilding his company with the same characteristic drive that had brought him to the fore in 1919. A year after resuming operations, KLM was already bigger than it had been in 1939. In 1947, Plesman's achievements were recognized with an honorary doctorate at the Technical University of Delft. At the ceremony it was stated that his "dissertation" consisted of three letters: K L M.

Yet this success took its toll. In the years after 1946 Plesman gradually became estranged from his rapidly expanding organization as it grew too big for

12.6. A weary-looking Plesman showed the effects of wartime experiences as he emerged from the makeshift terminal building at Amsterdam's Schiphol Airport in the fall of 1945. (Courtesy of KLM)

him to identify the many different faces around him. Besides, life had been tough on him. In 1944, his son Jan was shot down over France flying a Spitfire in the RAF; in 1948, his trusted friends and designated successors, Henk Veenendaal and Koene Parmentier, died when one of KLM's Constellations crashed near Prestwick; less than a year later, his second son, Hans, lost his life when another Constellation went down near Bari in Italy. Also, his trusted right-hand man, Hans Martin, who had been with the airline since 1921, left in 1949, after a bitter fight over Plesman's financial policies. Still, Plesman battled on from his increasingly lonely position at the top, making KLM one of the most prominent international airlines in the world, until his health finally began to fail in 1953. For a long time he had been suffering from arteriosclerosis, a condition he had always kept secret, but now he could deny it no longer. Many a workday afternoon he had to stay home and rest. Perhaps he already realized what was coming when he gave a big dinner party at Schiphol Airport for all of his KLM pilots to celebrate Christmas and New Year's on December 29, 1953. It was something he had not done before, and two days later, on New Year's Eve, he died after suffering arterial bleeding in the stomach.

In the private sphere, Plesman had few demands and claimed only a modest salary for himself. For a long time, he lived in an apartment over the store where he had been brought up. His lifestyle was spartan. Sports and physical exercise were important to him, and with his four children he was a demanding father in this respect. Too singular to be a family man, his wife Suze was his best, perhaps his only real, companion in life.

Plesman's upbringing and military background had profound influences on his character. Both at home and at KLM he was authoritarian, paternalistic, impatient—qualities that were enhanced by his stature and his curt, forceful,

12.7. Plesman speaking to an audience of KLM employees about KLM's expansion plans in 1952. (Courtesy of KLM)

12.8. Plesman and his wife, Suze van Eijk, before boarding one of KLM's Douglas
DC-4s. (Courtesy of KLM)

and unpolished way of speaking. Few of his employees felt at ease with him.
Most accounts by people who knew him mention that he had trouble accepting
differences of opinion, and more so admitting when he was wrong. What made
up for these shortcomings were his clear long-term vision, his earnestness, and
his single-minded devotion to the interests of KLM. Fittingly, "It's hard work,
living off the air," became one of his most famous sayings.

NOTES

1. *Enquêtecommissie Regeringsbeleid, 1940–1945*, vol. 2, *Verhoren* (The Hague:
Staatsuitgeverij, 1949), 335. Translation by Marc Dierikx.

2. Anthony van Kampen, *Plesman: Portret van een luchtreder* (Hilversum: De
Boer, 1960), 6.

3. Ibid., 14–15.

4. W. C. J. Versteegh, "De ontwikkelingsjaren," in *De Vliegende Hollander: In me-
moriam Dr. Albert Plesman* (Baarn: Wereldvenster, 1954), 9.

5. *Eerste Luchtvaart Tentoonstelling Amsterdam, de ELTA* (The Hague: KNVvL/Het Vliegveld, 1919), 60.

6. M. L. J. Dierikx, *Bevlogen jaren: Nederlandse burgerluchtvaart tussen de wereldoorlogen* (Houten: Unieboek, 1986), 77–78.

7. *Verslag der Commissie ter beoordeling van de vraag welke plaats Nederland en Nederlandsch-Oost-Indië zouden kunnen innemen in het internationaal luchtpostverkeer*, May 3, 1919, KLM General Archives, Schiphol Airport, Netherlands, "Documents of Historical Value," no. 60.

8. "Memorie van Toelichting bij Ontwerp van Wet tot wijziging van de Staatsbegroting 1919," in *Handelingen der Staten Generaal, 1918–1919* (The Hague: Staatsuitgeverij, 1920), Bijlage 504, no. 3.

9. Letter, König to KLM, Nov. 24, 1920, KLM Board Papers, Amstelveen, Netherlands, series R-502.

10. Official report on the company's financial development in 1921–39, KLM Board Papers, series R-5, 1939.

11. H. Hegener, "Een bewogen leven," in *De Vliegende Hollander*, 74.

12. Minutes 25th meeting of Delegated Board members, July 13, 1920, KLM Board Papers, series R-5. The going price for a DH-18 was 70,000 guilders. Compared to this, Fokker charged KLM no more than 27,500 guilders for his F.II airliner.

13. Minutes 42nd meeting of Delegated Board members, June 7, 1921, KLM Board Papers, series R-5. Translation by Marc Dierikx.

14. De Geer (finance minister) to Van de Vegte (minister of waterworks), Jan. 6, 1927, Archive of the Ministry of Traffic and Waterworks (hereafter V & W), The Hague, RLD, 2-II.

15. Subsidy agreement between the Netherlands government and KLM, June 4 and 7, 1927, in *Handelingen der Staten-Generaal, 1926–1927* (The Hague: Staatsuitgeverij, 1927), Bijlage 354, no. 2.

16. J. C. Koningsberger (colonial secretary) to A. C. D. de Graeff (governor-general of the Netherlands East Indies), May 24, 1927, Algemeen Rijksarchief (National Archives), The Hague, Collection 403, A. C. D. de Graeff, inv. no. 12.

17. See also M. L. J. Dierikx, "De positie van Nederlands-Indië in de internationale burgerluchtvaart, 1918–1942," in *Nederland in de wereld, 1870–1950*, ed. P. Luykx and A. Manning (Nijmegen: Taakgroep Nieuwste Geschiedenis, 1988), 121–39.

18. KLM, *Annual Report 1927*, pt. 1, *Het Vliegveld* 12, no. 6 (1928): 177.

19. M. L. J. Dierikx, *Begrensde horizonten: De internationale burgerluchtvaartpolitiek van Nederland in het interbellum* (Zwolle: W. E. J. Tjeenk Willink, 1988), 54–63.

20. Note Alexander Leeper on KLM's proposed trial flights to Batavia, Dec. 14, 1929, London Public Record Office, Kew, Foreign Office Papers, FO 371, 14095.

21. Dierikx, *Begrensde horizonten*, 85–99.

22. Brancker to Plesman, Sept. 14 and 17, 1928, Archive Netherlands Ministry of Foreign Affairs (hereafter BZ), The Hague, Ned. Indië, DEZ 151.

23. Plesman to the minister of waterworks, H. van de Vegte, Sept. 21, 1928, BZ, Ned. Indië, DEZ 151.

24. De Marees van Swinderen to the Netherlands minister of foreign affairs, Dec. 7, 1928, BZ, Ned. Indië, DEZ 151.

25. Plesman to the minister of waterworks, Dec. 18, 1928, BZ, Ned. Indië, DEZ 151.

26. De Marees van Swinderen to Netherlands Minister of Foreign Affairs Beelaerts van Blokland, Dec. 12, 13, 1929, V & W., RLD, Dossier "KLM, bestuur en directie."

27. Dierikx, *Begrensde horizonten,* 88–96.

28. Dierikx, *Bevlogen jaren,* 133–40.

29. Letter, Gullett to the Dutch consul-general in Sydney, Tom Elink Schuurman, July 7, 1939, BZ, Records Netherlands Consulate-General Sydney, 9A, S-1.

30. Second Report by the government-appointed Committee on the Aircraft Industry (Commissie van Doorninck) on the Fokker factory, June 21, 1935, Appendix 2, V & W, RLD, 14-III.

31. Minutes 100th board meeting, Sept. 27, 1932, KLM Board Papers, series R-5.

32. Minutes KLM board meeting, Nov. 28, 1933, KLM Board Papers, series R-5; memorandum, Lambert Slotemaker (KLM's company secretary) to the board, Sept. 17, 1934.

33. Letter, Plesman to the minister of waterworks, Nov. 9, 1933, V & W, RLD 14-II.

34. Albert Plesman, *Albert Plesman, mijn vader* (The Hague: Nijgh and Van Ditmar, 1977), 41–42.

35. Letter, Plesman to minister of waterworks, Nov. 29, 1933, V & W, RLD, 14-II.

36. Memorandum from Plesman to the KLM board, June 21, 1934, KLM Board Papers, series R-5.

37. Survey of the negotiations between KLM and Fokker concerning the Douglas DC-2, Mar. 14, 1939, V & W, RLD, 14-V.

38. Sealed, stamped statement by Donald Wills Douglas, May 23, 1935, KLM Board Papers, series A-9/A-950, R-506-2.

39. Minutes Board of Controllers, May 23, 1935: KLM Board Papers, series R-5.

40. Van Kampen, *Plesman,* 164–66.

41. KLM, Annual Reports, 1935–37.

42. Dierikx, *Bevlogen jaren,* 107–8.

43. KLM, *Monthly Report: December 1939, February 6, 1940,* KLM Board Papers, series R-5.

44. Minutes 212th board meeting, Oct. 10, 1939, KLM Board Papers, series R-5.

45. Van Kampen, *Plesman,* 170–95.

F. Robert van der Linden

Progressives and the Post Office

Walter Folger Brown and the Creation of United States Air Transportation

Monopoly. Trusts. Oligopoly. Traditionally, these words have acquired negative connotations throughout the course of the last century of American history. The concentration of wealth and power has always deeply disturbed Americans, who have been fearful of any loss of personal liberty and equality before the law, regardless of economic realities. How the federal government has reacted to the demands of its citizens for solutions to the questions raised by the concentration of economic power has driven political debate to this day.

As business historian Alfred Chandler has shown, the rise of large industrial concerns in the United States in capital- and energy-intensive industries followed rapidly the revolution in communications brought by the coming of the telegraph and, most important, the railroad, midway through the nineteenth century. As these firms exploited economies of scale and grew through expansion and consolidation of smaller competitors, economic power became concentrated in the hands of a few. The rise of cartels, then trusts, and later holding companies that produced industrial oligopolies generally known as "big business," was a rational reaction of business in capital-intensive industries attempting to stabilize prices and establish a business environment that precluded ruinous competition.[1] These actions were perceived, often correctly, as the exploitation of the strength of these firms to force out competition and raise prices at the expense of small business and the citizen consumer.

At the turn of the century, the Progressive movement arose in response to the question of how government was to deal with so-called monopolies. Previously, government had encouraged business expansion but refused to interfere by regulating this uncontrolled growth. Gradually, many citizens overcame their traditional fear of government power when confronted with the strength and often corrupting influence of concentrated wealth and sought local and, later, federal relief from the excesses of big business.

Reform-minded individuals of both major parties swept into political office following the turn of the century. Beginning with President Theodore Roosevelt, Progressives began to form a national strategy to control the excesses of oligopoly. Roosevelt and Progressive Republicans accepted the presence, even the necessity, of large industrial enterprises as part of economic progress, provided they cooperate and conform to the administration's requirements. These requirements involved the supervision of big business's practices, a degree of economic planning, and the protection of less fortunate groups. Under Roosevelt's New Nationalism program, excessive competition was seen as unduly wasteful of resources. Instead, it was believed that a system of national controls would ensure that economic growth would be justly distributed and all would benefit. The tangible result was the beginning of a concerted effort to break up those trusts that refused to cooperate and support the efforts of those industries that did.

In contrast to the cooperative nature of New Nationalism toward the question of monopoly was the program of President Woodrow Wilson's New Freedom program. Heavily influenced by the work of Louis Brandeis, the New Freedom saw all monopoly as bad and sought through regulation and antitrust action to break up large combines. This was a concerted effort to abolish all allegedly unfair business practices and promote all competition, especially from smaller concerns. The practical result was a wave of legislation controlling numerous industries and the establishment of several regulatory agencies.

It has been generally assumed that Progressivism died after 1914. Work by Ellis Hawley and other recent historians has demonstrated that this is not entirely true.[2] While traditional, probusiness Republicans took office with President Warren G. Harding in 1921, many former Progressives remained in Congress. Government still maintained an interest in the workings of business and sought ways to benefit the public while encouraging new economic growth. In certain industries, in fact, especially aviation, the federal government led the way. What is not widely known or understood is the federal government's leading role in the creation of the air transport industry and its consequent and deliberate fostering of the giant new aviation industry.

Because of the primitive technological state of aeronautics, the government realized early on the necessity of external incentives if this new industry were to succeed. A rational, coherent system of air routes crisscrossing the country was envisioned as a worthy goal for national defense, but more important, also for the improvement of civilian transportation. The government, through its primary agent, the post office, sought to make this industry practical, and, both directly and indirectly, guided its development in the hope of building a new system of passenger and freight travel in a much more orderly and socially responsible way than in the unfortunate case of the railroad industry.

From 1918 until 1926, the post office flew the mail itself and developed the most efficient service in the world, pioneering new routes and new technologies. Nevertheless, despite this impressive accomplishment, the post office, during these days of Republican government, had no intention of operating a permanent service, wanting only to lay the foundation of a new industry and steer it in the right direction.[3]

With that in mind, beginning in 1925, the first steps toward creating a commercial airline industry were taken with the passage of the Contract Air Mail Act. Sponsored by one-time Progressive Congressman Melville Clyde Kelly, the law called for the transfer of the airmail service to private operators under contract. The Kelly Act, as it was popularly known, was the major catalyst in the creation of commercial airlines. Subsequently, the Air Commerce Act of 1926, which was part of a massive civil and military aviation legislation program, gave the Department of Commerce authority to regulate the airways, license pilots and aircraft, organize air navigation, promote air safety, investigate accidents, and encourage research and development. Most of these responsibilities fell on Assistant Secretary of Commerce William P. MacCracken, Jr.

With this new governmental infrastructure in place, the post office began to divest itself of its airmail routes. It did not, however, give up control, for it was the post office that determined the winner of the contract bidding, set the rates, and established and extended the routes. The contract carriers could fly nowhere without the postmaster general's permission and depended upon his largess for their survival. The contract airmail carriers began flying in February 1926, and by April 1927 all were in operation. These winning companies were formed exclusively to take advantage of the lucrative offer from the post office. Each airline was generously paid on a per-pound basis, thus ensuring profitability for most of the new companies.

Largely in response to these actions, the aviation business was booming by the late 1920s. Following Charles A. Lindbergh's daring solo flight across the Atlantic in 1927, the United States burst forth with a frenzy of aviation mania. Almost overnight, the country became "air-minded." With this wave of enthusiasm came an outpouring of money from the centers of finance seeking to exploit this new interest and especially the opportunity offered by the government's enticing airmail contracts. A torrent of capital deluged the existing aircraft builders, airline operators, and associated enterprises as Wall Street professionals opened the way for massive investments at hitherto unheard of amounts and for tremendous profits.[4]

Soon, three major holding companies emerged. The first, in 1928, was Clement Keys's North American Aviation, which controlled Curtiss Aeroplane and Motor and National Air Transport. The second, and by far the largest, was United Aircraft and Transport Corporation (UATC), founded in 1928 by Frederick Rentschler of Pratt & Whitney and William Boeing. This huge combine included the carriers that eventually comprised United Airlines. The Aviation Corporation of America, better known as AVCO, came into being in 1929 and was the parent company of what would soon be American Airways. All three established a network of airlines that traversed the country to carry the mail.

Concurrent with the expansion of North American, United Aircraft, and AVCO was the passage of important legislation destined to shape the course of commercial aviation for decades to come. On April 29, 1930, the Third Amendment to the Air Mail Act of 1925 was passed. Named after Progressive Republican Senator Charles D. McNary of Oregon and Republican Congressman Laurence H. Watres of Pennsylvania, the bill, popularly known as the Watres Act, offered contractors ten-year route certificates in exchange for their previous contracts, which were due to expire soon, provided the airlines had at least two years of operating experience. The rights of the pioneering companies would be respected. Furthermore, the postmaster general could expand or consolidate any route if, in his judgment, such an action was in the public interest. The bill was the brainchild of President Herbert Hoover's ruthlessly determined new postmaster general, Walter Folger Brown.[5]

Postmaster General Brown was an unassuming individual of great intelligence who avoided publicity, preferring to work quietly and effectively behind the scenes. He has been described by several historians as "a Toledo attorney." Indeed he was, but he was also much more. Brown was a political animal of great influence in the Ohio Republican party. President Hoover referred to him as having "a greater knowledge of the federal mechanism and its duties than any

13.1. Postmaster General Walter Folger Brown. (Courtesy of National Air and Space Museum; 87-11946)

other man in the United States."[6] Brown brought to the government the old Progressivism of Theodore Roosevelt's New Nationalism with regard to business and monopoly.

Brown came of age politically at the beginning of the Progressive era. Before entering Harvard Law School, he worked on behalf of William McKinley during the latter's successful gubernatorial campaign. After his graduation in 1894, Brown joined his father's law firm and quickly reentered politics. By 1897, he was elected chairman of the Republican central committee of Toledo. His political acumen ensured the election of noted Progressive reformist Samuel M. ("Golden Rule") Jones as mayor of Toledo, from whom he eventually broke.[7] Brown allied himself with the powerful camp of Senator Marcus Hanna and continued to exert his growing influence, first by controlling Toledo through his strength in the Republican party and later, from 1906 to 1912, as chairman of the Ohio state Republican central committee.[8]

A major turning point in Brown's political career came in 1912. A friend of Theodore Roosevelt, Brown bolted the Republican party to support Roosevelt's Bull Moose bid for the White House as chairman of the newly formed Progressive party. Brown, a supporter of Roosevelt's New Nationalism, had broken with Taft because he felt the president was overly zealous in antitrust prosecution, particularly of the steel industry.[9]

After Roosevelt's defeat, it took Brown several years to regain his power base after he rejoined the Republican ranks. But his influence remained prodigious. Through his careful work, Brown managed to secure the nomination of dark horse Senator Warren G. Harding at the 1920 Republican national convention. Despite losing his only bid for elected office that year, Brown declined Harding's offer of the ambassadorship to Japan but did accept a presidential appointment as chairman of the joint congressional committee on the reorganization of the executive branch of the government. This committee sought to rearrange government along principles of business management to improve efficiency. Harding's untimely death, coupled with bureaucratic intrigues, stymied any attempts at change.[10]

During this time in Washington, Brown forged a friendship with then-secretary of commerce Herbert Hoover. In 1927, Brown accepted an offer from Hoover to become assistant secretary of commerce, a move widely seen as Hoover's unofficial announcement of his presidential candidacy for the upcoming 1928 Republican nomination. Once again, Brown excelled in his role as president-maker. Hoover easily won the election, rewarding his campaign manager, Brown, with the top patronage position of postmaster general.[11]

Assuming office in 1929, Brown, charged with the task of promoting commercial aviation as well as efficiency in the post office, wished to bring reason to the rapidly growing yet still fledgling industry. Many small airlines had been created overnight and flew haphazard, disorganized routes in many areas of the country. Passenger traffic, in particular, was confused and sporadic. The existing situation offered little chance for improvement if left uncontrolled and was significantly similar to that of the railroads in the nineteenth century. After studying the problem for several months, Brown took action.[12] And action was necessary; following the burst of merger mania in the aviation industry, the nation's economy collapsed in late 1929. By the late spring of 1930 a tentative recovery stalled, and stocks began to plummet once again. The nascent airline industry's survival hung in the balance. Coupled with this catastrophe, the previous airmail contracts awarded under the Kelly Act were due to expire soon. Brown realized that by exercising dictatorial control over airmail contract awards, which were really thinly disguised subsidies, he could force the airlines to do his bidding.[13]

Much work was yet to be done, in Brown's opinion. He required additional tools to realign the air routes to his satisfaction. Other large corporations, such as AVCO and North American Aviation, operated a plethora of unrelated schedules and routes that ignored the needs of much of the country. Now, in early 1930, Brown persuaded the administration to back his plan to foster improved airmail service and promote passenger travel with appropriate legislation. A committee of private aviation experts, determined to eliminate unnecessary competition by abolishing competitive bidding, hammered out the Watres bill in late 1929 and early 1930. Carriers were to be selected based on their fitness to operate and paid on a space-per-mile rather than a pound-per-mile method. This would directly encourage the carrying of passengers on regularly scheduled service. Bonuses would be paid for operating at night and in difficult weather.

The postmaster general was given absolute authority to award the routes. Loud protests came from many members of Congress, particularly Clyde Kelly, the author of the original act, and the comptroller general, John McCarl, who was deeply concerned about Brown's freedom to award contracts without competitive bidding. This opposition resulted in a compromise that allowed the postmaster general to award only extensions of existing routes.

As modified, the Watres Act passed on April 29, 1930.[14] Accordingly, between May 15 and June 9, Brown held a series of open, though unpublicized meetings, later derisively called the "Spoils Conferences," to award the new contracts. Representatives of the leading aviation enterprises were invited and instructed to divide the contracts among themselves in such a manner as to produce a rational transcontinental system with appropriate connecting routes. Of the twelve major routes, the conferees could only decide on seven, leaving the decision up to William P. MacCracken, Jr., the chairman of the group of participants; and the postmaster general himself for the remaining five. The comptroller general thwarted Brown's attempt to award extensions. Undaunted, with MacCracken's guidance, Brown rewrote the rules to allow only those airlines with over six months' experience in night-flying over routes longer than 250 miles to "bid" on the new routes.

This measure effectively excluded all of the independent operators, who were not officially asked to attend.[15] Brown reasoned that only the large corporations had the resources to fulfill his ambition to fashion a coherent and cohesive transport system. In fact, his opinions concerning the efficacy of monopoly enterprises reflected his earlier New Nationalism views. Brown bluntly favored monopoly as the best and fastest way to ensure a profitable national air transport network. To him, commercial aviation was a public utility regulated in the public's interest by the actions of the post office. Before Congress, Brown stated:

> I do not believe in competition in public service. I think competition in public
> service simply adds to the burdens borne by the public. Monopoly in public ser-
> vice under very definite regulation is my idea, and I think that is what will come
> here ultimately. We will have air systems knit together giving a competitive ser-
> vice. . . . These big organizations with spare equipment and a variety of equip-
> ment—passenger and mail planes—are much better able to do a job than a
> fellow with two or three planes and no money, with the sheriff just one leap be-
> hind him all the time.[16]

In his sincere desire to foster a major United States airline route network,
the postmaster general had little interest in supporting the claims of smaller
operators.

Walter Brown's desire to reshape and rationalize air transport into a system of
transcontinental routes with complementary north-south routes came to fruition
in late 1930. Despite the reluctance of Harris Hanshue, the president of Western
Air Express, Brown decided that an amalgamation of Clement Keys's Transcontinental Air Transport (TAT), which had the strong financial backing of the
North American Aviation holding company, and Western would best serve his
vision of creating a practical transcontinental line to compete against UATC's
Boeing Air Transport and National Air Transport. Brown forced Hanshue to
surrender his interests or risk losing money from his other mail contracts. After
fighting off a lower bid from a recently formed and underfinanced independent
United Avigation group, Brown completed the "shotgun marriage," producing
a new airline, Transcontinental and Western Air, better known as TWA.[17]

The results of Brown's efforts were impressive, but also controversial. Airlines began to acquire the latest aircraft and equipment to satisfy the post office's new requirements for speed and safety and immediately expanded their
service to carry far more passengers. Indeed, though these actions occurred in
the midst of the general economic crisis of the Great Depression, the airlines
and holding companies thrived, returning to profitability as ridership rose dramatically. It was also clear that Brown favored the claims of the three major
holding companies at the expense of the little operators. Of the 22 contracts
awarded at the "Spoils Conferences," 20 went to the four airlines controlled by
the oligopoly of the so-called Big Four—United, Eastern, TWA, and American
—who in turn were controlled by the three holding companies.[18]

American Airways was the newest addition to this elite group. Brown encouraged its formation through a conglomeration of several small airlines flying in the southern and central United States. Because American was the operating agent of the Aviation Corporation, it had sufficient resources to provide a
third transcontinental route. Brown's night-flying requirement ensured that

American won the necessary contracts over the lower bids of several independents, including Paul and Thomas Braniff, and drove several firms out of business.[19]

Though grateful for the contracts, the Big Four, like the other, smaller companies, did not care for the postmaster general's abrupt manners, high-handed tactics, and the pressure he exerted to create a modern air transport network. More important, Brown's abrasiveness and dubious methods gained him enemies in the halls of Congress, where, unlike in aviation, he did not reign supreme.[20]

Agitation against Brown and the aviation combines began to be heard in 1931, beginning with the recently jilted Braniff brothers, who began an orchestrated campaign with the help of other suffering independents. In response to growing public outrage at the high level of payments given to the combines when millions of citizens were out of work, Rep. James A. Mead opened hearings in 1932 to consider a bill reducing the level of airmail payments. A report written for Mead's House Committee on the Post Office and Post Roads by Harvard professor John B. Crane recommended a significant reduction of $1 million for the coming fiscal year. Crane also uncovered massive, questionable accounting procedures among the airlines, particularly American, in reporting their costs to the post office and strongly suggested changes. The report criticized Brown's unbridled power in awarding routes and especially in route extension without competitive bidding.[21] Despite voluminous testimony, however, little was done, and Brown emerged unscathed. As it resulted, Brown's apparent victory was merely a reprieve.

When Franklin D. Roosevelt swept into the presidency following his election in November 1932, he brought a rejuvenating wave of reform with him. Roosevelt was a former member of the Wilson administration and brought to the White House a readiness to effect change. After flirting unsuccessfully with his version of Hoover's associationalism with the legalized cartels of the National Recovery Administration (NRA), Roosevelt returned to his New Freedom Progressive roots by early 1934, turning his attention to the old question of monopoly. Like Wilson and Brandeis before him, Roosevelt lashed out against the trusts and, not coincidentally, the discredited Hoover administration.

During the waning days of the Hoover's term in office, Brown had arbitrarily attempted to extend eight routes, despite the pleas of Congress. It was the process of route extensions that placed Brown's hitherto well-planned strategy of commercial air transport in jeopardy. The granting of route extensions revealed the weakness in the Watres Act, which gave the postmaster general too much authority. Brown arbitrarily created additional lines and awarded high rates for service to remote areas because of the political pressure from congressional interests, among others. Disliked by both business and Congress, in January 1933 Brown incurred the wrath of the House when he attempted to extend more routes without competitive bidding.[22]

Senate Democrats had already agreed to cut the airmail subsidy to $10 million before the postmaster general's actions, but Brown's effrontery infuriated them to the extent that they struck out the $19-million expenditure altogether. The Democrats, led by Sen. Joseph Robinson of Arkansas, successfully thwarted Brown until Roosevelt could take office in March and establish his own airmail policy. "There would be plenty of time," Robinson stated, "to supply the necessary appropriations after the new administration comes into office."[23]

Although peeved at the postmaster general, the House made an unsuccessful attempt to persuade the Senate to reconsider its actions. Clyde Kelly, who had sponsored the original Contract Air Mail Act seven years earlier, proposed a revision to his bill and subsequent legislation intended as a protest against Brown's actions and philosophy. Supporters hoped to restore the original pound-per-mile basis for payment in place of the space-per-mile system, which encouraged the development of larger aircraft but often resulted in the inefficient underutilization of equipment. The bill was designed to cut costs and waste, and eliminate some forms of what was perceived as corruption.[24] The latter point was especially significant when reviewed in light of the Crane Report. On behalf of the House Post Office Committee, Professor Crane argued for the complete cessation of airmail subsidies and for allowing the airlines to compete on their own. Most important was his condemnation of the power of the three major holding companies, stating that despite their youth, the aviation combines were as complex and intricately developed as the railroads and utilities, and dominated 98 percent of the airmail system.[25]

The revelations of the Crane Report, the hearings on Kelly's new bill, and remarks by Col. Lewis Brittin condemning the oligopolies did not pass unnoticed in the Senate. As early as February, Democratic Sen. Hugo Black of Alabama had been calling for a sweeping investigation of all postal contracts. In particular, he demanded an inquiry into the organization and financial conditions of the contracting companies and their efforts to reap federal subsidies.[26] On September 28, the Special Committee on Investigation of the Air Mail and Ocean Mail Contracts, under Black's chairmanship, began its work.

By New Year's of 1934, with its work completed on the ocean mail, the Special Committee turned its attention to aviation and promised sensational revelations. On January 8, Black reconvened his committee. What followed was both serious drama and comic opera, generating garish daily headlines across the country. A succession of witnesses came forth who outlined Walter F. Brown's complicated machinations during the Hoover years. Few were complimentary. Amid much fanfare, they documented Brown's high-handedness and virtual dictatorship over the airlines. Keyed to the revelations of forced mergers, preferential treatment, and noncompetitive awarding of route extensions was the testimony of several small independent operators about the series of clandestine meetings between Brown, aided by MacCracken, and the representatives of the three holding companies at the "Spoils Conferences." Especially controversial were the remarks of Thomas H. McKee, former operator of the Wedell Williams Air Service of Louisiana, who recalled that his brief encounter at the meeting "gave me the definite impression that Mr. Brown had placed this whole transport operation in the hands of a fixed group with an axe to grind."[27]

Black pressed other witnesses concerning the events of these secretive conferences and underscored the participants' ties to the interlocking directorates. Col. Paul Henderson, vice-president of United Airlines, confirmed that thousands of miles of new route extensions were never opened to bidding and admitted that the United States air map was drawn up at these meetings. Henderson did correctly assert the crucial fact that as discriminatory as these practices may have seemed, they were within the law.[28]

Compounding the damage done by these allegations was the revelation of potential illegal activity within the post office. James Maher, a post office clerk, testified that he had burned potential evidence on the orders of the postmaster general's secretary just two days before Brown left office.[29] The plot took a strange twist ten days later when Brown returned to Washington. On January 19, he arrived with a large suitcase, proceeded immediately to his successor's office, and deposited the contents with James Farley, Roosevelt's new postmaster general.[30]

With this crisis resolved, attention turned again to the dealings of the holding companies, producing a series of nasty shocks. First, America's greatest hero, Charles Lindbergh, was implicated in the stock manipulations of North American. At that time Lindbergh was a valuable advertising commodity whose services were desired by every airline. An astute businessman, Clement Keys enticed Lindbergh to lend his name as technical adviser to TAT. Senator Black revealed that in addition to a generous $10,000 annual salary, the "Lone Eagle" received 25,000 shares of TAT stock worth $250,000. As expected with anything associated with Lindbergh, the stock's value soared, and Keys advised Lindbergh to sell his new shares quickly and turn a tidy profit. He was also advised by Keys to keep the stock manipulation quiet.[31] Like Brown's activity, Lindbergh's profit-taking may have been questionable, but it was legal.

The loudest bombshell was yet to come. On January 16 and 17, officials of UATC, the largest by far of the holding companies, were summoned before Senator Black. Subjected to ardent questioning, Fred Rentschler, UATC vice-chairman, revealed that by 1929 he had turned his modest $254 investment in his new company into a startling $35,575,848. Despite the subsequent collapse of the market, Rentschler still held $2.1 million worth of stock in various companies while continuing to receive a huge salary of $192,500, which had actually increased by 92 percent since 1927, despite the ravaged economy.[32] Black and other committee members were appalled and infuriated by the profit-taking that had originated from the use of federal funds.

Believing he had confirmed his suppositions, Black was ready to call for the cancellation of all the contracts. Speaking to a radio audience over NBC, he stated that the evidence his committee had gleaned over the past five months showed that the government should either give up subsidies, fly the mail itself, or completely revise the system of awarding contracts. Recalling the revelations of several witnesses, Black concluded that "when the air mail map had been redrafted it was found that the eighteen or more million dollars of taxpayers' money annually paid for the carriage of air mail was controlled more than 90 percent by four companies."[33]

More fireworks were yet to come. On January 30, several witnesses attempted to implicate Walter F. Brown in illegal stock dealings. While eventually disproved, the allegations cast further doubts on the former postmaster general's integrity, and, though legal, his possession of 3,000 shares of International Mercantile Marine appeared questionable at the very least. Further testimony claimed that some vital correspondence between Brown and Secretary of the Treasury Andrew Mellon concerning the latter's interest in TAT was missing from Brown's recently discovered files.[34]

By this time, President Roosevelt was becoming increasingly concerned about the recent events. In a private luncheon with Roosevelt, Senator Black outlined his findings and reminded the president that it was within the chief executive's authority to cancel the contracts. Receiving Roosevelt's full support, Black was urged to press on.[35] Events began to move more quickly. Postmaster General Farley also spoke with Roosevelt and conferred with Attorney General Homer Cummings but refused to discuss the growing crisis with the press.[36] The reason for his silence became clear the next day. On February 9, the president issued Executive Order 6591, which canceled all existing domestic air mail contracts and ordered the Army Air Corps to fly the mail.[37]

Charges and countercharges followed in an excited press as the administration was both vilified and praised for its action. Quickly, though, public opinion began to turn against Roosevelt because of unforeseen developments. Roosevelt had asked the army to assume all responsibility for flying the airmail with only ten days' notice. Lack of preparation, flying equipment inferior to the airlines', the worst winter weather in decades, and several fatal accidents brought the matter to the forefront of public attention. Within a few weeks, 12 pilots were killed (8 in training), prompting Eddie Rickenbacker, then vice president of North American Aviation Corporation, to condemn what he called "legalized murder."[38] The overwhelming public outcry forced Roosevelt to suspend the air corps' operation on March 10. Nine days later, the air corps renewed its mail flights on a greatly reduced schedule.[39]

Roosevelt, an astute politician, realized that a better solution was needed immediately—but one that preserved the integrity of the administration and accomplished important reforms yet placated the airline industry and kept it alive. His practical solution was to reopen bids on essential routes for the airlines. Under this interim arrangement, the commercial carriers would return to carrying mail, thus ending the crisis.[40]

At noon, April 20, on the fourth floor of the Old Post Office Building in Washington, 150 representatives of the airlines crowded into the private office of Superintendent of Air Mail Stephen A. Cisler. They gathered to hear the results of 45 bids for the first 17 airmail routes returned to civilian operation. Present were Postmaster General Farley and assorted government officials. Not present were the individuals who had attended the "Spoils Conferences" four years earlier. Also not present in name were the airlines these individuals represented. As part of the agreement, these people and organizations were forbidden to participate. The Big Four, however, were there, but under new names, reflecting their corporate reorganization. American Airways, for instance, became American Airlines, and Eastern Air Transport was renamed Eastern Airlines. The others made similar superficial changes. United kept its original name, but became an operating airline, not a name for a holding company. TWA remained unchanged in name but had been reorganized from within.[41]

Despite the desperate pleas by the independents in the Black committee hearings, few showed up that day. Not unexpectedly, the awards were given essentially to the same airlines that had won them before.[42] These airlines had the equipment, personnel, money, and infrastructure already in place on these routes, as Walter Brown had always asserted. Realistically, no independent airline stood much of a chance to fly the mail more efficiently or safely. The irony was not lost on many observers. United, American, Eastern, and TWA still essentially flew their old routes. Brown's program had been validated, albeit reluctantly.

The most significant and last act in this drama would profoundly and permanently reshape the face of the American aviation industry and clearly reflected

Wilsonian New Freedom attitudes. While Farley was giving out three-month temporary contracts, Senators Black and Kenneth McKellar were preparing legislation that would assimilate the findings of the Special Committee and the needs of the post office into a coherent plan for the airmail and the route network across the United States. After much work and revision, the Air Mail Act of 1934 became law on June 12. The act made the temporary contracts permanent and thus reestablished Brown's system.[43]

Of even greater significance, the act reflected the administration's New Freedom roots concerning monopoly. The vertically integrated holding company was now forbidden. The terms of the new Air Mail Act were clear, making it unlawful for any person holding an airmail contract to hold any shares of stock or other interest in any firm involved in aircraft manufacture.[44]

After December 31, 1934, all aviation holding companies were forbidden from receiving federal subsidy through the airmail, thus effectively destroying these organizations, which were heavily dependent upon the government for funding. The combine companies soon divested their interests. UATC gave up United Airlines and Boeing Aircraft Company, and became United Aircraft Corporation. Likewise, American was divorced from AVCO, and TWA became independent from North American, although General Motors retained control of Eastern for a time.

Thus, a brief but turbulent period in American air transportation reached a watershed. Today, the monopolistic holding companies are gone, but the oligopoly of airlines and manufacturers that was permitted to exist in the aftermath of the events of 1934 remains virtually intact, even in this day of deregulation. The foundations built in those difficult depression-era years has served the nation and its citizens well, with the federal government, as it was from the beginning, ultimately in control.

Clearly, the actions and reactions of both Republican and Democratic administrations reflected old Progressive values, placed within the context of a nascent aviation industry. These ideals profoundly affected the shape of American air transportation and guaranteed its success during the most difficult of times, thereby ensuring its growth in the future.

Progressivism did not die in 1914. It remains in the skies above us today.

NOTES

1. Alfred D. Chandler, Jr., *The Visible Hand: The Managerial Revolution in American Business* (Cambridge, Mass.: Belknap Press, 1977).

2. Ellis W. Hawley, *The New Deal and the Problem of Monopoly: A Study in Economic Ambivalence* (Princeton, N.J.: Princeton University Press, 1966), 4–8.

3. Ibid., 27.

4. Frederick W. Gill and Gilbert L. Bates, *Airline Competition: A Study of the Effects of Competition on the Quality of Service and Price of Airline Service and the Self-Sufficiency of the United States Domestic Airlines* (Boston: Harvard University, 1949), 43–52.

5. Ronald E. G. Davies, *Airlines of the United States since 1914* (Washington, D.C.: Smithsonian Institution Press, 1984), 114.

6. Harvey S. Ford, "Walter Folger Brown," *Northwest Ohio Quarterly* (summer 1954): 205.

7. Ibid., 201–2.

8. Anne Hard, "Uncle Sam's New Mail Man," *New York Herald Tribune,* Apr. 7, 1929.

9. Theodore G. Joslin, "Postmaster General Brown," *World's Work* 59 (August 1930): 39–40.

10. Eugene P. Trani and David L. Wilson, *The Presidency of Warren G. Harding* (Lawrence: University Press of Kansas, 1977), 83–84.

11. Ford, "Walter Folger Brown," 204.

12. Henry Ladd Smith, *Airways: The History of Commercial Aviation in the United States* (New York: Alfred A. Knopf, 1942), 156–57.

13. Davies, *Airlines,* 111.

14. David D. Lee, "Walter F. Brown," in *Encyclopedia of American Business History and Biography,* ed. William M. Leary (New York: Facts on File, 1992), 83–86.

15. Ibid., 86–87.

16. U.S. Congress, House, *Hearing before the Committee on the Post Office and Post Roads,* Mar. 1–4, 23, 1932, 199.

17. Lee, "Walter F. Brown," 86–87; Davies, *Airlines,* 89–93.

18. Smith, *Airways,* 169–70.

19. Ibid., 187–94.

20. Ibid., 138–41; Davies, *Airlines,* 125.

21. John B. Crane, *An Analysis of the Air Mail System in the United States* (Cambridge, Mass.: Harvard University, 1932).

22. *New York Times,* Jan. 27, 1933.

23. Ibid., Feb. 2, 1933.

24. U.S. Congress, House, Committee on the Post Office and Post Roads, *Report: A Resolution Authorizing an Investigation of the Expenditures of the Post Office Department,* 72nd Cong., 2nd Sess., Feb. 21, 1933.

25. Crane, *Analysis,* 36.

26. *New York Times,* Feb. 16, 1933.

27. U.S. Congress, Senate, Special Committee on Investigation of Air Mail and Ocean Mail Contracts, *Hearings: A Resolution Creating a Special Committee of the*

Senate to Investigate Air Mail and Ocean Mail Contracts, 73rd Cong., 2nd Sess., Sept. 26, 1933, to May 25, 1934, pt. 6, 1442.

28. Ibid., 1462.

29. Ibid., 1438.

30. *New York Times,* Jan. 20, 1934.

31. Letter, C. M. Keys to C. A. Lindbergh, June 6, 1928, *New York Times,* Jan. 16, 1934.

32. G. R. Simonson, ed., *The History of the American Aircraft Industry: An Anthology* (Cambridge, Mass.: M.I.T. Press, 1968), 87–93.

33. *New York Times,* Jan. 25, 1934.

34. Ibid., Feb. 1, 1934.

35. Ibid., Jan. 26, 1934.

36. Ibid., Feb. 9, 1934.

37. Samuel I. Rosenman, ed., *The Public Papers and Addresses of Franklin D. Roosevelt,* vol. 3 (New York: Macmillan, 1938), 93.

38. *New York Times,* Feb. 19, 1934.

39. Rosenman, *Public Papers,* "The Army Stops Flying the Mail," 141.

40. Ibid., 142 n.

41. "Spring Opening: Formal Prelude to an Air Mail Shuffle," *Aviation* 33 (May 1934): 135.

42. "Up from Chaos," *Aviation* 33 (Nov. 1934): 339.

43. "A New Law for Air Transport," *Aviation* 33 (July 1934): 205.

44. Ibid., 206.

Leigh Edmonds

Edgar Johnston and the Empire Men

Commonwealth Government Control of Australian Civil Aviation in the 1930s

Edgar Johnston spent most of his life working in and for aviation. He became a fighter ace during World War I, spent the 1920s shaping Australia's network of airfields, and through most of the 1930s guided the development of the civil aviation industry in Australia. For the rest of his working life he was a senior official in Australia's civil aviation administration and then adviser to Australia's international airline. Yet his name is not among those that come to mind when recalling the pioneers of Australian aviation.

Memory of Johnston has faded because of the things that happened in a few heady years from 1932 to 1938, when he was in charge of Australia's civil aviation administration and thus the development of Australia's aviation industry. He may not have been perfect—few people are—but he achieved much and tried for even more. And, unlike such adventurers as Charles Kingsford Smith, Bert Hinkler, and Charles Ulm, Edgar Johnston achieved things that have had an effect on Australian aviation lasting to the present. Those exciting years were also difficult ones of radical change, when new technologies challenged old values. Johnston defied the old order in trying to help Australia's civil aviation industry flourish, and, despite his achievements, it cost him a greater place in our memories. He paid the price that the vanquished usually pays.

14.1. A pioneer aviator, Edgar Johnston headed Australia's civil aviation administration from 1932 to 1938. (Courtesy of Edgar Johnston Archive, Australian Civil Aviation Administration)

In the sixth volume of his *History of Australia,* Manning Clark develops the idea of Australia as a divided nation. By the 1920s there was, he says, a clear distinction between those who supported British culture in Australia and those who looked to the development of an indigenous Australian culture.[1] The conflict between these cultures had been openly declared in the conscription debates of 1916 and 1917 and continued, sometimes overshadowing other issues, throughout the 1920s, the 1930s, and beyond. Clark says it was a battle between Empire men, those who saw Australia as a province of British civilization; and Australian nationalists, who believed that most Australians were "dupes of the British and lackeys of British imperialism."[2]

The division between Empire men and Australian nationalists ran deep and found its way into every corner of Australian life: politics, the arts, religion, and sports. It became a part of the air that Australians breathed and central to what they thought and believed. Even those who were not at the extremes of the division knew well all its nuances and how it shaped their daily lives. But the old Empire values prevailed. Schoolchildren stood under southern skies, saluted a British flag, and, with their hands on their hearts, pledged allegiance to a northern monarch and northern values.

There was a good reason, many said, why this should be so. Australia depended on Britain for its defense. At the beginning of the first conscription debate, the prime minister, William Morris Hughes, told Australians they "were only free as long as Australia remained part of the British Empire and Britain was unconquered."[3] Seven years later, the next Australian prime minister, Stanley Melbourne Bruce, told Australians there were two reasons to be part of the Empire: naval defense and imperial trade.[4] The conviction that the Royal Navy would protect Australian shores and that trade with the "mother country" and the other British dominions was the foundation of Australian wealth ran deep in Australian society. But those beliefs were countered by equally strong views about Australia's need to find its own identity and place in the world. Perhaps most Australians held an amalgamation of both views—being proud of Australian achievements in war and on the playing fields but yet feeling the emotional ties of the Empire and owing some kind of loyalty to Britain. In 1929, 98 percent of Australia's population was said to be British.[5]

Edgar Johnston was probably like most Australians in holding middle views. The growth of aviation as a viable transport technology during the 1930s, however, put him in a position where the conflicts between Empire interests and Australian loyalties became focused. His attempt to put local Australian aviation interests before the interests of the Empire led him into conflict with Empire men.

Manning Clark also notes the increasing importance of aviation to Australia after World War I. In 1919, Prime Minister Hughes offered a prize of £10,000 to the first Australians to fly between Britain and Australia, but his opponents denounced it as another "stunt to tighten the fetters binding Australia to the British, and their colonial past."[6] Clark classes the aviation adventurers, such as Ross and Keith Smith, Bert Hinkler, and Charles Kingsford Smith as Empire men because their actions and beliefs strengthened the bonds of empire.[7] The air link to Britain was founded in December 1934 when that symbol of the Empire, Prince Henry, the duke of Gloucester, inaugurated the first scheduled airmail service from Britain to Brisbane,[8] showing Australians that aviation was bound to the development of the Empire.

Some background will be useful in understanding the context of these problems and issues. Australia is the large island continent at the bottom of Asia. Its western coast faces the Indian Ocean, and its eastern coast faces the Pacific Ocean. It has about nine-tenths the area of the United States but five times that nation's arid areas. White settlement of Australia started from Britain in 1788, and by 1836 British colonies had been established at most habitable places around the coast. By the end of the 1850s all of Australia was under the control of largely self-governing British colonies except for Western Australia, which did not achieve self-government until 1890. During the 1890s, all the Australian colonies agreed to join a federation to create the Commonwealth of Australia, founded on January 1, 1901. The former colonies became states of the Commonwealth, and a Commonwealth parliament was established along Westminster lines.

By the 1930s, Australia had a population of about seven million, mostly concentrated in the southeastern corner of the continent. Australians were xenophobic and particularly afraid of Asians. The "White Australia" immigration policy was designed to keep the Australian continent safe for the white race. To the north and northwest, and between Australia and Britain, lived 750 million Asians, half the population of the world and about 150 times Australia's white population.[9] Australia's foreign, defense, and immigration policies reflected this isolation and fear, and it can be argued that all these factors contributed to Australia's early and enthusiastic adoption of aviation.[10]

The first heavier-than-air flight took place in Australia in 1909, but civil aviation did not become established until 1919, when many men returned to Australia at the end of the war with flying experience and a desire to remain in the flying business. But, despite early promise, civil aviation was in decline by mid-1920. Hughes, the air-minded prime minister, who called himself "a fanatic" in his belief in aviation, and the like-minded minister for defence, George Foster Pearce, restored the early momentum of Australian aviation development.[11] In 1921, they oversaw the creation of the Royal Australian Air Force and the establishment of a civil aviation industry through the Civil Aviation Branch of the Department of Defence.

The Civil Aviation Branch had three main functions: to ensure aviation safety by enforcing the Air Navigation Regulations, to advise the government on civil aviation policy, and to supervise expenditure on civil aviation.[12] A major part of this expenditure was on subsidized air services established to encourage the growth of civil aviation and assist in developing Australia's remote areas. Three weekly air services were established in the early 1920s. The first operated along the Western Australian coast from Perth to Derby, another between the state capitals of Adelaide and Sydney through isolated areas, and the third linked a number of isolated railhead settlements in outback Queensland.[13] These routes were extended or altered during the 1920s, but no new subsidized routes were introduced until 1929, when a weekly airmail service was established between Perth and Adelaide.

H. C. Brinsmead was the first controller of civil aviation, with superintendents of airworthiness, flying operations, and aerodromes under his control.[14]

Edgar Johnston was the first superintendent of aerodromes, and, in the late 1920s, he also became the assistant controller of civil aviation. It seems that there was some tension between Brinsmead and Johnston over matters of policy and personality, but when Brinsmead was seriously injured in a flying accident in 1931 and could not resume his position, Johnston replaced him as the controller of civil aviation.[15]

Edgar Johnston was born in Western Australia in 1896. He was the son of a prominent family. One of his brothers became a well-known Western Australian senator in the Commonwealth parliament, and another became the surveyor-general of the Commonwealth.[16] Edgar Johnston was also a surveyor but became a pilot during World War I, when he was credited with nine and a half kills.[17] He returned to civil life as a surveyor but was only one of two men in Australia who held flying qualifications and a surveyor's ticket, the necessary qualifications for the job as superintendent of aerodromes.[18] Johnston spent most of the 1920s touring around Australia, selecting airfield sites and surveying air routes. In 1928 he made the first flights along the north coast of New Guinea while surveying New Guinea and the northeastern coastline of Australia.[19]

Johnston was a man with enormous energy and determination, but he also had faults. On the one hand, he was said to be courageous, loyal, tenacious of purpose, possessing unbounded energy and zeal, a man of good mental capacity and some force of character. On the whole, he commanded the respect of his staff, particularly those with whom he had been associated for a long time. He was dedicated to the development of civil aviation, and his "energies were devoted entirely to what, in his view, were the best interests of Civil Aviation." On the other hand, he was said to be egotistical, dogmatic, and unyielding in his views, unable to order his work according to a definite program or bring matters to a final conclusion. He was also said to be reluctant to delegate authority and restricted in his ideas of the administrative qualities necessary to deal with a rapidly expanding organization.[20] The last criticism is easy to understand because the once insignificant position of controller of civil aviation had grown in importance and complexity around Johnston, but he had little experience of public administration. Nevertheless, those who worked for him said he was a gentleman and seem to have admired his ability for hard work and his thoroughness.[21]

Perhaps this vigorous, tenacious, and yet dogmatic and untrained personality contributed to the mood of the times. Conflict and growth were the main features of Johnston's administration because he found himself in a position of power at the center of a network of conflicting interests. This conflict came about because the Commonwealth government had tight control over Australian civil aviation through its system of regulations and subsidies.

Although the Constitution of the Commonwealth of Australia did not give the Commonwealth any legal authority over civil aviation, the interest shown in it by Hughes and Pearce, and the lack of interest from the state governments, meant that the Commonwealth took control of civil aviation legislation and administration from December 1920 on. The Commonwealth claimed its authority through the powers it had been given over international and defense issues when it had been created in 1901.[22] For this reason the civil aviation administration was located in the Department of Defence, and the Air Navigation Regulations were closely based on the rules of the air promulgated by the International Convention for Aerial Navigation (ICAN), which Australia had signed. Although these arrangements were not made strictly legal until the late 1930s, almost every aviator and aviation company in Australia supported Commonwealth administration of civil aviation because they did not relish the likelihood of six separate sets of state aviation regulations that might replace unified control.[23]

The Commonwealth supported air services by paying subsidies for the carriage of airmail. Until the late 1930s it was not possible to operate profitably without subsidies, and by granting or withholding them the government could control the provision of all Australian air services. Initially subsidies were calculated on the basis of miles flown, but later subsidies were sometimes calculated on the weight of mail carried. The first subsidies paid in Australia, in 1922, were at the rate of 4 shillings a mile for the airmail service in Western Australia, but by 1940, Australia's major airline company, Australian National Airways, was being paid to carry mail at the rate of .055 shillings per pound/mile.[24] On some occasions subsidies were granted after a rigorous tendering process; at other times tenders were granted to airlines already operating on particular routes; and at other times again subsidies were granted following negotiation between the Commonwealth and individual operators.

Australian civil aviation grew rapidly in the 1930s. In 1932, Australian regular air services flew about a quarter of a million route miles. By 1935, this figure had grown to 2.3 million, and by 1938–39 it had reached 9.6 million.[25] These changes came from two important developments, besides the gradual recovery from the worldwide depression.

In 1936, a consortium of British, Australian, and New Zealand shipping companies formed Australian National Airways (ANA), which took over or developed an extensive network of air routes in Australia.[26] By 1939, in association with another major company that it had bought, ANA operated almost all the major domestic air routes in Australia.[27] It was virtually a monopoly, and the long-term goals of the company to develop a strong airline led to a vigorous program of expansion affecting all other aviation developments.

One of the keys to ANA's success was its use of Douglas DC-2 and DC-3 airplanes. In 1928, the Commonwealth government had decided to ban importation of all airplanes that did not have an ICAN certificate of airworthiness. This bureaucratic measure was intended to protect Australia as a market for British airplane manufacturers by blocking the importation of American and German airplanes lacking ICAN certification, because neither the United States nor Germany was an ICAN signatory.[28] By 1935, it was becoming clear that the restriction on importing American airplanes was hampering the development of the civil aviation industry, and Johnston, who was about to visit the United States, Britain, and Europe, was instructed to examine the subject.[29] When he returned he recommended lifting the ban, and the government did so. This approval did not mean that the government agreed with the use of American airplanes in Australia, but it took note of Johnston's comments that the British manufacturing industry was not, at that time, able to provide airplanes to meet Australian needs.[30] Within weeks, the first DC-2 was on the way to Australia, and it and those that followed immediately improved air service. In particular, the service between Perth and Adelaide, which had previously taken two days, could now be flown in one.[31]

The government acknowledged the growth of the aviation industry in 1935 by upgrading the Civil Aviation Branch, which was by then 15 years old, to the Civil Aviation Board, with the same powers as the Navy, Military, and Air boards in the Department of Defence.[32] The staff of the civil aviation administration grew from 59 in July 1934 to 99 in 1936.[33] Johnston became the chairman of the board, with the title of controller-general of civil aviation, and three other public servants or service officers sat with him. Johnston also wanted a representative of the civil aviation industry on the board, but that was not allowed by the government.[34]

The most important impetus to the development of Australian civil aviation sprang from its part in the British Empire. In 1929, Imperial Airways first approached the Commonwealth government about the possibility of an imperial air service from Britain to Australia via India and Singapore.[35] The depression halted any serious planning, and it was not until 1932 that the subject became a matter for serious consideration. Pearce, who had returned to the post of minister for defence after a decade, said he saw the establishment of an imperial air link as fundamental to Australian civil aviation policy because all the domestic air routes could be tailored to carry the imperial airmail from Darwin in the north to the centers of white habitation in the south of the continent.[36]

The government set up an interdepartmental committee to recommend a

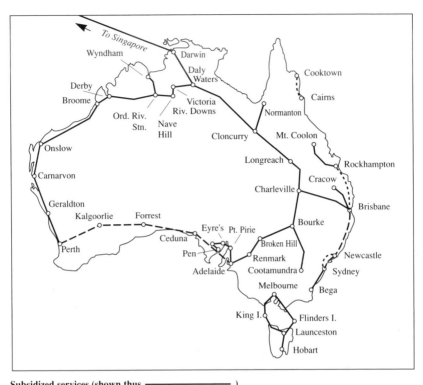

Subsidized services (shown thus —————)

Brisbane – Darwin – Singapore	4, 361 miles
Charleville – Cootamundra	629
Perth – Daly Waters	2,252
Cloncurry – Normanton	216
Ord River – Wyndham	147
Bourke – Adelaide	590
Melbourne – Launceston – Hobart	460
Brisbane – Cracow	250
Rockhampton – Mount Coolon	330
Sydney – Bega	205
Adelaide – Eyre's Peninsula	475
Total mileage	9,915

Unsubsidized services (shown thus — — — — — — — ·)

Sydney – Brisbane	500
Perth – Adelaide	1,453
Total mileage	1,953

Unsubsidized services not carrying mails (shown thus · · · · · · · · · · · · · · ·)

Sydney – Rockhampton	325
Sydney – Newcastle	80
Cairns – Cooktown	100
Total mileage	505

Total mileage all regular services	12,373

Note: Although included herein, the subsidized services Bourke–Adelaide and Ord River–Wyndham did not commence operations until after the award of contracts early in 1935.

14.2. In 1934, more than 12,000 miles of air routes were regularly scheduled in Australia. (Courtesy of Civil Aviation Authority, Australia, and Australian Archives)

course of action. Johnston was chairman of the committee and played a key role in shaping its decisions. As a result of its recommendations, the Commonwealth government decided to recreate its existing air transport services completely.[37] The existing air services were put up for tender, and tenders were also called for proposed new services, the most important of which was the route from Singapore to Australia's eastern states. Those that won were guaranteed five-year contracts.[38]

Edgar Johnston was a member of the committee that examined the tenders for these services and made recommendations on the new services. The committee's most important recommendation was that the major contract be awarded to Qantas Empire Airways (QEA), a fifty-fifty partnership between QANTAS and Imperial Airways.[39]

Even before the first imperial air service was inaugurated in December 1934, the British government approached the Commonwealth government with a proposal, known as the Empire Air Mail Scheme, which would have important implications for the development of Australia's domestic civil aviation. Some of the most important points in the British scheme were that Imperial Airways would operate a complete air service between Britain and Sydney using Short flying boats and that Australia's major contributions to the air service would be large annual subsidies and providing landing areas. All first-class mail posted in the Empire would fly free of charge on these services so that the large volume of mail would guarantee the viability of the service.[40]

Johnston and other important members of the Department of Defence disagreed with these proposals, leading to a fight that lasted almost four years with the Australian Postmaster-General's Department and the British government. Later Johnston said that it was "quite well known that those were negotiations of a highly difficult nature."[41] The controversy highlighted the powerful attachment of Empire men to their British roots, and those who resisted the Empire proposals were charged with putting their own small interests before the larger interests of the Empire.[42]

After some initial doubts, the Postmaster-General's Department supported the British proposal to carry all first-class airmail free because it strongly agreed with the British postmaster-general about the primacy of airmail services. The British proposal was unsound, however, because it did not take into account Australian conditions, which included sparse populations spread across wide distances. If airmail were carried *into* Australia free of charge, it would have to be carried free *within* Australia too. The existing airmail charges held down the use of air services to a manageable level, but if all first-class mail were carried free into and within Australia, there would be a huge increase in loads but also a dramatic decrease in revenue.[43]

Johnston fought the Postmaster-General's Department, and he did not fight fair. He used simple tactics like not showing his opposition to the proposals going to the government until it was too late for them to put up any defense, keeping them ignorant of his advice to his minister, and playing down the importance of interdepartmental committees established to foster cooperation between civil aviation and the postmaster-general.[44] Eventually he was successful on the surcharge issue, and, although the British government flew first-class mail into Australia free of surcharge, all mail leaving Australia carried a 3-shilling surcharge.

Even then the fight was not over because of the Postmaster-General's Department's apparent belief that the main role of air transport was to carry airmail. The department tried to take control of civil aviation administration, forcing Johnston, the Civil Aviation Board, and the Department of Defence to defend themselves in a struggle that seems to have reached its height in the middle of 1938.[45] They were successful: the Postmaster-General's Department was forced to withdraw, and civil aviation for the time being remained under the wing of the Department of Defence.

Johnston was partly successful in his opposition to other British proposals that would have seen the end of Qantas Empire Airways as one of Australia's major airlines and the loss of Australia's international air route to Singapore.[46] Just as controversial was the British proposal to use flying boats on the service to Australia, mainly because they were considered slow by the standards of the mid-1930s, even though the British argued that speed was not their primary concern.[47] The proposal was announced not long after the MacRobertson air race from London to Melbourne, in which a KLM DC-2 operating a scheduled route finished second, covering the distance in about three days. The British proposed to fly the service from Britain to Sydney in 12 days, initially, which seemed outrageously inefficient.[48]

Johnston had seen the new American airliners in operation during an overseas tour and saw no reason why Australia should lose its international air route and endure an inefficient service when a better one could be provided. He proposed that the lumbering flying boats of Imperial Airways would be met at Singapore by a fleet of fast Australian-owned American-manufactured airplanes that would fly the mail through to Australia.[49] This would provide a much quicker service without the need for expensive special-support facilities for flying boats. Britain rejected Johnston's suggestions because, it said, the economic operation of the service depended on using one type of airplane over the whole route.[50] Unstated was Britain's objection to the proposal because the use of DC-3-type airplanes on part of the imperial air routes would support the

American aviation industry rather than the British and because the type of operations Johnston proposed were similar to the KLM service from Europe to the
Netherlands East Indies—a service the British said was inferior to the service
provided by Imperial Airways to Singapore.

In addition to opposition from Britain, Johnston also found himself opposed
by members of the Australian government whose greatest loyalty was to the
Empire. The Empire Air Mail Scheme became a major political issue. In the
43 months from late 1934 until the completion of the intergovernmental negotiations in June 1938, the government considered the Scheme on 29 separate
occasions and other related aviation matters on a further 28 occasions.

As the 1930s progressed, emotions in the government became spread along a
spectrum of support for Britain, and aviation became a focus in the fundamental
structure of Australian society. The prime minister, Joseph A. Lyons, seems to
have entertained some independence from British domination, but others, in
particular the attorney general, Robert G. Menzies, were staunch Empire men.
At first Johnston and the minister for defence argued successfully against the
British proposal, and this culminated in a flat rejection of it at the beginning of
1936.[51] When the British softened their initial line, the Australian government
did likewise, but Britain also emphasized Empire loyalty to bring the Dominion
government into line. Britain said that the Scheme was vital to its aviation supremacy against the major threat of the United States and Pan American Airways, "which the United States Government have made their chosen instrument
for external air development, and on which they are spending many millions of
public money."[52]

Just as important to the Australian change of heart was a gradual shift in the
balance of power in the government as Lyons declined and Menzies grew in
strength. Menzies already supported the British Scheme and had probably done
so from the beginning.[53] He was in Britain for two months while negotiations
were at their most critical, and in June 1936 he and the deputy leader of the
government recommended that an amended form of the Scheme be adopted.[54]
Eventually a compromise was reached in which Qantas Empire Airways remained in charge of the route to Singapore, but the entire route to Britain was
operated with a common fleet of flying boats shared with Imperial Airways.[55]
The British also made major concessions in cost and other arrangements, but
they had won a major victory. They, and the Empire men in Australia, had defeated Johnston's proposal for an independent air service between Singapore
and Australia's major cities to suit Australian economic, social, and political
aspirations.

Johnston's opposition to the British proposals made him unpopular with many people. He received one of the worst criticisms possible at the time—he was said to be "un-British" (though he would not have considered himself so). The British men who met him at this time were not impressed, and G. E. Woods-Humphrey wrote that he was "a stubborn rather than a strong man."[56] Menzies (who, Johnston believed, would have been quite happy to hand over civil aviation entirely to the British)[57] seems to have disliked Johnston—if not the man, at least his attitude. At a high-level meeting in London in 1935 chaired by Menzies, he offered no assistance as Johnston attempted to defend his position against a number of Britain's most influential civil aviation leaders single-handed.[58] (Perhaps this dislike continued through to the 1950s and early 1960s, when Menzies was prime minister of Australia. When other pioneers like Hudson Fysh and Norman Brearley were being given imperial honors for their services to aviation, nothing was given to Edgar Johnston). Neither Johnston's stubborn personality nor his conviction that he was doing the right thing in the interests of Australian civil aviation helped lessen his unpopularity. In August 1938, the secretary of the Department of Defence severely reprimanded him for his actions in relation to the Postmaster-General's Department, and the minister for defence issued direct instructions to force Johnston to do things that he did not want to do.[59]

As a result of these confrontations, by mid-1938 Johnston found himself facing hostile interests in many high places of Australian political life. Although he had not achieved all that he wanted, he had managed to protect what he saw as important Australian interests against empire demands. But the men he had offended were not ready to forgive such disloyalty easily.

The late 1930s were a hectic time in Australian civil aviation. Traffic was increasing rapidly, and the development of the imperial air link placed heavy burdens on the limited resources of the Civil Aviation Board. None of this was helped by the condition of the board itself, which did not function efficiently because Johnston and another board member, A. H. Cobby (who happened also to be a World War I fighter ace), could not work together. Relations between board members were far from cordial, and open expressions of hostility were based on personal animosity rather than opposing opinions. It was, in fact, surprising that the board was able to function at all for so long.[60] Instead of having board meetings, the practice developed that the initials of all board members on a minute represented a board decision regardless of whether or not a meeting had taken place.[61] The long and difficult negotiations over the Empire Air Mail Scheme, the provision of ground facilities for the flying boats, and the complete reorganization of all of Australia's domestic airline services to meet the new demands took up most of the board members' time, leaving little for less de-

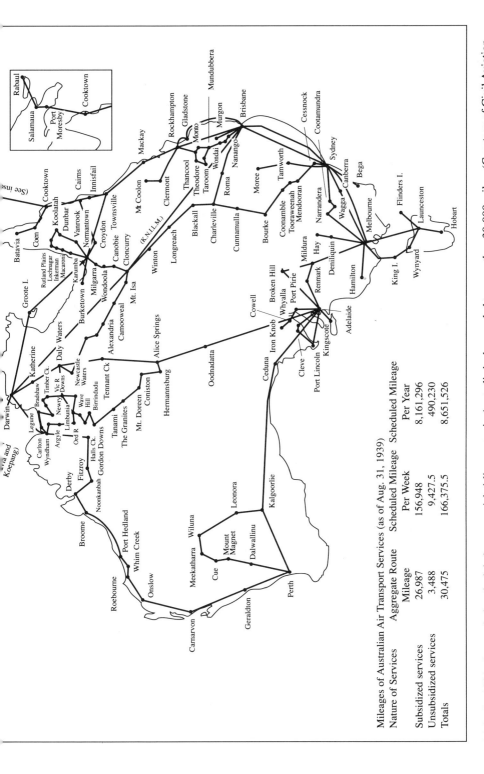

Mileages of Australian Air Transport Services (as of Aug. 31, 1939)

Nature of Services	Aggregate Route Mileage	Scheduled Mileage Per Week	Scheduled Mileage Per Year
Subsidized services	26,987	156,948	8,161,296
Unsubsidized services	3,488	9,427.5	490,230
Totals	30,475	166,375.5	8,651,526

14.3. By 1939, the regularly scheduled commercial airline routes in Australia had expanded to more than 30,000 miles. (Courtesy of Civil Aviation Authority, Australia, and Australian Archives)

manding matters of day-to-day administration. Also, the difficult and distracting intergovernmental discussions and negotiations with the Dutch over the extension of their air service from Batavia in the Netherlands East Indies to Australia taxed the board's resources.[62]

Another serious problem developed in establishing infrastructure to support the rapidly growing industry. To provide radio navigation aids for the fast American airliners, the Civil Aviation Board decided to establish a chain of ultra high-frequency radio beacons on the major air routes, but the equipment was at the forefront of the existing technology and therefore difficult and costly to get operating.[63] A crucial delay arose in testing the beacons because when the board asked the government for permission to buy an airplane capable of doing the work effectively, it received unworkable directions. On three occasions (March and June 1937 and March 1938) the board was told that it had to buy a British airplane. When the board advised the government that no suitable British airplane existed, the government replied that the board was to find one.[64]

In the end a British airplane of adequate performance was bought and an American Lockheed leased to test the beacons. But by then the damage had been done. In October 1938, an ANA DC-2 became lost in fog as it tried to land at Melbourne Airport, and all on board were killed when it crashed.[65] The press and some aviation interests said that if the new navigation beacons had been in service the accident would not have happened, leading to a general outcry for an inquiry into the administration of Australian civil aviation. The usually confidential Air Accidents Investigation Committee inquiry, which was held after every accident, was opened to the public, and the committee's membership was increased from three to five.[66] Despite these changes, the committee was strongly criticized because it was prohibited from investigating problems in civil aviation administration.[67]

Critics called for a thorough investigation that would include the government's role and the testimony of the minister for defence.[68] R. M. Ansett, an airline operator, said that civil aviation's most pressing need was for a complete change in the government's attitude towards it and that, while the public inquiry might be helpful, the problem was that "the Government does not appear to appreciate fully the importance of the industry to the country."[69] Sir Henry Gullett, a prominent politician, said that it was not the Civil Aviation Board but the Department of Defence and the government as a whole that was on trial.[70]

The public inquiry lasted over a month, including 23 days of hearings. Edgar Johnston, as the man in charge of civil aviation administration, was the principal target of criticism, and within days of the accident, there was a behind-the-scenes movement to replace him.[71] Although some severe criticism of the government attitudes and policies were made before the investigation committee, the suggestion that the minister for defence appear before it was rejected, and Johnston was the highest government official examined.[72]

While the long and difficult investigation into the accident was going on, Prime Minister Lyons found himself in a tough political fight with members of his government who thought he was not being strong enough in preparing for the coming war. Menzies, his major opponent, was publicly critical of the Lyons administration.[73] The prime minister was eventually forced to reorganize his cabinet to meet the demands of the hard-liners. He also had to maintain the balance of the coalition between the two parties making up the government. At the center of the dispute was the minister for defence, H. V. C. Thorby, who was said to be too weak to reorganize Australia's defenses for war. He was, however, also the deputy leader of the smaller of the parties in the coalition, so he could not be unceremoniously dumped from the ministry, and an important but out-of-the-way position had to be found for him.[74] The prime minister did this by creating a new post for a minister for civil aviation and works and giving it to Thorby, who was not well regarded by many.[75] One report said he proved that "intolerance, incompetence and unpopularity are the necessary qualities in a Minister."[76] Nonetheless, his new position was important for the survival of the Lyons government, and while Thorby was shielded, Johnston received the full brunt of the Accident Investigation Committee's adverse criticism.[77]

From October to December 1938, Australia's civil aviation administration was completely overhauled. The new Department of Civil Aviation was created on November 24, 1938, and took over the duties of the Civil Aviation Board in early 1939.[78] From the start it was clear that Johnston would not become director-general of civil aviation, partly because he was judged to lack some of the capabilities necessary to lead a government department,[79] and partly because his reputation had been destroyed when he was made the scapegoat by the Air Accidents Investigation Committee. After his disagreements with many politicians and bureaucrats he had no supporters left among important government members to defend him. Had he been prepared to acquiesce to the desires of the Empire men in the previous four years, he might have been spared, and some other person found to take the blame. A year and a half later the new director-general of Civil Aviation wrote: "No doubt Johnston has been the subject of political personal hostility in certain quarters. From my experience of close personal contact with him for over twelve months, I think this political attitude resulted from ill-informed criticism and malice."[80]

Other choices made in creating the Department of Civil Aviation showed that Johnston had not yet paid in full for what had happened. In a move suggesting that the earlier struggle for control of civil aviation was not over, A. B. Corbett, a senior officer in the Postmaster-General's Department, became the first permanent director-general of civil aviation.[81]

Johnston's problems arose primarily from the political antagonism that he created for himself. But that was not the entire cause. His difficulties exemplify what can happen when a form of technology such as civil aviation moves from being fairly insignificant to playing an important national role. By 1940 it was recognized that allowing the introduction of new high-performance airliners without providing the necessary ground facilities had been asking for trouble—like "introducing new 400 ton locomotives to a railway without upgrading the track from 100 ton capacity."[82] Johnston noted that because the United States led the world in civil aviation "in many respects," its practices were more highly developed, and Australia, as a much less prosperous and progressive nation, found it difficult to "keep abreast of the latest American practices."[83] In such circumstances politics becomes as important as technological innovation in deciding an outcome. When old organizations and systems are put under pressure, some people are likely to get hurt.

Edgar Johnston remained at the highest levels of the civil aviation administration for the next 17 years as the assistant director-general and director of air transport and external relations. Despite the appointment of three new director-generals, Johnston remained in the secondary position until he retired from the department. From this job, however, he played a major role in the development of Australian civil aviation. He attended the Chicago Convention in 1945 and led the Australian delegation to the first General Assembly of International Civil Aviation Organization in 1948. Johnston also led most overseas civil aviation delegations and oversaw the negotiation of Australia's first bilateral international air service agreements. In 1957, he left the department to take up the position of adviser on international affairs with QANTAS.[84]

Perhaps Johnston was struck down because he was an aviation man first and a public officer second. His enthusiasm had sometimes brought him ridicule and condescension: "It appears to me from the discussion with the Controller that he had rather an exalted view of the importance of Civil Aviation, based largely on the grounds that it is comparatively new and that he and his officers are pioneers in Civil Aviation administration, and that he was, therefore, inclined to make somewhat extravagant claims."[85] Almost everything he did was aimed at improving civil aviation, and he worked tirelessly to do what he thought was best for the industry. Civil aviation in Australia today owes as much to Johnston as it does to anyone, and it is a tragedy that his name is so little known.

In the early 1980s, members of the Department of Aviation (the successor to

14.4. Edgar Johnston led the Australian delegation to the International Civil Aviation Organization in Montreal in 1948. (Courtesy of Civil Aviation Authority, Australia, and Australian Archives)

the Civil Aviation Board and the Department of Civil Aviation) formed the Civil Aviation Historical Society and recognized Johnston's importance. They established the Edgar Johnston Lectures and the Edgar Johnston Archive of Australian Civil Aviation Administration. Before he died in 1988, Johnston saw his achievements and importance start to be recognized.

NOTES

1. C. M. H. Clark, *A History of Australia*, vol. 6 (Melbourne: University Press, 1987), 41.
2. Ibid., 207, 461.
3. Ibid., 34.
4. Ibid., 210.
5. Ibid., 293.

6. Ibid., 153.

7. Ibid., 273, 441.

8. Ibid., 475.

9. Speech by W. M. Hughes in *Commonwealth Parliamentary Debates* 93:4389–90.

10. Leigh Edmonds, "Problems of Defence, Isolation and Development: What Civil Aviation Could Do to Help," *Aviation Historical Society of Australia Newsletter* 6 (1990): 50–55.

11. Hughes, 4393.

12. *Commonwealth of Australia Gazette* 94 (Nov. 4, 1920): 2037.

13. Stanley Brogden, *The History of Australian Aviation* (Melbourne: Hawthorne Press, 1960), 76–82.

14. G. A. Shearer, "The Foundation of the Department of Civil Aviation, 1919–1939," M.A. thesis, University of Melbourne, 1970, 20.

15. *Aircraft*, Feb. 28, 1929, 240; Shearer, "Foundation," 48.

16. F. M. Johnston, *Knights and Theodolites: A Saga of Surveyors* (Sydney: Edwards and Shaw, 1962), 118.

17. Keith Isaacs, *Military Aircraft of Australia, 1909–1918* (Canberra: Australian War Memorial, 1971), 154.

18. Interview with E. C. Johnston, May 20, 1986.

19. James Sinclair, *Wings of Gold: How the Aeroplane Developed New Guinea* (Sydney: Pacific Publications, 1978), 259.

20. These comments come mainly from reports prepared for the minister for civil aviation by a special investigating committee, Dec. 30, 1938, Australian Archives (hereafter AA), CP 372/1; and a letter from the director-general of civil aviation, Apr. 12, 1940, AA, CRS A447, item A39-2890.

21. K. N. E. Bradfield, "Captain Edgar Johnston—His Role in Australian Civil Aviation, 1921–1957," Edgar Johnston Memorial Address, presented to the Civil Aviation Historical Society in Melbourne on May 20, 1992.

22. Tadao Kuribayashi, *The Basic Structure of Australian Air Law* (Tokyo: Nogaku-Kenkyu-Kai, 1970), 17.

23. *West Australian*, Nov. 14, 1936, 17.

24. Minute, Dec. 4, 1928, AA, CRS A705, item 192/12/569; letter, May 24, 1940, AA, MP 347/1, item 192/139/55.

25. Figures are drawn from the civil aviation annual reports for the period, AA, MP 391.

26. *Aircraft*, Oct. 1, 1936, 24.

27. Ibid., Aug. 2, 1937, 7.

28. Press statement, Nov. 29, 1935, AA, CRS A461, item E314/1/1.

29. Cabinet decision, Feb. 7, 1935, AA, CRS A2694, vol. 13, pt. 1.

30. Minute, Nov. 13, 1935, and cabinet decision, Nov. 27, 1935, AA, CRS A2694, vol. 14, pt. 3.

31. *Aircraft,* Mar. 1, 1937, 19.

32. Interview with E. C. Johnston, May 20, 1986.

33. Memorandum, July 7, 1937, AA, CRS A447, item A-36-1319.

34. Interview with E. C. Johnston, May 20, 1986.

35. Letter, Jan. 29, 1929, AA, CRS A458, item W314/3, pt. 1.

36. *West Australian,* May 27, 1932, 16.

37. Cabinet decision, Nov. 29, 1932, AA, CRS A2694, vol. 4; cabinet decision, July 12, 1933, AA, CRS A2694, vol. 9.

38. "Air Communications within and beyond Australia, Report of Inter-Departmental Committee," Oct. 1932, AA, MP 273/1, item 1939/11122.

39. "Tenders for Overseas and Internal Air Services, Recommendation of Air Contracts Committee," Mar. 1934, AA, CRS A461, item B314/1/5.

40. "Empire Air Mail Scheme—A Scheme for the Carriage of All First Class Empire Mail by Air on Existing Empire Air Routes," AA, CP 402/1, bundle 2.

41. "Report of Proceedings of Inquiry re Disaster to Airliner 'Kyeema' at Mt Dandenong on Tuesday 25th October 1938," AA, CRS A467, Special File 30, bundle 65, 1042.

42. *Sydney Morning Herald,* Feb. 3, 1936.

43. Memorandum, Feb. 14, 1935, AA, CRS A461, item G314/1/5.

44. For example, see letter, May 31, 1938, AA, MP 131/1, item 192/101/347.

45. *West Australian,* June 18, 1938, 20; and June 22, 1938, 13.

46. "Empire Air Mail Scheme."

47. *Aircraft,* Apr. 1, 1935, 5.

48. "Civil Aviation Aspects, Air Mail Scheme," AA, MP 131/1, item 192/119/258.

49. "Empire Air Mail Scheme—Conclusions of the Defence Department Representative on the Inter-Departmental Committee," June 12, 1935, AA, CRS A571, item 37/3481, pt. 2.

50. Draft letter, July 1935, AA, MP 131/1, item 192/119/258.

51. Cablegram, Jan. 31, 1936, AA, CRS A2694/XM1, vol. 15, pt. 1.

52. Cablegram, Feb. 13, 1936, AA, CRS A461, item G314/1/5, pt. 1, AA.

53. Letter, July 23, 1935, AA, MP 131/1, item 192/119/258.

54. Cablegram, June 26, 1936, AA, CRS A461, item G314/1/5, pt. 2.

55. Cablegram, Dec. 31, 1936, AA, MP 131/1, item 192/119/499.

56. John Gunn, *The Defeat of Distance: Qantas, 1919–1939* (St. Lucia: University of Queensland Press, 1985), 261.

57. Ibid., 309.

58. Letter, Aug. 10, 1935, AA, MP 131/1, item 192/119/258.

59. Letter, May 25, 1938, and minute, Aug. 22, 1938, AA, MP 131/1, item 192/101/424.

60. Letter, Dec. 30, 1938, AA, CP 372/3, bundle 1.

61. "Report of Proceedings of Inquiry," 512.

62. Ibid., 1043.

63. *Aircraft,* June 1, 1937, 12, and May 1, 1937, 8.

64. Cabinet minute, Mar. 14, 1938, AA, Agenda 204, CRS A2694/XM1, vol. 18, no. 2.

65. "Report by Air Accidents Committee on Fatal Accident of Douglas DC-2 Aircraft VH-UYC 'Kyeema,' the Property of Australian National Airlines, Which Occurred at Mount Dandenong, Victoria on Tuesday 25th October 1938," AA, CRS A461, item Y314/1/1.

66. Minutes of Cabinet meeting, Oct. 26 and Oct. 27, 1938, AA, CRS A2694, vol. 19/1.

67. *Sydney Morning Herald,* Oct. 28, 1938, 11.

68. *Argus,* Oct. 26, 1938, 12.

69. *Melbourne Herald,* Oct. 26, 1938, 3.

70. Ibid., Oct. 27, 1938, 1.

71. Sir Hudson Fysh, *Qantas at War* (Sydney: Angus and Robertson, 1968), 75.

72. "Report of Proceedings of Inquiry," 1262.

73. *Sydney Morning Herald,* Oct. 25, 1938, 11.

74. *Age,* Nov. 5, 1938, 297; *Argus,* Nov. 5, 1938, 1.

75. *Argus,* Nov. 8, 1938, 1.

76. *Smith's Weekly,* Dec. 7, 1938, 12.

77. For example, the headline in *Argus,* Dec. 9, 1938, 1.

78. *Commonwealth of Australia Gazette* 70 (Nov. 25, 1938): 2751.

79. Letter, Dec. 30, 1938, AA, CP 372/1, bundle 1.

80. Letter, Apr. 12, 1940, AA, CRS A447, item A39-2890.

81. C. A. Butler, *Flying Start: The History of the First Five Decades of Civil Aviation in Australia* (Sydney: Edwards and Shaw, 1971), 46.

82. "Report on Civil Aviation in Australia and New Guinea, 1939–40," Department of Civil Aviation, 6.

83. "Report of Proceedings of Inquiry," 1038.

84. Bradfield, "Captain Edgar Johnston."

85. Memorandum, Nov. 16, 1933, AA, CRS A447, item A34-1316.

R. E. G. Davies

Conclusion

Facing the Transport Gridlock
of the Twenty-first Century

Excluding the embryo stage, say from 1919 to 1925, the history of air transport can be divided into five eras or dynasties: the pioneer years, the DC-3 era, transoceanic and intercontinental service, the first jet age, and the wide-bodied jet era. Successive generations of transport aircraft, representative of these five eras, have progressively made spectacular advances. Seating has increased from 14 in the Ford Tri-Motor to an average of about 400 in the Boeing 747; cruising speed has increased from 100 to almost 600 miles per hour; and—less recognized or appreciated—average annual aircraft utilization has risen from no more than 1,000 hours in the air per year by the Ford to about 4,000 hours by today's long-range aircraft, which spend almost half their existence in the air.

The combination of these three parameters of technical excellence results in the standard measure of aircraft productivity, seat-miles per year, which has increased from about one and a half million with the Ford to a formidable one billion with the Boeing 747. To put this latter figure in perspective, it is about ten times that of a luxury ocean liner such as the *Queen Mary*. A further refinement is the average percentage of seats occupied, or the load factor, which has risen from about 40 percent in the 1930s to about 80 percent in these days of mass air travel.

This level of efficiency has led to enormous benefits to the traveling public. The airlines have reduced operating costs from about half a dollar per seat-mile in the 1920s to a few cents per seat-mile today. The big breakthrough was the introduction of jet airliners, which brought the cost of air travel sharply downwards, not—contrary to popular assumption—simply because of their speed (although this was a contributory factor), but because of their productivity.

One other vital technological achievement was, by engine development and design efficiency, the enormous increase in range. The Ford could not fly far without refueling. Nonstop transcontinental or practicable transoceanic travel was achieved only after World War II with the ultimate development of four-engined airliner design. Today, even twin-engined types can fly around the globe with only two stops.

The Pacific route illustrates the effect of this range capability. From Pan Am's China Clipper of 1936, which could carry a maximum of only eight or nine people on the San Francisco-Honolulu leg and took almost a week to cross the ocean, 25 airlines compete for this lucrative traffic market today. Most of the aircraft that fly this route are 747s, and more than half of them make the crossing nonstop in about 12 to 14 hours. (And this is the market that Pan Am sold for the price of five 747s!)

Let us look at some other aspects of the amazing developments in air transport. In addition to the technical innovations introduced by the manufacturers, summarized here in a Gompertz curve (Fig. 15.1), there have been corresponding operational and commercial innovations, summarized in a parallel Gompertz curve (Fig. 15.2). Gradually, air travel infiltrated, then superseded, passenger rail traffic in the United States (though not entirely elsewhere) and replaced passenger traffic across the world's oceans. The jets permitted economy fares, and innovative minds in the airline industry discovered that a substantial segment of the traveling public did not demand scheduled service. In Europe, thanks to inclusive group air tours, nonscheduled traffic exceeded the business-oriented scheduled total by the mid-1970s.

After 70 years of endeavor, the airline industry has thus grown from a transport curiosity to an all-powerful world industry. It has, by its sheer efficiency, brought the cost of air travel within the reach of the ordinary citizen. As a means of going from one place to another—as opposed to taking a cruise—it has eliminated sea traffic, as this chart of North Atlantic travel (Fig. 15.3) shows.

You may wonder why I have not mentioned supersonic transport (the SST) and called this another generation. The operating costs of a supersonic airliner, not to mention the astronomic development costs, are so high that they rule out commercial application except for a tiny, elite fraction of the market. This can

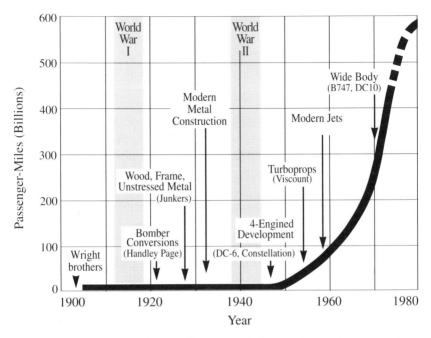

15.1. Gompertz curve showing the effect of technical innovation on air transportation as a function of passenger-miles over time.

easily be demonstrated by some calculations on the back of an envelope (Fig. 15.4). This piece of arithmetic leans over backwards to favor the SST, but whether considering the Concorde, the United States SST (which was never built), or the hypersonic figment of current theoretical imagination (HST), the market is so small that it does not bear thinking about.

So let us abandon stratospheric fantasy and ask the manufacturers, operators, and regulators of this great industry: *Where should it go, how should it expand, and what are the problems that confront it?* I submit that the problem can be summarized succinctly: Aircraft productivity has almost reached its maximum. All the elements of productivity have reached operational maxima, so that the only way to meet continued air traffic growth is to put more aircraft into the skies.

But is such an outcome inevitable? Can it be that air transport, like other transport modes before it, and like other products and industries, has reached the zenith of the economist's Gompertz curve and is now reaching a plateau of maturity, or—dare we contemplate—even entering a decline? This has cer-

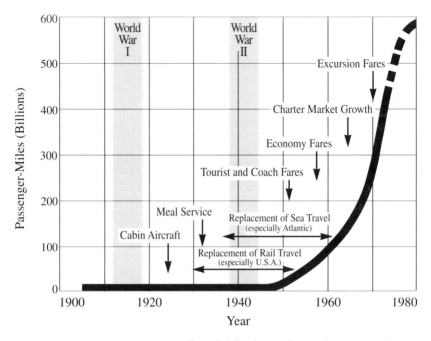

15.2. Gompertz curve showing the effect of airline innovation on air transportation as a function of passenger-miles over time.

tainly happened with other industries and their products. In Britain, in my lifetime, I can remember when the coal mines were the biggest single employer of any heavy industry. But only a handful of pits remain in full production today.

In manufacturing, the sound reproduction industry clearly illustrates the pattern of rise and fall. Within a single century, there have been three major technical revolutions, and in each case, a new technology has completely superseded the incumbent method. Berliner's disc records eliminated Edison's cylinders; long-playing records made the 78-rpm record obsolete; and today I cannot even buy an LP.

Now I do not wish to assert that air transport as a whole is threatened with decline, although the world's air transport statistics of late do suggest that some kind of plateau has been reached. This leveling off may have a great deal to do with the state of the world's economy; but it may also have something to do with the fact that the market for new travelers—those who have never flown

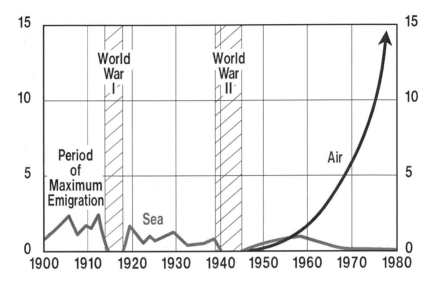

15.3. This chart of North Atlantic travel by sea and air shows changes over time in millions of passengers per year.

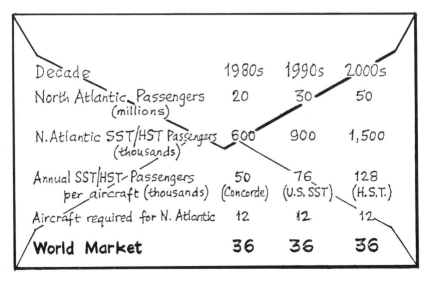

Decade	1980s	1990s	2000s
North Atlantic Passengers (millions)	20	30	50
N. Atlantic SST/HST Passengers (thousands)	600	900	1,500
Annual SST/HST Passengers per aircraft (thousands)	50 (Concorde)	76 (U.S. SST)	128 (H.S.T.)
Aircraft required for N. Atlantic	12	12	12
World Market	36	36	36

15.4. The world market for the SST and the hypothetical HST between 1980 and 2010.

before—is dwindling, because almost everybody who wishes to fly already flies, and that businessmen are actually beginning to use their fax machines to save the expense and time-consumption of travel.

I would venture to suggest, however, that the old Gompertz theory may be evident in the short-haul segment—say up to about 400 miles—of the airline market. Intercity travel began to feel the effect of the introduction of high-speed rail service in 1964. For the Shin Kansen (or Bullet Train) was not merely a faster train service; it was effectively a new form of transport. The Japanese Tokyo-Osaka express service was followed by further construction of new straight-and-level lines that permitted *average* 100-miles-per-hour (160-kilometers-per-hour) speeds between city centers. Today all the major cities of Japan and even most of the secondary ones are connected by high-speed trains, and they account for at least 80 percent of the intercity market in Japan today.

Thus the high-speed train is a factor to be reckoned with today, simply because it has doubled the competitive effectiveness of rail travel as a whole against travel by air. Whereas orthodox rail could compete with the airlines over distances of up to about 150 miles, high-speed rail competes up to at least 300 miles.

Europe has already recognized the potential of high-speed rail. In spite of

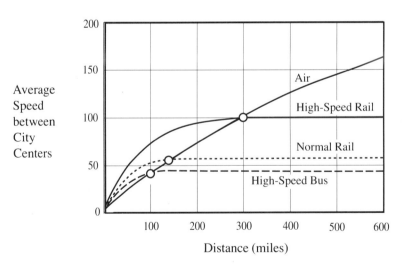

15.5. A comparison of the average speed of various modes of transportation between city centers.

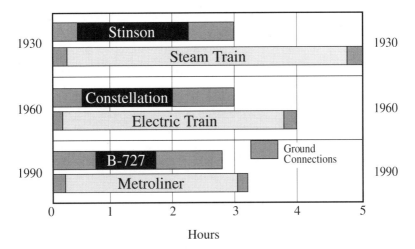

15.6. Reduction in travel time between Washington and New York (city center to city center).

political separation, for many years all the main cities of continental Europe have been within a few hours' comfortable train ride of each other. Except for cross-channel routes to Great Britain (and this has been rectified by the "Chunnel"), times between city centers up to about 200 miles apart are already as quick by surface rail as by air. At present, almost all the business air routes in Europe are short. By the next century, these same routes will be operated by rail, by trains like the French TGV, even faster than the Japanese Bullets.

A high percentage of the world's densest air routes are over distances of less than 400 miles, even including those in Japan, in spite of the Shin Kansen. Routes radiating from all the main population centers of Europe, in England, France, Italy, Spain, Germany, Scandinavia, and the Low Countries—not to mention the banking center of the continent, right here in Switzerland—are almost all less than 400 miles. In Australia, the big cities are similarly placed, and we must not forget that the world's first air shuttle service, from Rio de Janeiro to São Paulo, was over a distance of 250 miles (400 kilometers).

So what about the United States? On the Washington-New York route, once one of the busiest air shuttles in the world, the travel times have not changed significantly since 1930. But Amtrak's Metroliner has halved the time of the old Pennsylvania steam trains, and increased speed in the air has been wiped out by airport congestion.

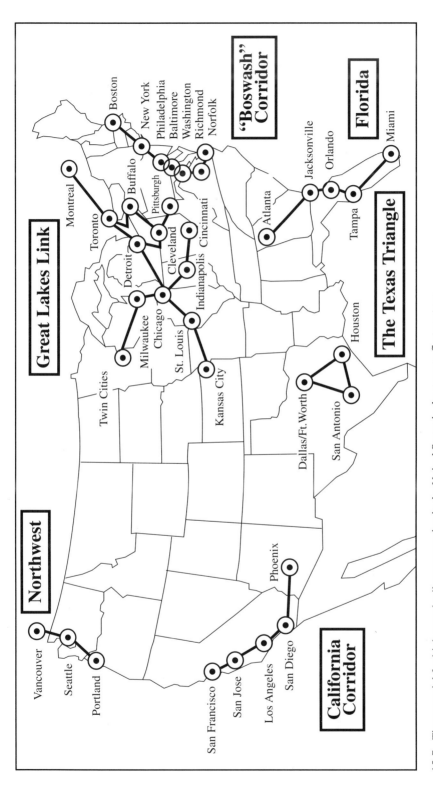

15.7. The potential for high-speed rail transportation in the United States in the twenty-first century.

Such factors apply equally to the London-Paris route, the busiest air shuttle in Europe, and a number of others. But this familiar and fairly obvious comparison involves only one criterion: speed. It ignores another important factor: comfort. With rail service, the extra space, absence of restrictions of movement, and lack of fuss and bother getting to and from, and maneuvering within, the terminal airports, are dispensed with.

I believe that, sooner or later, the United States will either come to its senses or be shamed into reviving what it had in the late 1930s: the best passenger trains in the world. Were the next president, perhaps, to announce a New Deal for the railroads and spend only half as much money on putting people on trains as it took to put people on the moon, the high-speed rail map of the country could look something like this (see Fig. 15.7) as we move into the twenty-first century.

Here, then, are my answers to the questions of where air transport should go, and how it should expand: (1) For distances up to 300 miles, high-speed rail is the sensible answer. (2) Airlines should cooperate rather than compete with surface modes (as in the old days!). (3) Air and rail should be coordinated, following the example set by Lufthansa when it opened its Airport Express a few years ago, with immediate connection and incorporated air-rail ticketing from Frankfurt Airport to Cologne, Düsseldorf, and other cities. (4) To relieve congestion between airports and downtown areas, there must be a form of high-speed urban transit, such as an elevated monorail, not a metro system that is little better than the commuter railroads or intercity lines of the nineteenth century.

In the future, therefore, the airlines must concentrate on what they do best: carrying people and cargo over long- and medium-haul distances of at least 300 miles, leaving the short-haul work—where most of the financial losses are incurred—to high-speed rail. I foresee that air traffic, which has traditionally peaked at distances between 200 and 400 miles, will undergo a fundamental change. High-speed rail will take over in this area, the airlines will discard the loss-sustaining routes and become more economical, and the traveling public as a whole will reap untold benefits.

◼◼◼
◼◼◼
◼◼◼ W. David Lewis

Epilogue

Three-point Landing

All flights must end. The laws of gravity are inexorable, and nothing ultimately eludes their grasp. At the close of a scholarly adventure that began with a slow takeoff roll in the summer of 1989, all that remains is for me to say that an earthbound orientation was implicit in the underlying plan of this conference from the beginning. Nothing could have brought ICCA 92 to a more fitting conclusion than the challenging message provided by R. E. G. Davies in his final address, "Facing the Transport Gridlock of the Twenty-first Century." It is notable for its emphasis on thinking carefully about what aerial operations can do best and being more discriminating about combining them with other modes of land-based travel, which, at least in the United States, have languished for want of a well-integrated national transportation policy.

In tracing the history of civil and commercial aviation, it behooves us to recognize that flight, like every other human activity, is tightly bound within a political, economic, and cultural context that inescapably brings our attention back to ground level, however much our imaginations may revel in images of freedom that have long been associated with aeronautics and astronautics. More, perhaps, than any other type of technology, human flight has been invested with messianic symbolism that makes it difficult for us to approach it rationally. We must therefore be careful not to let our imagination outstrip our capacity for exercising good judgment.

"Oh! I have slipped the surly bonds of earth," proclaimed John Gillespie Magee, Jr., in one of the most widely quoted poems ever conceived about flying. His words, written in September 1941, echoed themes long treasured among devotees of what Joseph J. Corn has aptly called "the winged gospel." Twenty-five years earlier, Alfred W. Lawson, one of the greatest prophets of civil and commercial aviation, had predicted the ultimate rise of "Alti-man," a superhuman creature who would "live in the upper stratas of the atmosphere and never come down to earth at all." Such disdain for terrestrial realities, woven into the fabric of aviation from the start, was epitomized by Icarus, who suffered the inevitable consequences of his recklessness by plunging to his death after flying too close to the sun. Magee himself had a similar fate, dying in a flight-training accident only three months after writing his stirring words.[1]

Slip the surly bonds of earth? Not for long. Any just assessment of the history of civil and commercial aviation must conclude that airline pioneer Clement A. Keys was correct in asserting that "ten percent of aviation is in the air, ninety percent on the ground." That is why this conference began with a session devoted to airports, the most conspicuous components of the earthly infrastructure that alone makes flight possible. That is why the next session dealt with technical developments in such areas as radio and air traffic control, which utilize ground-based installations to keep aircraft on course and guide them safely back to the landings that their pilots must inevitably execute.[2]

For a time, simply to drive home the point that aviation is firmly tethered in earthbound realities, I thought of devoting no sessions whatsoever to airplanes, which dominate so much of the literature in which the history of aeronautics is discussed. Abandoning that idea as unduly heretical, I deliberately focused a session on *constraints* affecting the development of commercial aircraft. My purpose in doing so was not to question our deep psychological need, as members of a highly creative species, to push constantly against the farther limits of what may seem possible at any given time. Magee's poem beautifully expresses an aspiring spirit, without which we would not be fully human. But our zest for further conquests in the air and in outer space must always be balanced by a realization of the price to be paid for our ceaseless urge to innovate and a consciousness of basic physical, political, economic, and social realities from which we cannot escape.

Every paper given in the opening sessions emphasized the underlying contexts that have heavily affected the development of aviation. Think, for example, about the way in which political and economic forces thwarted efforts to locate a third international airport near London. Consider, also, how the uses to which Berlin's Tempelhof Airport were put reflected changing political and ideological objectives in the Weimar Republic, Hitler's Third Reich, and the cold war. Ponder the dense web of business and governmental policy that surrounded the emergence of American airports in the 1920s and 1930s. One could go on, session by session, to trace the same pattern, but my point is by now sufficiently clear. In trying to understand the history of civil and commercial aviation we may momentarily lift our eyes to the heavens, but our attention must be directed mainly to what takes place on terra firma.

When our focus shifted from the first main topic of the conference, "Infrastructure and Environment," to the second, "Pioneers and Operations," the underlying concept remained the same. We observed, for example, that mundane impediments have severely limited both lighter-than-air and heavier-than air operations. Few of the slides that accompanied the presentations impressed me more deeply than one showing German work crews laboriously shoveling snow off the roofs of the gigantic structures needed to house and service dirigibles. The need for such sheds and the problems of maintaining them were among the circumstances that brought the age of the Zeppelins to a close. We also saw how carefully the physiological nature of the human organism itself, resulting from eons of evolution on Planet Earth, has had to be taken into consideration in planning every forward step in aerial operations.

In one paper after another, the same story was told. We saw how dreams that every United States citizen might fly his or her own airplane collapsed in the face of stubborn economic and social realities after World War II. We learned how nationalism affected the interface between civilian and military aviation, and how political attitudes in the Progressive era lay at the heart of regulation imposed on airlines by such administrators as Walter Folger Brown. We were told how differing convictions about Australia's place in the British Empire bore heavily on the development of aviation in that huge territorial land mass.

Slip the surly bonds of earth? Magee's poetic eloquence must not cloud our judgment about the real nature of our conquest of the air. Everything that happens in the sky as aircraft make their transitory journeys from one earthbound point to another reveals how tightly they are enmeshed in what takes place beneath their wings. That is why the thoughtful analysis presented by Davies, emphasizing costs, markets, and relative distances, strikes home with such force as we consider the illusory nature of the freedom that aviation symbolizes. Greek mythology makes the same underlying point by contrasting the heedlessness of Icarus with the wisdom of his older, more experienced partner, Daedalus.

Instead of entertaining heroic fantasies, historians of civil and commercial aviation must emulate Daedalus by probing as scientifically as possible the problems and paradoxes that this subject reveals, so that our findings can help informed citizens and government officials decide what possibilities to pursue in the future. Perhaps, as Davies suggests, we will find that breathing new life into older forms of transportation, such as the railroad, is preferable to making lavish investments in supersonic flight and discovering that these outlays have only intensified the problem of moving about on the surface of the earth, where we live and work and have our being. Whatever the answer at which we arrive, we must balance creativity with objectivity.

More than most products of human ingenuity, the capacity to fly has elevated our spirits and evoked images of transcendence over physical limitations. We justly celebrate the courage it has taken to overcome one of the most fundamental of all natural forces—gravity—and soar in an element long closed to us. We are instinctively aspiring creatures and must never lose Magee's urge to "dance the skies on laughter-silvered wings." But we are also blessed with rational faculties, and we must use them. Perhaps someday we will hold conferences at which scholars will give papers about the history of enterprises that have mined the asteroids and pioneered interplanetary passenger travel. If so, let us hope that the hidden costs of such ventures have been carefully scouted in advance, that visions of transcendence have been balanced by respect for our limitations, and that euphoria has not prevented our descendants from making wise and rational choices. Let us hope, also, that such a conference will be held in as beautiful a place as Switzerland, and that it will be hosted by an institution as able and well-equipped to meet its needs as the Swiss Transport Museum.

NOTES

1. A. H. Lankester, "John Magee: The 'Pilot Poet,'" *This England*, Jan. 1978, copy at National Air and Space Museum; Joseph J. Corn, *The Winged Gospel: America's Romance with Aviation, 1900–1950* (New York: Oxford University Press, 1983), 41.

2. On Keys's axiom, see R. E. G. Davies, *Airlines of the United States since 1914* (Washington, D.C.: Smithsonian Institution Press, 1982), 51. Papers from the opening four sessions of the conference are printed in the first volume of proceedings, *Infrastructure and Environment*, edited by William M. Leary.

Contributors

RUDOLF VON BAUMGARTEN received his medical degree from the University of Freiburg in Germany and has taught physiology at the University of Göttingen, the University of Michigan, and the University of Mainz. From 1986 to 1991, he was president of the German Society of Aviation and Space Medicine. Since 1992 he has been professor emeritus at the University of Mainz. He has been a pilot for more than 50 years and was the principal investigator or coinvestigator on five manned space missions.

ROGER E. BILSTEIN is professor of history at the University of Houston, Clear Lake. He received his Ph.D. at Ohio State University and has taught at the University of Wisconsin-Whitewater and the University of Illinois-Urbana. He was Lindbergh Professor of Aerospace History at the National Air and Space Museum in 1992–93.

KLAUS-RICHARD BÖHME attended Kiel University in Germany and received his Ph.D. from the University of Uppsala in Sweden. He taught at the Universities of Stockholm and Uppsala, where he is an associate professor, and is military historian at the Swedish Staff and Defense College.

R. E. G. DAVIES, who had a lengthy career in aviation economic research in Great Britain and the United States, is curator of air transport at the National Air and Space Museum.

MARC DIERIKX received his Ph.D. from the Catholic University of Nijmegen in the Netherlands. He has taught and held research positions at Nijmegen University and the London School of Economics. He has also held a research fellowship with the Royal Netherlands Academy of Arts and Sciences. In 1993–94, he was visiting professor of history at Auburn University.

LEIGH EDMONDS is research officer for the Centre of Western Australian History at the University of Western Australia in Perth. He has published numerous articles on civil aviation in Australia in *Aviation Heritage*, the *Journal of the Australian War Memorial*, *Sabretache: The Journal of the Military History Society*, and the *Aviation Institute Journal*.

RICHARD P. HALLION is historian of the United States Air Force. Among his books are *Test Pilots: The Frontiersmen of Flight* (rev. ed., Smithsonian Institution Press, 1988), *Strike from the Sky: The History of Battlefield Air Attack* (Smithsonian Institution Press, 1989), and *Storm over Iraq: Air Power and the Gulf War* (Smithsonian Institution Press, 1992).

ALEXANDRE HERLEA is a professor at the Conservatoire des Arts et Métiers in Paris. He specializes in the history of aviation, the internal combustion aircraft engine, the transfer of technology, and industrial research laboratories.

LEE KOLM, a doctoral candidate at Brown University, thanks the National Air and Space Museum and the National Aeronautics and Space Administration for their support of this research.

NICK A. KOMONS is a research collaborator for the National Air and Space Museum. He received his Ph.D. from George Washington University. He has worked in the Office of Aerospace Research and headed the history office of the Federal Aviation Administration.

W. DAVID LEWIS is Distinguished University Professor at Auburn University. He is the coauthor, with Wesley Phillips Newton, of *Delta: The History of an Airline* (1979) and the coauthor, with William F. Trimble, of *The Airway to Everywhere: A History of All American Aviation, 1937–1953* (1988).

F. ROBERT VAN DER LINDEN is curator of aeronautics at the National Air and Space Museum. He received his bachelor's degree from the University of Denver and his master's degree from George Washington University. He is presently completing his Ph.D. at George Washington with a dissertation on Progressives, the post office, and the airmail.

WOLFGANG MEIGHÖRNER-SCHARDT has been director of the Zeppelin-Museum, Friedrichshafen, since 1991. He studied modern history, medieval history, and classical archaeology at the Ludwigs-Maximilians University in Munich, receiving his master's degree in 1984 and his Ph.D. in 1991. Before coming to the Zeppelin-Museum, Dr.

Meighörner-Schardt was head of the exhibitions department of the capital of the Federal Republic of Germany in Bonn and head of the department of history/ archives/museum of the Luftschiffbau Zeppelin GmbH.

JOHN H. MORROW, JR., is associate dean of the College of Arts and Sciences at the University of Georgia. He was Lindbergh Professor at the National Air and Space Museum in 1988–89.

GENRIKH V. NOVOZHILOV is general designer and academician for the Ilyushin Aviation Complex in Moscow. He graduated from the Moscow Aviation Institute and has worked for Ilyushin since 1948. Among the aircraft he had principal responsibility for were the Il-18 turboprop and the Il-62 turbojet, both mainstays of Russian aviation in the 1960s and 1970s. In more recent years, he led the design teams on the Il-76 and the wide-body Il-86 airliners.

DOMINICK A. PISANO is curator and deputy chair of the Department of Aeronautics at the National Air and Space Museum. In addition to his principal responsibility for collections management and exhibitions, he is author of *To Fill the Skies with Pilots: The Civilian Pilot Training Program, 1939–1946* (University of Illinois Press, 1993) and coauthor of *Legend, Memory and the Great War in the Air* (University of Washington Press, 1992).

JOHN PROVAN is historian at the Historical Aviation Collection at the Frankfurt/Main International Airport in Frankfurt. He is a graduate student at the Technical College in Darmstadt, where he has recently completed his master's thesis on the use of the German rigid airship in World War I. At Frankfurt/Main, Mr. Provan has been responsible for exhibits on the Berlin airlift, Count Zeppelin, and Otto Lilienthal.

EIICHIRO SEKIGAWA graduated from Kyoto University with a major in Sanskrit literature. He was editor-in-chief of *Aireview* magazine before becoming a free-lance aerospace journalist and public commentator.

WILLIAM F. TRIMBLE is associate professor of history at Auburn University. He is the author of *Admiral William A. Moffett: Architect of Naval Aviation* (Smithsonian Institution Press, 1994), *Wings for the Navy: A History of the Naval Aircraft Factory, 1917–1956* (Naval Institute Press, 1990), *The Airway to Everywhere: A History of All American Aviation, 1937–1953* (with W. David Lewis; University of Pittsburgh Press, 1988), and *High Frontier: A History of Aeronautics in Pennsylvania* (University of Pittsburgh Press, 1982).

ALFRED WALDIS was the first director of the Swiss Transport Museum in Lucerne, the most popular museum in Switzerland. He was instrumental in raising funds for the museum and overseeing its expansion since its opening in 1959. He has served as a director of the Swiss Federal Railways and a member of the Federal Commission for Swiss Transport Planning. Since 1981, he has served as president of the Swiss Transport Museum and has been the museum's honorary president since 1990.